CHANGE
AND
CONFLICT

A Study of
Community Work
in Glasgow

CHANGE
AND
CONFLICT

A Study of
Community Work
in Glasgow

Barbara and Richard Bryant

ABERDEEN UNIVERSITY PRESS

First published 1982
Aberdeen University Press
A member of the Pergamon Group
© Barbara and Richard Bryant 1982

British Library Cataloguing in Publication Data
Bryant, Barbara
  Change and conflict
  1. Social group work—Glasgow (Strathclyde)
  2. Community development—Glasgow (Strathclyde)
  I. Title   II. Bryant, Richard
  361.8′09411   HV249.S

  ISBN 0-08-028475-2
  ISBN 0-08-028480-9 Pbk

PRINTED IN GREAT BRITAIN
THE UNIVERSITY PRESS
ABERDEEN

CONTENTS

ABBREVIATIONS

ACW	Association of Community Workers
CDP	Community Development Project
CCTESW	Central Council for Training and Education in Social Work
DHSS	Department of Health and Social Security
GAG	Govanhill Action Group
GTRA	Govanhill Tenants Rehousing Association
SNP	Scottish Nationalist Party
SWSG	Social Work Services Group

ACKNOWLEDGEMENTS

Many individuals and organizations helped us with the preparation of this study. The Central Council for Training and Education in Social Work (CCTESW) financed the research and were patient in waiting for a long overdue report. The Applied Social Studies Course at Ruskin College and the Department of Social Administration and Social Work at Glasgow University provided work space and study facilities. Crossroads Youth and Community Associations tolerated us, with humour, as ex-employees turned researchers. Our greatest debt is to those Crossroads staff, management committee members, students and the local residents in Gorbals and Govanhill whose work provided the inspiration for this study.

The interviews were the most enjoyable part of the research. Almost without exception, everyone we approached for personal interviews agreed to participate. We would like to thank local residents, Crossroads members, local government officials, politicians and academics who contributed in this way.

Shirley Price and Sue Hearne typed the drafts and final report. We thank them for their skill and hard work.

The final responsibility for the study is entirely that of the authors and does not necessarily reflect the views of CCTESW, Crossroads or local organizations in Gorbals and Govanhill.

FOR RUTH AND FIONA

Chapter One

INTRODUCTION

In November 1969 Scotland's social work services were reorganized. The previously fragmented and separate services for
child care, welfare and home helps, mental health, day nur-
series, probation and after-care were brought together into
one single local authority department. On paper, the Social
Work (Scotland) Act 1968 was a more comprehensive and radical
piece of legislation that its English and Welsh counterparts.
The Scottish legislation initiated not only an administrative
reorganization, but also stretched the traditional boundaries
of social work beyond the individual and the family to embrace
the community at large. Section 12 of the 1968 Act gave local
authorities a duty to 'promote social welfare' and a key element in this promotional philosophy was the community development role of the new Social Work departments.[1] The implementation of the 1968 Act was beset by a formidable array of
financial, organizational and political problems. Much needed
finance was not immediately forthcoming from central government
and this resource famine was compounded by the parsimonious
attitude of some councils. The preventive and promotional
philosophy of the Act was only partially appreciated by many
local power holders, who tended to focus their attention on
the nuts and bolts of the administrative reorganization rather
than on the social policy implications of the new legislation.
Staffing was also a recurrent problem, both in terms of manpower availability and, more importantly, in terms of the
availability of staff with the imagination, commitment and
risk-taking abilities to test out the scope of their new
responsibilities. Nowhere were these problems more evident
than in Glasgow, the city which poses the acid test for any
social reform in Scotland.

[1]References start on p.231

As in England and Wales the staffing difficulties and short-
falls of the new Scottish social work departments were almost
exclusively defined in the terms of the need for more qualified
social workers and, consequently, there was a spawning of new
and expanded social work courses in the wake of the 1968 legislation. As with the developments in the field, the demands
which were generated on the training courses could not be
handled merely by providing 'more of the same' for a larger
number of consumers. The philosophy of the reorganized social
work services called for the training of a new type of social
worker who could operate within a generic framework and who
could move beyond, in day to day practice, the traditional
casework approaches. Many of the Scottish social work courses
lacked the teaching and fieldwork resources to immediately
respond to these demands and this shortcoming was particularly
apparent in the community work dimension of social work education. During the late 1960s community work was not taught on
the majority of Scottish courses, and only one course provided
a community work element as an integral part of the curriculum.
In 1970, the social work course at Glasgow University, recognizing these shortcomings, began to take steps to develop
teaching and fieldwork training in community work. Supported
by the Scottish Social Work Services Group (SWSG) the University appointed a staff member, Richard Bryant, to develop
teaching in community work and also began to take steps to
establish a student training unit in Glasgow. This fieldwork
unit, which was the first community work training unit to be
established in Scotland, was eventually located with Crossroads
Youth and Community Association (Crossroads), a Gorbals-based
voluntary organization which had been operating since the late
1950s.

The Unit opened in February 1971, and, three years later, the
SWSG agreed to sponsor a second fieldwork Unit with Crossroads.
This study is concerned with the history and experiences of
the Crossroads fieldwork Units from 1971 to 1978, an arbitrary
time period which reflects our years of direct involvement with
Crossroads. Between 1971 and 1977, Barbara Bryant worked as a
fieldwork teacher in both Gorbals and Govanhill and this
involvement was maintained in a voluntary capacity until late
in 1978. Between 1974 and 1978 Richard Bryant worked as a
fieldwork teacher with the Gorbals Unit and, for four years
previously, he had been the community work tutor at Glasgow
University and the academic link between the units and the
university social work course.

AIMS OF THE STUDY

The research which we have undertaken has three related aims:

*i) To document and evaluate the Community Work Practice
    of the Crossroads Staff*

Here the community work staff and their employing agency are
the major objects of study; the organizational and political
contexts in which they operated; the policies, values and goals
which informed their work; the roles and functions which they
performed in local situations and the assessments which they
made about what constituted 'good' community work practice.
Reflecting a concern about the lack of consumer perspectives
on community work in the British literature, we have included
in the evaluation of community work practice, assessments made
by local activists, politicians and 'informed' outsiders as
well as those made by the Crossroads staff themselves.

ii) To document and evaluate the Community Work Programme

Here the perspective broadens from a focus on the theory and
practice of community work to embrace the collective activities
which were initiated and supported by the Crossroads staff; the
campaigns, action groups and self-help schemes which were supported in Gorbals and Govanhill and the achievements, shortcomings and defeats which were experienced. Again we have
attempted to incorporate perspectives which derive from a
range of participants - local activists, politicians and students, as well as the Crossroads staff.

*iii) To document and evaluate the Educational and Training
     Programme which was organized for Social Work Students*

Here the focus is on the experiences of the students who undertook fieldwork placements with Crossroads; what was the value
of the placements within the context of social work education;
what were the expectations of courses and what were the experiences of the local activists who worked with students? These
and related questions are examined from the perspectives of
the students, course tutors and local activists, as well as
from the perspective of the staff.

STUDY METHODS

In terms of the literature on community work research we have
been concerned with what Thomas has defined as 'Knowledge -
development research' and 'evaluation research'.

Knowledge development research in community work seeks
to extend understanding, for example, about practitioner
activities, roles and skills and about the various
settings and sponsors of community work. Evaluation
research would be concerned with monitoring and assessing the product and process of community work interventions.[2]

While a distinction can usefully be drawn between these two
approaches we would suggest that both are required if studies
of community work interventions are to avoid a partial and lop-
sided perspective. Evaluation research can underplay the contribution made, for good or ill, by professional workers and
the community work agency. The workers remain as shadowy
figures in the background, their contribution, or lack of it,
to the promotion of local action being obscured by an emphasis
on the activities of local residents, community organizations
and campaigns. On the other hand, knowledge development
research can have the reverse effect. We gain an insight into
the theory and practice of community work, but tend to learn
only a limited amount about the outcome of collective action,
particularly in terms of the achievements and shortcomings of
the groups with whom the community workers are involved.

Any attempt to evaluate a community work programme is fraught
with methodological difficulties and, as Kay, Hudson and
Armstrong point out,[3] the selection of a research design will
be influenced by the programme of the agency which is being
evaluated, the funds which are available, the audience for the
evaluation and the choices which are made by the researchers.
The nature of the community work programme is especially
problematic, as the goals of community work agencies are often
vague, and are shot through with different value assumptions
which are open to conflicting interpretations and which are
difficult, if not impossible, to quantify. For instance, there
are no widely agreed yardsticks and norms for measuring the
development of 'community self-organization' or, in social
work education terms, the development of 'practice skills'.
The very nature of community work is not - and, indeed, should
not be - a predictable activity in terms of its processes and
outcomes. Attempts to encourage the articulation of felt needs
and the stimulation of collective action are very much journeys
into the unknown; interventions on one issue may lead to action
being taken on other problems, and goals and strategies can be
redefined as circumstances and personalities change. Also,
professional workers and local activists act and make decisions
on the basis of intuition, anger and prejudice as well as on
the basis of accumulated knowledge and empirical data. The
vagueness and value conflicts which can surround objectives,

and the unpredictability of process and outcome, pose serious
dilemmas for research designs which are based on classical
scientific or social engineering models of evaluation. Key,
Hudson and Armstrong suggest that 'broad-aim programmes' are
not easily evaluated by 'hard-line' research approaches.

> The essence of the goal model - the classical model for
> evaluation - is that a programme of action is planned
> and later assessed in strict relation to stated general
> aims and to the objectives that are specified in order
> to contribute to the achievement of those aims. In so
> far as aims are narrow, objectives can be turned readily
> into statements of behaviour that should occur if those
> objectives have been achieved. This behaviour is then
> taken as a sign by the evaluator that there has been
> some progress toward the achievement of the aims. When
> programme aims are broad, specified objectives are less
> likely to be meaningful and the goal model becomes
> correspondingly more difficult to follow.[4]

Critics of the classical model of evaluation have proposed
alternative approaches for community work research. Peter
Marris has argued that research into community action is
'contemporary political history' and that its methodology
should involve:

> To be everywhere, know everything that happened, and
> how it happened, to record all this - and then, behind
> the mass of details and the accidents of personality,
> to discern the general pattern of issues which
> determined these events. In many ways, it is more
> demanding than the interpretation of scientific experi-
> ment, because so little can be taken for granted.[5]

Key, Hudson and Armstrong also suggest that 'soft line' approaches, which employ techniques such as impressionistic
inquiries and opinion surveys, are more appropriate to 'broad
aim' community work programmes:

> The enquirer talks to staff and clients, sits in on
> occasions, reads relevant material etc. After the
> collection of information in this way he or she pro-
> duces a report on the basis of observations and
> impressions. The enquirer may be an insider to the
> programme but is often an outsider.[6]

These alternative approaches share certain common features.
There is an emphasis upon examining the process as well as the
outcome of community work interventions. There is a recognition

of the importance of gathering qualitative material – however
subjective it might be – in building up an overall picture of
experiences and there is an explicit recognition that value
perspectives will shape evaluation, and that competing views
are likely to be held of the same events, depending upon the
vested interests and opinions of the participants. Rather
than attempting to impose a structured research design upon an
often complex and confusing reality, the role of the researcher
becomes that of a 'narrator' and 'story teller', attempting to
document and elucidate the various processes, contexts and
circumstances which shaped the development of collective action.
Given the 'broad aim' nature of the Crossroads community work
programme we opted for the impressionistic model of inquiry.

SOURCES OF MATERIAL

The data and material have been derived from the following
sources.

Personal Experience

We have drawn on our experiences of being employed as fieldwork
teachers with the Crossroads Units in Gorbals and Govanhill.
In some of the local initiatives which are described in the
study we provided the main source of full-time community work
support and, in all cases, we had a good working knowledge of
the projects described.

Interviews

We carried out a series of tape-recorded interviews with other
Crossroads staff members (seven interviews), local community
activists (sixteen interviews), social work tutors (two interviews), local politicians (six interviews) and informed 'outsiders' who were familiar with the activities of Crossroads
(seven interviews). These interviews – which were normally of
$1-1\frac{1}{2}$ hours duration – attempted, through open-ended questions,
to elicit the interviewees' opinions on local organizations
and Crossroads community work practice. The transcript of the
personal interview was sent to all participants, to afford them
the opportunity to check and amend the material. Many of the
quotations used in the case studies and elsewhere in the study
are drawn from these transcripts. The SWSG declined to comment
on the training programme of the student units.

Questionnaires

Material on the student experiences of placement was derived
from a postal questionnaire, devised by Barbara Bryant, and

amended slightly after a pilot survey involving six students.
All students who completed a placement between Oxtober 1971
and Summer 1977 (one hundred students) were sent a lengthy
postal questionnaire in January 1978 which invited them to
review and reflect upon their placement experiences (see
Appendix 1 for details). A follow-up reminder was sent six
months later to those who did not reply. The response rate to
the questionnaire was low - 30%. This can be attributed to a
combination of factors, including the time period which had
elapsed since some of the students had completed their placements (up to six years in some cases), the length and detail
of the questionnaire and the general problems which are often
associated with the use of postal questionnaires, such as
changes of address and the lack of personal contact with interviewees affecting the motivation to respond to the survey.

Material on the experience of social work courses was derived
from a second and much shorter questionnaire, which was sent
to twenty-nine tutors on six of the Scottish based courses
which regularly used Crossroads for placements. (See Appendix
2 for details). This survey produced thirteen replies - a
response of 45%.

Written Sources

There is a considerable amount of written material on the
history of Crossroads and community organizations in Gorbals
and Govanhill. This literature included previous publications
by Crossroads staff, placement reports prepared by students,
the management minutes and annual reports of Crossroads, staff
recordings and reports from the 'View', a monthly community
newspaper for Gorbals and Govanhill which has been published
since 1967.

While we have attempted to build up a narrative and evaluation
which incorporates a variety of perspectives, it should be
emphasized that the control, filtering and editing of this mass
of material has been our sole responsibility. Inevitably, our
own values and experiences have shaped the research process and
have stamped an impression on the end product.

PLAN

The study is divided into three parts. In Part One we are
concerned with defining and detailing the context in which
Crossroads has operated; the social and political location of
Gorbals and Govanhill within the City of Glasgow; the local
organizations and outside bodies which have provided the sponsorship and organizational structure for the fieldwork Units;

the approach and policies adopted by the staff in undertaking
their local community work and fieldwork training activities.

In Part Two we are concerned with examples of local community
work. These are presented in the form of case studies and
incorporate details on the role performed by the staff and
reflections on outcomes made by both staff and local participants. In the last chapter of this section we comment upon
the staff practice of community work, in the light of their
experience with Crossroads.

In Part Three the evaluative perspective is extended to examine
what makes a good community worker and what constitutes a successful community work project, from the perspectives of local
activists, politicians and informed outsiders. Their experiences and the yardsticks they adopt for assessing outcomes are
compared with those of the Crossroads staff. Also, we consider
what social work students gained from community work placements
and this is discussed from the viewpoint of the students, local
residents and course tutors. In the light of these findings,
we discuss whether social work training needs community work.
Finally, in the last chapter, we present some personal reflections on current debates about the value, limitations and
shortcomings of different approaches to community work.

PART ONE

THE SETTING

Chapter Two

GORBALS AND GOVANHILL

The neighbouring districts of Gorbals and Govanhill are situated on the south side of Glasgow - a mere ten minute bus ride
from the city centre and the Victorian grandeur of the City
Chambers in George Square. Even someone who is unfamiliar
with Glasgow is likely to have heard of the Gorbals and the
image, which the name invokes, is invariably associated with
slum housing and gang violence. The more literary minded
stranger may also be familiar with the area through innumer-
able press articles, a best selling novel ('No Mean City'),
several plays and even a ballet ('Miracle in the Gorbals').
Govanhill is unlikely to prompt such instant and stereotyped
recognition. Indeed, it is an area which outsiders often
wrongly associate with another of Glasgow's historic south-
side communities, Govan, which is situated some miles away
down the Clyde. Our stranger might also be surprised to
learn that, by the mid 1970s, it was Govanhill rather than
Gorbals which figured prominently in the official league
table of 'deprived' Glasgow communities.

GORBALS

The Gorbals has a long and, in human terms, cruel history.
In the mid-18th century a village settlement called Gorbals
developed at the southward approach to the old Stockwell
Bridge over the river Clyde. The village housed a small
community of weavers, numbering some 5,000 by 1790. By the
early 19th century Gorbals had become a residential suburb
for the rich merchants of the city. These 'town houses' of
Glasgow were large sandstone tenements, complete with servants'
quarters. With the expansion of the city's colonial trade and
the development of heavy industry on the Clyde, Glasgow's
population began to rapidly expand, partly through the

extension of the city's boundaries (The Barony of Gorbals was
incorporated in 1846) but mainly through immigration. The
growth rate was phenomenal and the city's population increased
from 30,000 in 1770 to 359,000 in 1851. Gorbals, with its
proximity to the city centre and ready access to the Clyde and
the rapidly developing railway system, was at the heart of the
early expansion. The immigrants were lowland Scots, dis-
possessed Highlanders, Irish peasants escaping from the famine,
and, later on, Jewish immigrants from Europe. They were the
proletariat for the new textile and heavy engineering industries, part of what Johnston has described as the 'great mas-
sacre'[1] of colonial trade and industrialization which produced
wealth for a few and deprivation and premature death for many.

As industrialization gathered momentum, the merchant class
retreated to greener pastures and conditions in Gorbals dete-
riorated. Bathrooms were removed from many of the 'town-
houses' to facilitate sub-letting and the new tenements for
the incoming workers were built to a very inferior standard.
The upsurge of population generated a demand for housing
which the private market and the limited public provision
made by the City Improvement Trust could not handle. Gross
overcrowding and intolerable living conditions, 'vile almost
beyond belief',[2] were an inevitable consequence. By the turn
of the century parts of the Gorbals, especially Crown Street,
Rose Street and Thistle Street, were notorious for overcrowding on a scale which was unimaginable in the larger English cities. They were places which, as Checkland observes,
were 'dense and festering, having the power of debilitation
and death'.[3]

Community Militancy

The period prior to the First World War witnessed the emergence of militant working class movements in the West of Scotland. John Maclean, whom the Bolsheviks named as the Russian
Consul in Glasgow after the 1917 revolution, unsuccessfully
contested parliamentary and municipal elections in Gorbals.[4]
Although the Gorbals never returned a revolutionary socialist
candidate, it was an area which was known for its left-wing
support and sympathy. Harry McShane comments:

> The South Side, Govan and Gorbals, was a very lively
> place for socialist propaganda. We sold literature,
> we held meetings, and for a big event we bill-posted
> everywhere. You couldn't walk through without seeing
> the pavements chalked with socialist slogans.[5]

It was the war years and the aftermath which established much
of the reputation of the 'Red Clyde'. The working class
action of this period embraced community conflicts as well as
the better known industrial struggles against the provisions
of the Munitions Act and the campaign for a forty hour week.
Slum housing, increased rents and a decline in new home building, sparked off a series of rent strikes in Clydeside between
1911 and 1920. The key action, both in terms of mass involvement and political impact, occurred in 1915, when the women
in Govan, supported by workers from the munitions factories,
refused to pay rent increases and faced eviction. On 17
November, 1915, the day when the tenants appeared at the
Glasgow Small Debts Court, they were supported by a 10,000
strong demonstration. At the same time rent strikes were
occurring in other Glasgow areas, including Govanhill and
Gorbals, and it has been estimated that, in all, some 15,000
Glasgow tenants were on strike during this period.[6] The mass
community agitation, allied to the threat of industrial action
by munition workers, eventually forced Lloyd George to inter-
vene and was an influential factor in the passing of the first
rent control legislation in 1915. The introduction of this
legislation represented a major victory for the Glasgow
tenants although, as Ginsburg and Corrigan[7] point out, the
bargaining power of the munition workers enabled the tenants
to exercise a degree of political muscle which was rare, if
not unique, in the history of British community struggles.

Agitation over rents, poor housing conditions and evictions,
continued well after the end of the war. Wal Hannington, in
his history of the unemployed workers movement, describes how
Harry McShane and Gorbals tenants organized resistance to an
eviction in South York Street.

> About 7.30 on the morning of the 17th May, 1922, one
> of the Glasgow leaders of the unemployed called upon
> Harry McShane to inform him that an eviction had taken
> place in South York Street in the Gorbals district.
> McShane, Duffy and another worker immediately pro-
> ceeded to the scene. They found that furniture had
> already been placed on the stairs and the door of the
> house had been nailed up. One was sent to rouse
> other supporters and McShane and Duffy forced open
> the door and replaced the furniture in the house.
> Crowds quickly gathered at the call of the movement
> and mass meetings were held in the street outside the
> house....[8]

The police eventually broke in but at the subsequent trial
the accused was discharged and the jury returned a verdict of
'not proven' to charges of sedition made against McShane.
The successful fight against this eviction led, according to
Hannigan, to the Glasgow City Council having to set up a
special rent fund to relieve tenants who were in danger of
eviction. It is rather ironic to note that, over fifty years
later, Gorbals tenants were still having to take direct action
to resist evictions, this time against the Local Authority
rather than a private landlord.[9]

Redevelopment

Until the First World War, public intervention in Glasgow's
housing was largely limited to the demolition of the worst
slums and the control of overcrowding in the remainder.
After the First World War, private building slumped and the
Local Authority, encouraged by new Central Government subsidies, began to take a more direct role in the provision of
council housing. During the inter-war years Glasgow Corporation, first under the 'moderates' and then from 1933 onwards
under the Labour Party, began to develop an extensive programme of council housing. Between 1919 and 1939 out of the
76,360 houses which were built in the city all but 9,106 were
in the public sector, the majority being developed on green-
field sites on the outskirts of the city. The city's new
council schemes were not, however, all of a common standard
and status. Glasgow Corporation recognized important differences between sections of the housing stock.

> Ordinary houses built under the 1919, 1923 and 1924
> Acts were confined to 'respectable' skilled and semi-
> skilled artisans and lower paid white collar workers.[10]

When slum clearance started in the 1930s, a 'rehousing' cate-
gory was introduced at lower rentals and with fewer facilities. The slum clearance housing became stigmatised as being
for the 'less respectable' tenants and contributed, in Govanhill, to social tensions within the area which exist to the
present day.

> When we formed one tenants' association for the whole
> of Govanhill, we managed to bring a certain group of
> people together from this area but never really amal-
> gamated with the other side. It used to be separate
> and I think it will always be like that. People on
> this side always think of that side as the slum clear-
> ance. I think it's a stigma that will always be there.
> (Govanhill tenant)

Despite the Council house building programme of the inter-war
years the city's housing problem remained acute. At the end
of the Second World War, Gorbals and the neighbouring district of Hutchesontown still remained grossly overcrowded and
deficient in housing facilities. Despite a loss of 20% of
its population between 1931 and 1951, mainly due to rehousing,
Gorbals was, in 1951, the second most densely populated ward
in the city. Nearly 42% of the population, which totalled
37,000, were living at more than two per room; nearly two-
thirds of the houses were of one or two rooms; less than
half of them had a lavatory of their own and less than one in
ten had a bath.[11] Historically, Glasgow had acquired new land
for house building and industrial development by expanding its
municipal boundaries but, by the post-second world war years,
this policy was becoming impracticable because of the physical
restrictions imposed by the city's geographic location.

Redevelopment was inevitable and was to involve the demolition
of 100,000 homes and the building of modern Council housing on
the cleared sites. The drastic thinning of the population in
the older parts of the city was designed to reduce overcrowding
and provide the major source of population for new outlying
housing estates and new towns (e.g. Cumbernauld and East Kil-
bride). Hutchesontown-Gorbals was the first area to be
selected for comprehensive redevelopment and it was as much
the reputation of the area, as the poor physical conditions,
which influenced this policy. The Counsel for the Glasgow
Corporation make this abundantly clear at the public enquiry
into the proposal:

> The very name of Gorbals has come to epitomise all
> that is worst in living conditions, not only in
> Glasgow, or indeed in Scotland, but in Britain.[12]

It was during the inter-war years that Gorbals acquired its
world-wide reputation as being Britain's classic slum; an
area of congested tenement housing, poverty-stricken families,
bored unemployed men and razor gangs which engaged in mindless
violence. As with all stereotypes, especially of working-
class communities, it was a distortion of the situation. If
there was any basis for the reputation is applied only to the
'reception zone' of Gorbals, especially the area around
Gorbals Cross which had, for many years, provided a temporary
or permanent base for newcomers to the city and for people
who had been displaced from other parts of the city. Ironically, the first area scheduled for redevelopment included
only a small part of this infamous district. Research by
Brennan clearly indicates that the population structure of
the first clearance area mainly comprised long-term families,

with bread winners who held skilled jobs. They were part of
a 'respectable and stable working-class area',[13] which bore
little resemblance to the reputation of 'The Gorbals'.
Brennan suggests that this indiscriminate labelling functioned
to minimize any organized public opposition to the drastic
nature of the redevelopment proposals.

> The fact that the scheme was concerned with the Gorbals
> explains the absence of opposition and at least partly
> explains the comprehensive nature of the clearance. It
> was widely felt that whatever might be acceptable else-
> where, in the case of Gorbals the only thing to do was
> to clear the site and make a clean start.[14]

The second part of the redevelopment, covering the Laurieston
Gorbals area, commenced in the mid 1960s and is still being
completed at the present time. The population of the Laurieston Gorbals area, which included the 'problem area' around
Gorbals Cross, was to be reduced from 18,000 to 10,000 and,
as in the Gorbals-Hutchesontown district, an area of mixed
housing, industrial and commercial uses was to be replaced by
mainly residential provision. The new housing provided in the
Laurieston area had one innovatory feature: 'decked' housing
blocks which, it was claimed, combined the high densities of
multi-storey flats without the social disadvantages of isolation. These 'streets in the air' were hailed, by the civic
authorities, as a major development in housing design.

The New Gorbals

Today, housing in the new Gorbals comprises high rise flats
(up to twenty-three storeys), medium rise deck access blocks
(seven storeys) and low rise three and four storey blocks.
Over 3,000 households in the area are now accommodated in
high flats with lifts, and included in this population is a
substantial proportion of pensioners, e.g., in the four block
high rise development at Stirlingfauld Place (Laurieston) over
25% of the population are over the age of sixty. In Glasgow
a high rise housing allocation is considered, because of the
presence of lifts, as a ground floor offer. This substantial
commitment to high rise housing in Gorbals reflected a major
trend in the city's housing and planning policies during the
late 1950s and the 1960s. The high rise policy, which resulted in the construction of over three hundred multi-storey
blocks throughout the city, reflected the influence of both
local and national factors. At the local level high rise
developments were viewed, by politicians and officials, as a
partial solution to the City's chronic shortage of building
land and a quick response to the urgent demands for new

housing. At the national level, generous central government
subsidies and the development of new building technology, in
the form of industrialized building systems, also created
conditions which were favourable to high rise developments.
One may also speculate that high rise developments, rather
like the ambitious and economically dubious Glasgow inner-city
motorway network, were politically attractive because they
projected a 'modern image' for a city which, in the minds of
many people, is still associated with the ugly legacy of the
industrial revolution. It was not until 1974 that Glasgow
abandoned high rise developments. This was many years after
other cities had stopped building, in the wake of the Ronan
point disaster, research evidence about 'social difficulties'
and, perhaps most significant of all, the recognition from
practical experience that high rise flats were economically
expensive to build and maintain. When Glasgow finally stopped
its high rise policy the then Labour leader of the Council,
Richard Dynes, engaged in a tour de force of criticism and
recrimination.

> In Glasgow we will not be building any more high flats
> after this. It is just not worth the candle. We have
> had a large number of complaints from both young and
> old people. The planners should have told us about the
> difficulties before they were built - but they did not.
> We had to find out for ourselves... They are socially
> undesirable.[15]

The social cost of these 'undesirable' housing developments
has been borne by the Council tenants and, during the 1970s,
Gorbals was to become a focal point within the West of Scotland for community struggles against the 'new slums' (see
Chapter 6). The 'streets in the air' were to become damp and
insanitary within two years of being built. Housing has not
been the only problem faced by the residents of the new
Gorbals. Throughout the 1970s unemployment in the area averaged over 10% and male unemployment averaged over 20%, in some
parts of the district. The deepening unemployment in the
region, allied to the not insubstantial local job loss due to
redevelopment, forced many families into poverty. We would
estimate that one in four of the present day Gorbals population are wholly or partially dependent on social security and
welfare benefits for their main source of income. The working
class families of Gorbals, as elsewhere in the city, are
locked into a system of institutionalized inequality.

GOVANHILL

Gorbals has a long, and in some respects, unique history.
The development of Govanhill is more recent and is typical of
much of the rest of the city. Govanhill is an example of the
speculative building which dominated the housing market between the 1860s and the First World War. Originally known as
'No Man's Land', because a former owner had fled from Britain
due to being heavily in debt, Govanhill was only developed
after 1864 when the coalmines had been worked out and ownership had passed to Mr Dixon, then owner of the coalmines and
ironworks immediately to the north of Govanhill. The land
was developed largely to house Dixon's workforce and the
engineers from Dub's Works in Polmadie. The houses, built
for rental, were small and had few facilities. They were
typical of working-class tenements throughout the city. Between 1862 and 1901, 18% of all the houses which were authorized to be built had only one apartment; 49% had two apartments and only 19% had three apartments. Public facilities,
when available, were donated through the patronage of the
factory owners; the bandstand in Govanhill park was a gift
from the manager of Dub's Engineering Works and the Dixon
Halls was a gift from Mr Dixon in 1879. It was intended to
provide 'proper meeting rooms where the inhabitants could
discuss their interests and have their social gatherings'.[16]

According to the 1971 census the population of Govanhill comprised 19,000 people living in 7,780 dwellings. Apart from
some small council schemes, built in the 1920s and 1930s, the
housing has changed little since the early 20th century. The
census indicated that 41% of the area's houses were without
exclusive use of hot water, bath and toilets, and local
authority reports have identified Govanhill as being one of
the most overcrowded and deprived areas in the West of Scotland. There is, however, a great attachment to the area.
Local surveys carried out during the 1970s consistently
identified, throughout the area, that most people wanted to
remain in Govanhill. The population structure is imbalanced,
partly because of the number of small housing units and the
lack of larger units for families. The area has more than
its fair share of elderly residents and a Crossroads survey
indicated that the elderly, especially those over seventy-
five, are more handicapped and disadvantaged than those in
other areas.[17]

Change and Decay

In such a large area there are, inevitably, physical and
social differences. Joan Shannon, a student who was brought
up in the area, gives a vivid account of Govanhill in the
early 1970s.[18]

> The area roughly divides into four, being cut East-
> West by Calder Street and North-South by Cathcart
> Road. The North-East sector comprises mainly four
> storey tenements built about seventy years ago. The
> houses are almost all rooms and kitchens with outside
> lavatories, usually a lavatory being shared by three
> families and no hot water. This area is deteriorating
> rather rapidly. This area includes the 'slum clear-
> ance' Corporation scheme. When I lived in the area
> families mainly from the slums in Gorbals were re-
> housed in this scheme. My memories of it are of a
> wild place, seething with weans and trouble. The
> kids from the slum clearance tended to be poor, un-
> kempt wee souls who solidly sat at the bottom of
> class throughout primary school. In a poor but res-
> pectable working-class area, they stood out. The
> North-West sector tends to be a better quality tene-
> ment, the houses having bathrooms. This area is the
> one which has shown the most evidence of the mining
> that went on in the area. This area also takes in
> Coplawhill, one of the A Category Corporation schemes.
> At one time you had to have your name on the housing
> list for twenty-five years before you had a chance
> of a house there. The South East area comprised
> mainly A Category Corporation housing, four in a
> block but with some good quality tenement housing.
> The South-West area is largely better quality tene-
> ment property. After the war, a large number of
> families were rehoused in the new schemes on the
> periphery of the city and the empty houses sold.
> Today the tenants of the tenements are a mixture of
> the old sitting tenants, owner-occupiers, and a
> recently increasing number renting furnished
> accommodation.

> Govanhill was, at one time, predominantly Protestant,
> but there are an increasing number of Catholic
> families; the older residents speak, not of Pakistani
> families filtering into the area, but of the increas-
> ing number of Catholics who are dubbed 'rough Irish'
> and blamed for the deterioration. That the area is
> deteriorating can be seen in pavements needing repair,

falling masonry and in the very poor condition of the
back courts. Some houses in the North-East area are
boarded up. On first arrival it gives the appearance
of being a thriving area mainly because Cathcart Road
is such an excellent shopping area. There are very
few empty shops, and everyone goes to Cathcart Road
for their shopping. Transport to the city is good,
but there are few recreational facilities. The three
cinemas, in which I spent a large lump of my childhood,
have all closed, and none even converted to a bingo
hall. The local professional football area went into
liquidation, and their ground sold for building. The
area is well off for churches, but has only two swing
parks, one of which is in the slum clearance and has
the dullest, dingiest collection of swings. It was
near where we lived, but none of us would go into that
territory. We risked crossing Cathcart Road to go to
the "wee swing park", which seemed more spacious, but
where ball games were and still are not allowed. In
this wee park, the old band-stand had been converted
into an "old man's hut". For about twenty years the
old men and women have campaigned for old women to be
allowed to use the old men's hut, but to date, for
reasons unknown they have been unsuccessful.

As children we played a lot of street games, but the
traffic today makes that impossible. We also played
in the backs and on the dykes but the backs are now
in poor condition with more often than not, drains
running. The dykes have mostly been knocked down as
so many of them were falling down. Children played
out in the backs from an early age and learned to be
sociable. Children of a wide age range played together, the big ones tolerating and looking after the
wee ones. We hung about and waited when the police
raided the bloke that ran a bookies in the close at
the bottom of the street. I couldn't see what the
kids today did for amusement. They seemed to hang
about at the close-mouth. None of the things we did
is available to them. I think I felt as sad about
this as I did about the general deterioration of the
area.

The official plan for Govanhill, drawn up in the 1960s, dec-
lared Govanhill an Outline Comprehensive Development Area
(OCDA). Approximately one third of the area, the northern
section, would be demolished between 1966 and 1980 to make
way for Council housing. Delays occurred and, by the early
1970s, Glasgow Corporation was reconsidering the outline plan,

and regarding housing improvement as a 'serious alternative
to clearance and redevelopment'.[19] Issues relating to house
improvement, rehousing and planning were to form the key
issues for the Crossroads community work interventions in
Govanhill during the 1970s.

GLASGOW - AN AREA OF NEED

How typical are Gorbals and Govanhill of the working-class
areas of Glasgow? Are they, as the historical reputation of
Gorbals might suggest, areas of exceptional need and social
priority? Research studies clearly indicate that the problems of Gorbals and Govanhill are not atypical; they are
shared by other Glasgow working-class communities and, in the
league tables of area deprivation which have been compiled
for the city, neither Gorbals nor Govanhill figure at the top
of the list. During the 1970s the scale and spatial distribution of deprivation in Glasgow was clearly documented in a
series of local authority reports. In 1972 the planning department of the then Glasgow Corporation produced a report,[20]
which analysed the spatial distribution of deprivation from
data derived from the 1966 Census. Using a measure of deprivation based on mainly social-physical factors - age structure,
unemployment, social grouping, retired persons, housing conditions, occupancy rates and household size - the report
concluded that the 'areas of need' in Glasgow, covered
approximately a third of the total area of the city (13,000
acres). A feature of this distribution was the inclusion of
council house estates as well as those inner city areas, like
Gorbals and Govanhill, which had been subject to redevelopment. In the mid 1970s the scale of deprivation was further
confirmed in a report produced by the newly created Strathclyde Regional Council.[21] Working on data from the 1971
Census and using a battery of criteria relating to social,
economic and physical factors, this report identified 1,014
ennumeration districts which were defined as being characterized by multiple deprivation. On the basis of this analysis
the Regional Council identified 'areas for priority treatment'
within the city. Fifty areas were classified as priorities
and their combined population was in excess of 480,000 - more
than half of the city's population! Only twenty-two of these
areas - including Govanhill, but excluding Gorbals - were
eventually included in the Region's programme of positive
discrimination for deprived areas.[22]

The relative deprivation of the Glasgow conurbation, when
compared with other parts of Britain, was reaffirmed by another report during the 1970s. In a national analysis of the
1971 census data, based on indicators relating to housing

facilities, overcrowding, employment and car ownership,
Holtermann concluded:

> The national picture is dominated by Scotland whose
> cities, particularly Clydeside, apparently contain
> areas of severe urban deprivation on a scale not
> matched in England and Wales.[23]

As these reports clearly demonstrate, Glasgow does not have
well defined pockets of deprivation which are located within
an otherwise prosperous and well housed city. All the city's
working-class communities are characterized, to varying degrees, by social and economic hardships. The scale of the
deprivation is striking to newcomers to the city.

> I've worked in Edinburgh and Manchester before, but
> the thing that really makes Glasgow stand out in my
> mind from these two other cities is the extent of the
> problem. The thing peculiar to Glasgow is the size
> of the problem, but I think you get blase about it.
> (Community worker)

The Industrial Base

Underpinning this deprivation is the economic structure of
Glasgow and Clydeside. The heavy engineering industries, the
traditional foundation of the region's economy, have been in
a state of contraction since the inter-war years. Decades
of foreign competition, erratic investment policies and a
lack of sustained technical innovation have eroded this industrial base. By the 1950s Clydeside was 'confronted with
creeping obsolescence on a massive scale'.[24] Between 1961
and 1971, the net employment in Glasgow fell by 78,000 jobs.
The loss of jobs was greatest in the manufacturing sector,
with the bulk of the loss being in the engineering industry.
As in the depression years of the 1920s and 1930s, rising unemployment and migration were the consequences of this decline
in employment opportunities. In the decade between 1961 and
1971, 190,000 Clydesiders left Scotland and 55% went overseas.[25]
Many of these migrants were young and economically active.
The contraction in the traditional industrial base has not
been compensated for by the emergence of new, vigorous,
alternative sources of production and employment. Indigenous,
Clydeside-based industry has failed to fill the gap. In the
decade between the late 1950s and the late 1960s, new job
creation in the region was mainly generated by externally
controlled firms; 33% of new jobs were created by firms which
were based elsewhere in Britain; 30% by overseas (mainly North
American) firms and only 37% by firms which were indigenous to

the region.[26]   Even the jobs created by the externally controlled enterprises were insufficient for the employment needs
of Glasgow, and, between 1958 and 1968, only 2,000 new jobs
were created in the city by incoming firms.

As the above figures suggest the control over decision-making
about the region's economy is increasingly in the hands of
external firms, many of which are part of multi-national comp-
anies based elsewhere in Britain or overseas.   By the early
1970s, over 50% of the region's total labour force were employed by non-Clydeside-based firms, and the figure was sub-
stantially higher for those large firms in the manufacturing
sector, which employed over 1,000 in their work force.[27]   Not
surprisingly, many commentators on the Scottish economy have
expressed serious concern about the satellite or branch line
nature of the region's industry and its vulnerability to
decision-making which is determined by commercial criteria,
undiluted by any historical, regional or national commitment
to the welfare of Clydeside.

City Management

The civic management of Glasgow has been the management of
deprivation.   In the absence of public control over market
forces the city managers, the senior officials and councillors,
are relatively powerless to directly shape and mould economic
developments.   They are faced with handling the social costs
of industrial decline without the resources and political
authority to halt this decline.   The response of successive
city administrations has been to adopt a vigorous and sustained policy of physical renewal, aimed at eradicating the
slums and modernizing the social and commercial infrastructure
of the city.   Comprehensive redevelopment, the building of
vast new Council estates, the creation of an inner city motorway network and the revamping of the City's shopping centre
are post war examples of policies which have had the dual intention of improving the quality of life for the citizens and
presenting to a sceptical outside world, especially to would-
be investors and industrial developers, a new forward-looking
image for the city.   However, as several observers have noted,
city managers cannot eradicate economic problems purely by
means of physical renewal or localized policies of positive
discrimination.[28]   If bread winners cannot obtain decent,
well-paid jobs, poor families remain poor even if they live
in modern council housing.   Investing extra social resources
in a handful of deprived districts, a policy which has been
pursued energetically by the Strathclyde Region, might improve
some local environments, but it will not, in the absence of
wider structural change, assist those poor people who live

elsewhere and may well only serve to redistribute public
money between the 'not so deprived' and the 'very deprived'
working-class communities. Also, the attraction of new capi-
tal investment from the private sector - a major plank in the
city's modernisation programme - will not be guaranteed by
providing improved communications, regional incentives and
the availability of cheap industrial sites. As Checkland
comments:

> The bitter lesson seems to be that the economy behaves
> largely according to its own rules: innovative and
> efficient management and a productive labour force
> have not been induced to any serious extent by infra-
> structure and regional incentives.[29]

These institutional limitations have been compounded by the
negative and largely unintentional consequences of some of
the city's physical renewal policies. Policies which were
intended to 'solve' problems have themselves created new problems. High rise flats have proved costly and have generated
additional social difficulties; some of the new Council
estates are now more deprived than the old tenement areas
which they replaced; the construction of the motorway network
has added to the environmental blight of the city centre and
has displaced many small factories and businesses. It is,
however, the management and allocation of the city's massive
council house stock which has generated the bitterest criticism and acrimony. In this case, an intentional policy of
allocating housing by the assessment of life style as well as
on the basis of social need - a policy which, as we noted
earlier, had its origins in the inter-war years - has created
a finely graded structure of tenant status groups and council
estates, which function to perpetuate and reinforce the
deprivations of many working-class families.

> The concentration of families 'at risk' into relatively
> small areas is occurring deliberately through the
> mechanism of the Corporation housing allocation policy.
> This concentration is not accompanied by any programme
> to alleviate the deprivation or to discriminate posi-
> tively in favour of these areas in the allocation of
> facilities and services.[30]

Some of the social and economic consequences of this long
established policy have been predictable. Estates labelled
as 'poor' have become stigmatised; mobility within the city's
housing system had been inhibited and even the job prospects
of some working people have been affected by the reputation
of their home area. The grading policy has also contributed

to the city's massive problem of 'hard to let' council housing.
A former leader of the Council, Richard Dynes, estimated in
1975 that, out of the city's council stock of 170,000 prop-
erties, some 70,000 were in areas where people 'are extremely
reluctant to go because of the poor environment'.[31]

Values

The development of this system of housing allocation did not
occur by accident. It has been a direct product of the values
which have informed the city's housing policies, especially
the concern to regulate and discipline the behaviour of those
sub-groups within the working-class who are felt to be anti-
social and potentially disruptive. Kay Carmichael has compared Glasgow's attitudes to 'people in need' with the poor
law philosophy of the 'undeserving' and the 'deserving' poor.[32]
Vincent Cable, a former Labour Party councillor, has also
commented on the apparent lack of concern for the city's
social casualties.

> Considering the city's political tradition, there is
> relatively little interest in the seriously deprived
> family. This shows itself only too clearly in the
> city's attitude to the problem of rent arrears cases,
> and problem families who are recycled in and out of
> slum tenements and the lowest amenity council schemes.[33]

The city's political traditions present an apparently paradoxical mixture of large scale programmes of public provision,
combined with responses to groups in need which are firmly
rooted in individualistic ideologies of welfare. Carmichael
suggests that the social backgrounds of the city's leaders
may help account for this situation. Self-made men and
working-class leaders, who have raised themselves out of
hardships, can be intolerant of people who fail to show similar personal initiative.

> There has in fact been very little difference in the
> philosophy of the Labour and Tory members of the Local
> Authority to those in need. Members of both parties
> tend to be self-made or self-supporting men and women.
> They have got on to the Town Council by having rather
> more drive and initiative than the average citizen,
> and this is the group with whom they identify. One
> might have expected the Labour Councillors to be more
> sympathetic than the Tories. With one or two notable
> exceptions, this has not proved to be the case.[34]

These factors may also underpin a paternalistic style of

political representation which emphasizes the ability of the councillor or MP to 'fix' problems for their constituents on an individual rather than a collective basis. The elected representative tends to act as a broker, arbitrator of need and entrepreneur for his constituents. His official status and powers of patronage is reinforced, especially in very safe Labour areas where the turnover of representatives is minimal, by an extensive network of personal contacts. This style of politics was described by a prominent Labour party member, from Gorbals and Govanhill, in the following terms:

> I believe in the kind of Tamany Hall business if you want things done - you speak to so and so to speak to so and so to manipulate situations rather than having open confrontations because it's my experience in life that you get things done better this way. It seemed to me anyway that the softly softly approach - the personal one - in the end is more effective, and I've always had it in my head that this is the way to influence people.

This approach can be effective in winning gains for individual constituents and in developing almost a type of social work advocacy and advice service, built around the elected representatives' 'surgery'. But, it can also function to undermine collective responses to problems and inhibit the development of participatory forms of organization and action. Collective responses to problems and calls for more participation in public affairs, whether they derive from within political parties or from community groups, can present a considerable threat to the 'Tamany Hall' style of politics. In Part Two we report on how this tension and the conflict it engendered was a characteristic of working-class politics in Gorbals and Govanhill.

CONCLUSION

The declining economic base of Glasgow, the history of public provision, and the values of the city's managers, are key elements in defining the framework for any form of community work intervention in the city. These forces also shape the limitations and potential for community work. There is the frustration of working locally on issues which are only really amenable to national solutions. There is also creative scope for helping to unleash capacities for self-organization and political expression amongst citizens who have been previously excluded from the public life of their city.

Chapter Three

CROSSROADS

THE GORBALS GROUP

The student units and their parent organization (Crossroads
Youth and Community Association), had their origins in the
pioneering work of The Gorbals Group.[1] The Gorbals Group
was formed in December, 1957, by five people, three of whom
were Ministers of the Church of Scotland. Inspired by the
worker-priest movement in France and experiences of the East
Harlem Church in New York,[2] the Group members came to live in
Gorbals with the intention of sharing in the problems of the
area and joining with local residents in attempting to seek
solutions. Their aim was:

> To establish in the Laurieston area of Gorbals a caring
> Christian presence which would assist where demand
> presented itself, in facing the problems of the area.[3]

Working from their own homes they made themselves available
to anyone and their primary commitment was to those members
of the local community who were labelled as 'socially
undesirable' by the authorities or, indeed, by their own
neighbours. In social work terms their approach was integrative and generic;

> We have always felt that it is important that social
> work in the area of casework, youth work, residential
> work, should always be complemented by social action,
> where possible, to change the situation in which
> problems arise.[4]

The early work of The Group was a 'family affair' in which
members became directly involved in service delivery in and

around their homes. They worked with small groups in a very
unstructured way, as this was regarded as the most effective
method of reaching those individuals and groups who were
outside of conventional organizations. They started informal
youth clubs in their houses after school; they allowed hard-
pressed mothers to 'park' their children for a day; their
open door policy resulted, more often than not, in someone
taking advantage of a 'bed for the night'. Direct action
was a central feature of The Group's work. There were no
local play facilities so Group members dug three sandpits in
the 'backs' and organized a junk playground on derelict ground.
They helped a group of women successfully resist the closure
of a public wash-house; they unsuccessfully petitioned with
their neighbours for traffic lights at a dangerous crossing
and they launched 'The Gorbals View', Scotland's first community newspaper.[5] The Group also fought against Rachmanism
in the area.

> In three houses, fifty-nine persons live; the lavatories
> have not worked for a year and have to be flushed with
> a bucket. Tenants cook either on their own spirit stove
> or on an open fire. The lighting was rigged up by the
> tenants and in one place repaired with a plastic head
> square. In houses where the light has failed the tenants
> have to do without it and are expected to pay their rents
> as usual.[6]

The action taken to challenge this situation included extensive advocacy work at Rent Tribunals and the Sheriff Court,
canvassing of politicians, the withholding of rent and the
use of the mass media. The local presence of Group members
facilitated speedy responses to crisis and other issues.
They were on the spot and available for assistance, twenty-
four hours a day. Also, without the continuity provided by
Group members, it might well have been impossible to build
and sustain neighbourhood organizations in a redevelopment
area which was losing population rapidly and was, both
physically and socially, falling apart at the seams. However,
it is also possible that this very availability, coupled with
the Group's policy of assuming leadership roles, may have
functioned to inhibit the growth of resident controlled
organizations in the Laurieston district. Local people
tended to rely on The Group members to express their
grievances.

> All we did was articulate certain things in the area -
> but we articulated them better than the average Gorbals
> punter. (Group member)

Despite the Group's innovatory history of self-help and direct
action the value which was placed upon community participation and local leadership tended to be subordinated to the
advocacy and activist roles of The Group members themselves.
This policy of leading from the front may also have been a
reflection of The Group's philosophy about the agencies and
forces which should provide the foundation for political
change. Group members tended to view long-term change as
being produced through established political structures,
especially the Labour Party, rather than through attempts to
build movements which directly involved the poor in extra-
parliamentary forms of political action. This philosophy of
attempting to influence established organizations involved
Group members in holding administrative office positions in
the local Ward Committees (Glasgow's forerunners of Community
Councils) and in the ward and constituency organization of
the Labour party. Initially, the Labour party involvement
did not extend to running for political office.

> Most people in the Party were careerists - our great
> strength was not putting in for political office -
> you have to toe the Party line once you're put
> forward. (Group member)

This policy was to be changed in the late 1960s and a founder
member of The Group, Geoff Shaw, was to later emerge as one
of Glasgow's most respected and influential Labour councillors.

CROSSROADS

The Group was never static. Like all organizations it altered
in response to outside pressure and changing membership.
Although most members remained for long periods of time, and
Geoff Shaw for his lifetime, there was a slow but continual
turnover of members. The Group's membership varied in size
from the original five to a maximum of fourteen. The middle
and late sixties saw a consolidation of many of the services
provided by The Group and a gradual withdrawal of Group
members from direct service to a 'planning and co-ordinating'
role. Originally, services were provided in homes and admini-
stered directly by discussion at Group meetings. The members'
homes had now become too small to accommodate everything.

> The sheer weight of administration made it desirable
> that these services should stand on their own feet
> and develop their own financial and administrative
> independence.[7]

Also, by the late 1960s, public funds and sponsorship were
slowly becoming more available for the type of community
based services which had been developed over a ten year period
by The Group. Some of the work promoted by The Group was now
becoming fashionable and legislation, such as the 1968 Social
Work (Scotland) Act, stressed the need for the 'promotion of
welfare' and defined a community work role for the newly
created local authority social work departments. Although
not using this terminology, Gorbals Group members had achieved
a very effective 'springboard approach' to service delivery.
They ran services themselves initially and then developed
satellite bodies to administer the activities or passed
responsibilities over to other organizations. The Group had
no constitution or office bearers, and could not directly
function, nor wished to, as an employing body. The day
nursery for non-working mothers who wanted to 'park' their
small children for one day per week was taken over by The
Save the Children Fund; the junk playground finally became
The Gorbals Adventure Playground; the odd jumble sale organized by a group of women ('the old hens') became a permanent
second-hand clothes shop - 'The Hen House'. In 1967 The Group
set up Crossroads to administer and employ two staff for its
youth work programme. The original Crossroads constitution
emphasized the priority of working with 'delinquent' children
and the executive committee was dominated by Group members
and volunteers, many of whom lived outside of the Gorbals,
who were associated with The Group. There were no public
meetings and no serious attempt was made to involve local
residents.

Crossroads became a useful umbrella organization for many of
the activities of The Gorbals Group. An Arts Centre, opened
in February 1969, provided pottery, art, library and folk-
singing, and also housed the playgroups which were once based
in the homes of Group members. In the same tenement, Crossroads House opened, providing short-stay accommodation for
young people who found themselves homeless. The executive
committee of Crossroads had acquired two members of staff
and some dilapidated buildings. Finance and the management
of buildings quickly became an obsession. For the first two
years Crossroads managed to find from trusts, and one very
generous donor, the £5,000 per year necessary to run their
programme and pay salaries. Glasgow Corporation contributed
only £200 in two years. By 1970, the need to fundraise 'in
a big way' was becoming urgent, because redevelopment was now
fairly far advanced in Gorbals and the Crossroads premises
were shortly due for demolition. The Gorbals Group and Crossroads were now planning for the 'new Gorbals', and their plans

were ambitious. They wanted a new youth and community centre
for the area, a permanent outdoor centre, and 'community
rooms' provided in the new high rise flats which were being
built at Stirlingfauld Place. The plan for the outdoor centre
never materialized but, on the local front, a 90% grant was
made available from Central and Local Government for the
youth and community centre ('The Playbarn') and Glasgow
Corporation agreed to the proposal to provide community
spaces under the Stirlingfauld flats.

THE STUDENT UNITS

As we noted in the introduction, the first Crossroads fieldwork Unit was established as the result of collaboration
between Glasgow University, the Social Work Services Group
(SWSG) and The Gorbals Group. The architect of the plan,
Donald Houston (Glasgow University), has noted the degree of
risk taking which was involved;

> A series of risks had to be taken about the viability
> of the scheme as proposed. At the beginning there was
> no framework available within which to locate the
> programme so that it might be developed on a controlled
> step by step basis. Three separate organizations had
> to come together to plan the setting-up of a fourth
> organization, which would be closely linked to all
> three and yet separate from each. The University
> had to recognize that eventually the student unit
> would take students from other teaching centres.
> The Gorbals Group had to recognize that eventually
> the Unit might develop activities which were different
> from those central to The Group's tradition, and the
> Social Work Services Group had to recognize that the
> unit would be providing services geared to meet the
> expectations of educational bodies and local community
> organizations.[8]

The Gorbals Group passed over administrative responsibilities
for the student Unit to Crossroads, and the first fieldwork
teacher was appointed in February 1971. After a six-month
settling-in period, the student Unit opened for business from
shop front premises in Crown Street, Gorbals. From the start
the staff sought to combine and integrate student training
with providing a local community work resource and this link
was symbolized, in the early days, by the fact that 'The
Gorbals View' newspaper used the student Unit premises as its
new administrative base. The first fieldwork Unit quickly
became locally known as the 'Gorbals View' shop, with the

paper's name boldly printed on its headboard and copies of
the paper displayed in the windows. Within eighteen months
the work generated by the first student Unit, both in terms
of student placements and local community work activities,
resulted in further developments. In 1973 Crossroads
negotiated successfully with the then Glasgow Corporation
Social Work Department for the appointment of a full-time
community worker, who was employed to back up the local
activities of the fieldwork teacher and students. This was
the first grant for community work, as opposed to youth work
activities, which Crossroads had received from the local
authority. In 1947 SWSG agreed to a request for the setting-
up of a second student Unit – a move which produced two new
full-time appointments (a fieldwork teacher and secretary)
and the funds for the setting-up of an additional office. By
this period the impact of redevelopment in Gorbals had forced
the first student Unit to vacate its original premises in
Crown Street and move to the nearby Govanhill area. This
change of location was of social as well as physical significance, as it extended the student Unit presence into a district which, despite its proximity to Gorbals, had rarely
figured in the previous activities of either Crossroads or
The Gorbals Group. The SWSG agreement to fund a second Unit
also coincided with the completion of the community rooms at
the Stirlingfauld flats in Gorbals. Crossroads decided to
locate the second Unit in one of the community rooms, a move
which retained a Crossroads community work presence in Gorbals
and dove-tailed, fortuitously, with the Association's long-
term plans for development work in the 'New Gorbals'.

By the mid 1970s Crossroads staff comprised two fieldwork
teachers, two secretaries, two youth workers and a community
worker. In addition, the full-time staff were complemented
by a regular intake of students who were expected to contribute directly to the local work of the Units. Within the
context of professional community work in Glasgow, Crossroads
had established itself as a major agency in the non-statutory
sector and, indeed, prior to the reorganization of local
government Crossroads actually employed more community work
staff than the City of Glasgow Corporation. This rapid
expansion was reinforced by developments on the youth work
side. In 1973 the Playbarn opened in Gorbals and, as noted
above, in 1974 the Community rooms opened at Stirlingfauld
Place, comprising five spaces which were under the management of Crossroads. This development prompted Crossroads to
seek additional resources for its youth work programme. In
1975 the Glasgow Corporation increased its grant and, a year
later, the Gulbenkian Foundation approved a grant of £4,000

to help with the equipment and running costs of the Stirlingfauld rooms. The Association now managed two student Unit
offices, which doubled up as local resource centres, ran a
large youth club and was responsible for the administration
of five small community rooms. The annual income, which
largely derived from central and local government grants, was
£35,000. - a far cry from the days when The Gorbals Group
financed, on a shoestring, their innovative youth and community projects.

MANAGEMENT

Crossroads had originally been established as an administration convenience for The Gorbals Group and its operation
depended, heavily, upon the close involvement and local
knowledge of Group members. Accountability to either outside
bodies or local residents was minimal and management affairs
were conducted on a personalized and very informal basis.
Bills were paid when someone remembered. Staff salary cheques
arrived at unpredictable intervals. Reports were rarely
written on time. No systematic records were kept or filed.
This cavalier disregard for administrative convention was
perhaps acceptable when Crossroads was operating on a modest
budget, but it began to generate stresses and strains when
the Association expanded its commitments in the 1970s. Also,
the appropriateness of the Crossroads structure for handling
the enlarged scale of work was further complicated by the
decline of The Gorbals Group as an active social force and
presence in the local area. By the early 1970s a number of
key Group members had moved away from Gorbals; The Group's
community work activities were being taken over by the student
Unit staff and even Geoff Shaw, who still lived in the heart
of the Gorbals redevelopment area, was finding that his political commitments were leaving less time for his role as the
lynchpin in both The Group and Crossroads.

Crossroads staff, especially those attached to the student
Units, began to press for the creation of a 'new Crossroads',
which would be more directly accountable to local residents
and would be more efficient in its administrative and financial
structure. In 1974 Geoff Shaw stepped down as Secretary of
Crossroads, due to competing work pressures. He was replaced
by Andrew Robertson, a lawyer with considerable experience of
voluntary work in Gorbals and elsewhere in Glasgow, who agreed
to take over the reins on the understanding that Crossroads
was committed to moving, as quickly as possible, to a locally-
based management structure. The new secretary defined his
role as guiding Crossroads through a transition period, and

within a year the Association's administrative and financial
structure had been successfully reformed. However, progress
in terms of local involvement in management was much slower.
The annual report for 1974 and 1975 noted:

> During the year the General Council have been concerned
> that the increase in level of activities has not been
> matched by an increased participation in management by
> people using the Crossroads facilities. We have been
> concerned that too many decisions have been made by too
> few people. We consider it essential to broaden the
> participation at all levels of the Association's
> management.

In Gorbals, the traditional stronghold of Crossroads, the
move towards local management was closely linked with the
running of the various services for which the Association was
responsible. In 1975, Crossroads established two local subcommittees to administer the Playbarn and the Community rooms
at Stirlingfauld Place. Involvement in these sub-committees
encouraged some residents to move into the Association's
Council of management and, in this manner, local participation in the Gorbals based activities began to gradually
develop. Also, in Gorbals, pressure from local residents
resulted in a significant change in the Crossroads constitution. The emphasis upon working with 'delinquent or potentially delinquent' children was dropped and was replaced by a
commitment to work for the welfare of all adults and children
in the area. This change reflected a local criticism that
Crossroads was only concerned with delinquent youngsters and,
also, recognized the fact that the Association's community
work activities in the area were mainly adult rather than
children based.

The management question was more complex and controversial in
Govanhill. Neither Crossroads nor The Gorbals Group had any
historical roots in the area; local residents viewed Crossroads as an exclusively Gorbals based organization and the
student unit staff in the area had increasingly defined themselves as a Govanhill organization, which had only formal
administrative links with Crossroads. In June 1976, the
Govanhill Unit organized a public meeting, which was attended
by over fifty residents, at which the staff outlined the
origins, funding and aims of the student Unit and argued
the case for a more democratic and locally-based management
structure. The staff did not propose a new management blue-
print and possible reforms were delayed for further public
discussion and consultation. But then events, in the shape

of a serious staff dispute in Govanhill, dramatically took
over and further highlighted the needs for the staff and
Crossroads to examine the thorny question of accountability.

Staff Dispute

In summer 1976 the fulltime secretary of the Govanhill Unit
decided to stand for the leadership position of Secretary with
a local community organization, in competition with a local
resident and against the wishes of other Crossroads staff.
After numerous discussions the staff reached an impasse.
Eight members of staff disagreed with the Secretary's decision.
The Govanhill organization publicly insisted that they had
the right to select their own Secretary, whether or not she
was employed by Crossroads. The Govanhill secretary refused
to change her position and the rest of the Govanhill staff
decided to withdraw from student work until a solution was
found. The decision to stop taking students on placements
was made because 'the present staff situation within the
Govanhill Unit makes it an unsuitable setting for student
placements'. (Staff paper) The Management Council of Crossroads, which was comprised of mainly Gorbals-based representatives, was faced with a dispute which was causing considerable
local controversy in Govanhill and which in their view posed
a direct threat to the future of the Govanhill Unit's funding.
They decided to dismiss the Govanhill Unit secretary – the
first occasion in the history of the Association that a member
of staff had been dismissed.

The sacking sparked off a storm of protest from the local
organization and it also provoked a critical reaction from
other community groups in Govanhill. A campaign to reinstate
the secretary was launched and several local groups decided
to boycott the work of the Govanhill Unit. The campaign was
abrasive, well publicized, but short-lived. It failed to win
the support of a majority of the community organizations in
Govanhill or to mobilize any significant support amongst the
local groups and Crossroad management members in Gorbals.
Although the local controversy was short-lived the dismissal
case continued through an industrial tribunal, which upheld
the Crossroads decision, and then proceeded to the Court of
Session which reaffirmed the industrial tribunal's decision.
The legal debate over the dismissal eventually came to a halt,
in 1978, when the ex-Govanhill secretary was refused the right
to appeal to the House of Lords. The experience was traumatic
and uncomfortable, but it was far from novel:

An interesting thing about neighbourhood groups – you

organize them as your constituency, hoping they will
give you the backing and support you need to conduct
your programme or push for reforms. But if you are
successful, if you give them their head, and help them
become really independent, they take a life of their
own. And they begin to put pressure on you just like
everyone else - even more so because you are the most
visible and easily accessible.[9]

The Govanhill dispute seriously damaged, for a time, the
credibility of Crossroads community work in the local area.
Although working relations with some of the community groups
who had opposed the dismissal were eventually re-established,
a number of local activists in Govanhill withdrew, on a
permanent basis, from any future contact with Crossroads.
Neighbourhood based community work invariably involves the
development of close personal as well as working relations
and, when serious disputes occur, friendships as well as work
ties can be shattered.

Staff Accountability

The Govanhill dispute highlighted a complex set of issues and
questions about management policy and staff accountability.
Did the staff, in both areas, exercise too much internal control over their work? Was it a basic community work principle
that staff should not accept permanent leadership positions
in local groups? And if so, should that principle be regulated
by staff or should it also be enforced by management? In the
wake of the dispute Crossroads embarked on a number of reforms
which focused on these issues. The management assumed a more
formal responsibility for regulating the staff's activities.

Crossroads has identified a growing awareness of the
responsibilities which their freedom at work in the
community must demand if the work is to retain the
necessary coherence, standard and discipline for not
only the community which it serves but also the students
which it supervises. If the Unit is to retain its
independent effectiveness and integrity it must not
be seen as in any way taking over responsibilities
in the community with particular reference to position
of leadership which would otherwise be filled by members
of the community.[10]

A new staff contract included a clause which gave the management powers to limit and control the activities of staff within
the local areas;

It is an essential part of employment with the
Association that staff members have a full commitment
to the Association's professional activities. In the
event of a staff member wishing to take up any occupation or appointment, whether paid or unpaid with
any other group or employer within the geographical
areas of the Association's commitment, he must receive
prior permission from the Association.[11]

Also, following lengthy discussion, the overall management
structure of Crossroads was reformed. On the pattern already
established in Gorbals, it was decided that the Govanhill
Unit should have a management committee which was made up of
representatives of local organizations who used the Unit and
a few individual local members, councillors and officials.
This subcommittee would be responsible for the day to day
running of the Unit. The Crossroads management structure now
comprised a Council of Management with three subcommittees
responsible for the running of the Govanhill Unit, the Stirlingfauld Place Community Rooms and the Playbarn youth club.
The Council of Management was comprised of representatives
from these subcommittees, representatives of local organizations who were affiliated to Crossroads, and individuals who
had an involvement with the Association's work but did not
represent an interest group. This new structure was designed
to increase local control over Crossroads. A number of these
reforms, such as the move towards subcommittees with managerial
functions, had been in the pipeline for some time. Other
changes, particularly those relating to the position of the
staff, had been prompted by the Govanhill dispute. The reformed structure was implemented in 1977. A local tenants
leader took over as the Association's Secretary and only two
members of the reconstituted Management Council were not
residents from Gorbals and Govanhill. The 'new' Crossroads
had finally been born. The birth had been painful.

Chapter Four

COMMUNITY WORK AND TRAINING

THE CONTEXT

From the early 1970s the community work activities of Crossroads
were promoted by the student Units. Both Units shared a similar
philosophy and work style and both were committed to integrating the role of student training with providing community
work support for local groups. In the case of the Govanhill
Unit this integration was symbolized by the association of the
Unit with the 'View' newspaper, an identification which had
been carried over from the Unit's early days in Crown Street.
In the case of the Gorbals Unit, which was situated in the
Stirlingfauld flats, the link between student training and
local work was expressed in the name which the Unit adopted
when it first opened in Autumn 1974 - the Unit was called the
'Laurieston Information Centre'. The Crossroads staff were
not free agents, but neither were they puppets controlled by
forces over which they were powerless to exercise any influence.
The pattern and style of their community work was shaped by
the interplay of several factors, all of which combined to
define the context and boundaries within which the staff
operated. These factors included the social and political
setting of Glasgow and the local areas (see Chapter 2); the
history and structure of Crossroads (see Chapter 3); the values
and community work approach of the staff (see below) and the
expectations of the sponsors of the fieldwork Units.

It is useful to distinguish between those forces which can
exert influence and those which have the power to demand com-
pliance. The support of residents is essential to successful
community work, but the support of the sponsor is a pre-
requisite for practice if the community worker is to remain in
his or her job. Few full-time community workers continue to

operate without financial reward. The Crossroads staff were
fortunate in the early days because the sponsoring organizations chose not to use their power to limit the activities of
the workers, but allowed practice to be defined by the values
of the fieldwork teacher and the local residents. As Donald
Houston noted;

> The meaning of 'community work' had to be left as
> widely defined as possible. The primary focus of
> the work undertaken has been determined by community
> demand, students' interests and the values of the
> fieldwork teacher.[1]

The major funder of the Crossroads community work programme
was the Scottish Social Work Services Group. They paid the
salaries of the two fieldwork teaching posts, the salaries of
two secretaries and also financed the equipment and running
costs of the two fieldwork offices. By the middle of the
1970s the SWSG contributed £20,000 towards the Association's
total income of £35,000. In return for this investment the
SWSG defined a basic set of mainly educational conditions about
the operation of the fieldwork Units. These related to the
number of 'student days' which should be completed each year
(600) and the stricture that the Units should only take students
from officially approved social work courses which awarded a
CQSW qualification. In practice, a blind eye was turned to the
Units taking students from non-social work courses, providing
that this additional commitment did not interfere with achieving
the target of 600 student days. Also, by convention rather than
written instruction, it was expected that the fieldwork teachers
would provide SWSG with a brief annual review of their student
work and keep them informed of any major changes in the organization of the units. SWSG were represented on the interviewing committee for fieldwork teaching staff and they retained
the power of veto over appointments. However, SWSG declined
to be represented on the Crossroads management council and the
Association was left to define its own priorities for community
work practice. For a number of years, the civil servants
adopted a liberal and benevolent attitude towards the Crossroads
units. This relaxed, conflict-free start was also politically
significant, because it allowed the Units the time and opportunity to establish a strong local base and a network of wider
support before having to handle a major sponsorship dispute,
such as the one which occurred between 1977 and 1978 after the
SWSG objected to the Crossroads support for 'militant' forms of
community action (see Chapter 9).

Crossroads was also fortunate in having significant areas of

agreement between staff, and, with the exception of the Govanhill dispute (see Chapter 3), the staff worked in harmony as
a team. This not only facilitated a consistent pattern of
community work practice, but also encouraged 'risk-taking'
because staff knew they could depend upon the support of their
colleagues. It also prevented the in-fighting which has
destroyed some community work projects.

> I wouldn't underestimate the support that comes from
> having eight staff. We may not always agree but it
> gives you a lot of support and stability; there's a
> lot of cooperation and a certain amount of like-
> mindedness. It's important politically too.
> (Staff member)

The framework of references is not fixed and the contextual
components can change over a period of time. During the years
covered by this study the Crossroads management structure
changed and local residents moved from a position of informal
influence to exercising an increasing degree of control over
the staff. The relationship with the major sponsor, the SWSG,
changed from one based on consensus to one based on conflict
and even the political control of the funding of the Units
changed in 1979, with the election of a Conservative government.
One observer has defined a community worker as a 'political
entrepreneur'[2] and it is a wise community worker who is aware
of the influences upon him and avoids antagonizing too many of
them simultaneously. Community workers have tended to dwell
upon the restrictions placed on them, by the contexts in which
they work, without considering the opposite side of the coin -
the opportunities which the employment setting may give them
and the support they can expect from interested parties. One
of the skills of community work is to follow other people's
expectations whenever it is possible. There are enough
situations of conflict without creating them unnecessarily!

> If we are going to get into sponsorship conflicts,
> let's make sure it's over a major issue of principle
> and not some minor administrative hassle. (Staff member)

APPROACH TO COMMUNITY WORK

The values and assumptions which informed the staff approach
to community work were made explicit at a public meeting held
in Govanhill in 1976.

> To explain what we are trying to do in the area we must
> point out two assumptions which inform our work. There

has to be a re-distribution of power and resources in
Society and a wide number of people are going to have
to demand these changes. For this reason, we support
local organizations and start new ones where a number
of people face the same problem, and organize to provide
facilities for the area. We also help these groups then
negotiate for money in order to achieve independence. A
lot of working class people in areas like Govanhill have
never had a chance to develop their potential. Working
class people have been told so often that they cannot
do things, that they begin to believe this. For this
reason, we help support local leaders. We do not see
us "Leading the revolution" whether this means trying
to over-throw society or whether this means demanding
a new nursery school. Working class people have to do
these things for themselves and make their own decisions.
They need the experience of power. (Staff member)

As Holman notes, the mention of 'power' and 'powerlessness'
gives an indication of the structural explanation of inequality
which underpins this approach.

Deprivation is not a consequence of the malfunctioning
of a few inadequates, not the grit in an otherwise
satisfactory machine, but inherent in the very nature
of society. The poor, or deprived, live in conditions
of deprivation because they lack the power to change
their situation. It is also assumed that changes of
the necessary magnitude will never be altruistically
conceded, but will only come as the poor themselves
can influence the system through collective power.[3]

It was consistent with this structural view of inequality that
the Crossroads staff favoured the community action approach to
community work;

Community action may denote a particular approach to
organizing local groups and welfare publics, an approach
in which the political impotence or powerlessness of
these groups is defined as a central problem and
strategies employed which seek to mobilize them for
the representation and promotion of their collective
interests...The central focus upon 'organizing for
power' and political definitions of problems predisposes community action to use conflict as a
strategy for achieving change.[4]

While the emphasis on the purposive use of conflict has been

frequently singled out as the hallmark of the community action
approach it is important to stress that organized attempts to
extend power to the powerless can, and do, involve the deploy-
ment of a wide range of activities, strategies and tactics. A
community action approach embraces not only collective
grievance-centred action which may involve confrontation with
established power structures (as, for example, in the case of
the dampness campaign described in Chapter 6) but can also involve working to establish community services which are under
the control and management of local residents rather than outside bodies. Crossroads staff pursued this goal with their own
employing body as well as with self help projects in Gorbals
and Govanhill. Organizing people and organizing services are
not incompatible bedfellows within a community action approach,
providing that in both types of activities the decision-making
about policies is firmly rooted in locally determined priorities
and is not merely a reflection of agency policies or the
professional worker's values and views.

The staff rejected social pathology and cultural explanations
of inequality. The basic community work goal was structural
change. If the poor in Glasgow were to improve their lot, they
would need to organize themselves. But within this framework
the staff also accepted the need for personal as well as
structural change.

> I suppose I see myself as having two sorts of objectives
> in community work - the structural change in society, and
> secondly, the educational side to enable any kind of change
> to come about. A change at political level isn't just
> what's needed - folk have got to learn the skills and
> opportunities to manage what they're given, or what they
> take or ask for, however it happens. (Staff member)

Although some staff put more emphasis on structural change and
others on personal change, the experience of community work in
Glasgow tended to bring the two sides closer together.

> Previously I tended to think more of structures and
> analysis than process but because of my Gorbals
> experience, I pay more attention to the process of
> community work and to the quality of the relationship
> you develop with local people. (Staff member)

> I'm basically a relationship person - I'm much more
> tuned into relationships than I am into structures, but
> community work in Glasgow has taught me how to face up
> to conflict - the realization that conflict won't go away

and therefore how to deal with it - more awareness,
not just at an emotional level. (Staff member)

For the staff the link between personal and structural change
was the local organization and the development of a politically
conscious local leadership. The workers' value-perspective
influenced the basis of the relationship with local residents.
One staff member pinpoints the question of authority and power.

> The work here gives students an entirely different
> experience with the client group. Most students have
> had some experience of case work when they come to the
> Unit, but the work with, for example, a tenants'
> association is entirely different from the usual one
> to one experience. The tenants' association is in a
> position of relative power compared to the individual
> in the casework situation.

Although staff struggle to describe their experiences by contrasting community work with social work, this is not, we would
suggest, the basic distinction. Conservative and paternalistic
relations between professional workers and client groups can
occur in community work, as frequently as they do in other
social work settings. It is the value perspective which the
worker holds on the causation of problems, irrespective of
whether they are employed as a community worker, fieldwork
social worker or a residential worker, which influences whether
a paternalistic or a more equal relationship is likely to be
established with client groups. As Holman argues, the structural perspective on poverty potentially creates the foundation
for establishing a more equal relationship than does the social
pathology perspective.

> In working with those whose problems stem from their
> socially depriving conditions, social workers can avoid
> the temptation to treat them in such a fashion that
> poverty is reinforced. This occurs when clients are
> cast into a therapeutic relationship, implying that
> their difficulties spring from personal or moral defects
> which the skilled worker will remedy. Appropriate as this
> approach may be to some clients, it does not help the
> poor. A more helpful stance entails a greater degree
> of equality between social worker and client. Of course,
> the former will still possess skills, powers and agency
> responsibilities not shared by the latter. The greater
> equality would issue from social worker and client
> perceiving that they are both attempting to counter
> external forces. In this relationship the client does

not have to see himself as an inferior person who has to
be treated, who is to blame, who can only take but cannot
contribute. Instead, he would see the possibilities of
working with others against those forces which maintain
poverty.[5]

A staff member commented that 'the greatest strength of the unit
is offering an alternative style of thinking'. This alternative
thinking, based upon a structural view of inequality, informed
practice and defined the relationship with local residents.
This relationship was an attempt, in Friere's terms, at creating
'dialogue'.[6] However, the staff were far from explicit about
the political agency through which their perspectives on community work could be developed and transformed into a national
movement for change.

Politics

As several writers have indicated, the community action model,
with its rhetoric of 'power to the people', is open to interpretation from several conflicting political perspectives.
These perspectives range from the 'community politics' of the
Young Liberals, the populism of a Saul Alinsky, the libertarian
anarchist tradition and the more orthodox socialist tradition
of the Labour Left and the Communist Party, which view community
action as a part, often a very marginal part, of the organized
Labour Movement. When seeking to relate these broad ideological
debates to Crossroads it is tempting to locate and define the
staff's approach within the libertarian tradition which, as
J. Smith[7] has noted, places a central emphasis upon the value
of self-determination and self-organization. The problem with
this type of political identification and pigeon holding is
that it assumes a high degree of ideological coherence, and the
existence of a collective philosophy which has been worked out
in considerable detail. Although there was a certain political
like-mindedness, the Crossroads staff, in common we suspect with
many community work teams, lacked such a coherent and clearly
formulated ideological stance. The libertarian influence co-
existed with ideas and activities which are more frequently
associated, in the literature, with the Labour Left-Communist
Party traditions. The staff's almost obsessive concern about
organization building, working to strengthen the internal unity
of local groups and forging links with trade unions was consistent with this perspective. However, the staff tended to
be suspicious of the 'vanguard' theory of the revolutionary
elite and were critical of what they considered to be the paternalism of some Marxist approaches to community work. Friere's
insistence on the need for the 'reflective participation' of
the oppressed struck a sympathetic cord.

Many leaders deny pedagogical action in the liberating
process and they use propaganda to convince: transformation for the oppressed rather than with them. It is
my belief that only the latter type of transformation
is valid. Attempting to liberate the oppressed without
their reflective participation in the act of liberation
is to treat them as objects and transform them into
masses which can be manipulated.[8]

Politically the staff did not articulate a collective and consistent philosophy. Indeed, some staff would have denied that
they had any 'politics' and maintained a sturdy individualism
which was cynical of any attempt to politically organize local
residents. All party politics, whether left, right or centre,
were a 'con'. As often as not it was an emotional commitment
to the local work, as much as any intellectual analysis, which
formed the common ground for the staff. A shared empathy with
the vicissitudes of life in Gorbals and Govanhill and a dislike
of paternalistic 'Daddy knows best' solutions forged links which
transcended individual differences in political views and ideological perspectives.

Implications for Community Work

The staff's ideas about community work predisposed them to give
a high priority to issue centred action and to service development which was based on local management. Their commitment to
community self-organization also resulted in a partisan identification with the local people - viewing the world through the
client's eyes and not those of the authorities. This partisan
identification imposed boundaries on the tasks which staff were
prepared to perform and there was a marked reluctance to assume
the roles of 'broker', 'linkman' and 'intermediary' between
outside agencies and local groups. Managerial and social planning models of community work were viewed with suspicion and
deep mistrust. Community development models offered interesting
insights into techniques and methodology, but were suspect in
terms of the neutrality of the 'enabler' role and bankrupt in
terms of guidance on how to respond to crisis issues. Any power
structure, public or private, which disturbed local people was
fair game for attack and this included the dominant political
force in Glasgow - the Labour Party.

STUDENT TRAINING

Between 1971 and 1978 one hundred students completed fieldwork
placements with the Crossroads Units. The average length of
the placement varied between three months on a block basis and

four months on a concurrent basis. The longest placement period
was a six months block and the shortest was a two months block,
which was the minimum period for which the units would accept
students. The majority of the students were drawn from social
work courses in Scotland, with the major intake being from
Glasgow University, Moray House College of Education and Edinburgh University. Occasional students were also drawn from
universities and polytechnics south of the border and, on two
occasions, studens came on placement from social work courses
in Sweden. A number of youth and community work students, from
courses at Moray House and Jordanhill College of Education, also
completed placements with the Units.

The Crossroads Units had certain distinctive and atypical features when compared with some of the other community work
training units which have been established by the SWSG and the
DHSS over the last decade. Being located in a locally based
and locally managed voluntary organization - as compared with,
for instance, being located within a town or a city wide agency
like a Council of Voluntary Service - resulted in the Crossroads
placements being focused almost exclusively on neighbourhood
work with self-help or interest groups within the Gorbals and
Govanhill areas. It was rare for a student placement to involve
working on a city wide project or for students to become engaged
in the managerial or social planning aspects of community work.
The Units never pretended to offer 'across the board' placement
opportunities. The focus was primarily on neighbourhood work
and the orientation of this work reflected the community action
approach. Also, the fieldwork teachers directly supervised all
placements and did not engage in shared supervision and shared
placements with the staff of other voluntary and statutory
agencies. The fieldwork staff never acted as co-ordinators and
brokers for placements which were organized across a range of
professional agencies and workers. This focus on direct supervision reflected the neighbourhood basis of the Crossroads work,
the absence of other full-time community workers in the local
areas and was also influenced by the fact that the teaching
staff were heavily engaged in direct community work tasks, as
well as acting as fieldwork teachers. In return, other Crossroads staff undertook many 'educational' responsibilities. The
fieldwork teaching staff divided their time between student work
and working with local groups and it was not unusual for students to be placed with local groups whose main link with the
fieldwork unit was through the community work role of the fieldwork teacher. Thus, on many occasions, staff and students
worked jointly together on the same local initiatives. Finally,
the local management structure of Crossroads and the use of the
fieldwork office as a local 'resource centre' exposed students
to considerable face to face contact with the residents of

of Gorbals and Govanhill. Students did not have to make visits
to meet 'the people'. They shared the same office with residents who were asking for advice, using the duplicator or competing with the students for the use of the same telephone.
The physical separation from clients and local groups, which
social work students sometimes complain about when on fieldwork
placements, was replaced, in the case of the units, by close
contact and regular encounters. Getting peace and time to
write, read and think was the major problem。

Aims of Placements

The fieldwork teachers identified two related objectives for
placements.[9] Firstly, community work placements provided social
work students with a basic introduction to how particular community work agencies operated and the types and range of issues,
problems and controversies which could influence the activities
of full-time workers and local residents. Here the educational
emphasis was not on the direct acquisition of practice skills,
but on the student gaining a knowledge of the mechanics and
functions of community work and acquiring insights which could
be of value in future work in a variety of social work settings。
Students could develop ideas about how local authority social
workers could link up more effectively with self-help groups
and gain practical insights into just how long-term and time-
consuming was the commitment required for the development of
local initiatives. The problems on which local community organizations were active could, at times, provide students with
first hand insights into wider political and social policy
issues: e.g. students with the Units were invariably in contact with, at some stage of their placement, the complex and
often bitter political debates about housing in the city.
Observational placements which provides students with an over-
view of an agency and some of its activities could be particularly useful for students, like many who worked with the Crossroads units, who had little or no previous experience of working
with community groups and community work agencies. Whether
this observational activity was, at some stage in the placement,
linked with more practice-centred tasks depended mainly upon
the length of the placement.

Secondly, fieldwork placements created opportunities for the
teaching of practice skills in community work. The move from
observational learning into the direct teaching of practice
skills took staff into a more problematic and potentially more
controversial area of fieldwork training。 When staff talked
about practice skills in community work, they were essentially
concerned with the basic ingredients of 'doing' community work;
the arts, techniques, information and insights community workers

workers needed, and how they organized and applied this knowledge and experience in action situations. How educationalists
conceptualize and define practice skills will be influenced by
a variety of factors, such as the value assumptions they hold
about the nature and function of community work, the work
experiences they have had in different organizational and social
settings and the perspectives they have on the relationship
between community work and other forms of planned interventions
(including casework).

Skills

It was over questions like the defining of practice skills in
community work that the vagueness and confusion about community
work which exists on many social work courses became very
apparent. The Crossroads staff rarely received from social
work or youth work courses a well-defined set of guidelines
for the teaching of practice skills which were geared specifically to community work placements. Normally they were based
on models derived from casework or youthwork experiences. While
some of the experiences and skills which are considered important in casework are certainly relevant to community work placements, particularly in the development of 'engagement skills',
it is very questionable whether conventional models of casework
skills can be projected, in a wholesale fashion, into the arena
of community work education. One obvious gap, which a number
of community workers have commented upon,[10] is the lack of
emphasis which is given to organizational, planning and political activities. Because of dissatisfaction with models which
conceptualized community work as casework multiplied by 'x',
the Crossroads staff attempted to identify a range of skills
which were more appropriate and relevant to community work.
These skills were defined under six related headings:-[11]

  Engagement skills: e.g. establishing working relations with
staff, local residents and community leaders; being able to
function in unstructured and sometimes chaotic situations; use
of self and self-awareness in action situations.

  Organizational skills: e.g. developing a grasp of the
mechanics and dilemmas of building organizations; work with
committees and organizing public events.

  Planning and policy skills: e.g. analysis of issues and
problems; ability to generalize from the specific; evaluation
of work completed.

  Action skills: e.g. ability to work towards specific

objectives; ability to make decisions in situations where all
the relevant information is never available; 'plotting out'
strategic and tactical options and their possible implications
for action initiatives.

Communication skills: e.g. communicating with others by
written and spoken word; ability to adjust style and manner of
communication according to different situational contexts.

Political skills; e.g. ability to view local initiatives
within a broader socio-economic framework of reference; a
knowledge of the sociology of political decision-making and a
grasp of different varieties of political ideologies and their
implications for change-centred action; ability to work within
a political framework.

These skills could obviously be used and applied in a variety
of community work settings. A key question arises over the
weighting which is given to the possible range and combination
of tasks which can be included under any of these headings.
For instance, under 'engagement' and 'organizational' skills,
the staff did not emphasize, in contrast to many community work
educationalists, the ability to perform mediator and broker
tasks between community groups and local or central government
departments. This reflected the view that community workers
should encourage the development of local organizations and
leadership and not act as 'go betweens'. No student or community
worker is ever likely to be of equal competence and ability in
all these skills. Thus, when it comes to passing judgement on
students - as, for instance, in the final evaluation and assessment of a fieldwork placement - the fieldwork teacher would,
almost inevitably, use a ranking order of practice skills.
Because of a bias towards community action the Crossroads staff
tended to place a priority on the development of organizing
skills and, in the words of C.W. Mills, the ability to relate
'personal troubles to public issues'.[12]

PART TWO

CASE STUDIES

Chapter Five

INTRODUCTION TO CASE STUDIES

Between 1971 and 1978 the Crossroads units were involved in
supporting a wide range of self-help, service provision and
issue centred activities. The Gorbals Unit worked directly
with nine different tenants' groups and housing campaigns; was
active in organizing opposition to new highway plans for the
area; supported the setting-up of a locally run playgroup,
pensioners' club and an annual summer playscheme; organized a
daily information service and a weekly welfare rights advice
service; helped to initiate a Gorbals wide survey of the chronically sick and disabled, and supported the activities of the
Playbarn youth club. The Govanhill Unit worked directly with
seven tenants' associations and housing campaigns; organized
opposition to expressway plans for the area and assisted a
local working party which considered future plans for Govanhill;
supported the formation of a locally run Housing Association
which modernized tenement flats and improved back courts;
carried out a survey of the chronically sick and disabled and
organized a daily information centre and a weekly legal advice
service. The Unit also supported self-help schemes. These
included two playgroups, summer playschemes, a locally run
youth and community centre and a Day Centre for pensions which
also inaugurated a street warden service. Jointly, the two
units provided administrative back-up for the 'View' community
newspaper and collaborated on city-wide community work, especially in relation to redevelopment and dampness issues.

Within the context of four case studies it is impossible to
accurately reflect all the types and varieties of community
work which were supported over a seven year period. The service development work has been omitted and readers will have to
refer to other publications for information on these activities.[1] Issue-centred collective action - organizing around

housing and planning problems - figures prominently in three
of the studies. The final case study comments on the politics
of sponsorship. The studies cover interventions which formed
dominant, recurring currents in the work of the units, and
reflect the mixture of success and failure, naive blundering
and competent organizing, depression and elation which is
typical of community work practice.

A FRAMEWORK OF REFERENCE

The dominant theme in the case studies is that of local community groups, supported by Crossroads, organizing to promote
or defend their collective interests. The key relationship,
which shaped the organizational and action process, was that
between the local community organizations and the external
organization which formed the target for their demands, campaigns and representation. Invariably, these external targets
comprised power groupings - councillors, MPs, local government
officials, civil servants - who were located within either
central or local government. The interaction between the community organizations and these formal power groupings exercised
a considerable influence over the timetable, process and content of the local community work. Also, the way in which the
'issues at stake' in these relationships were defined by the
parties involved shaped the selection of tactics and strategies
which were adopted by the community organizations. In attempting to understand and analyse the organizational process of
community work in Gorbals and Govanhill, we have singled out
this community group-formal power structure relationship for
particular attention. Drawing on work by Specht and Warren[2]
we have attempted to relate the case study material to a typology which indicates, in ideal type terms, the link between
local groups and external power structures. The typology
identifies four distinctive relationships.

A Collaborative Relationship

In this relationship the local group and the external power
structure are in a broad consensus over the 'issue at stake'.
Neither party in the relationship is afraid of losing face,
having its position undermined or being exposed to policies
which are detrimental to their collective interest. The strategies and tactics which are adopted by the local organization
are likely to be aimed at 'ironing out' minor difficulties or
disagreements, speeding up the timetable for the implementation
of agreed policies and strengthening the consensus through
undertaking joint initiatives. Discussion, getting the facts
straight and 'winning friends and influencing people' are the

preferred activities. The main community work role is that of
the 'developer'.

A Bargaining Relationship

In this relationship disagreement over the issues at stake does
exist, but the distance between the parties is sufficiently
narrow to offer the possibility of a solution being achieved
through compromise and negotiation. The interaction between
the local organization and the power structure occurs within
the framework of pressure group politics, and both parties ad-
here to the 'rules of the game'. They use established channels
for making representation and they do not engage in rule breaking, with regard to either the law or the violation of social
norms. Campaign strategies are the order of the day for the
community organization; lobbying, the use of the mass media,
petitions, delegations and demonstration projects. The aim is
to persuade the power structure to revise its position and
policy. The community work role can be that of the 'enabler'
or the 'advocate', although, as Barr[3] points out, different
values may underpin these roles.

Conflict Relationship

In this relationship a clearly defined clash of interests occurs
and the respective definitions of the issue are sharply polarized. Working through normal pressure group channels is perceived, by one or both parties, as being counter-productive to
the pursuit of their cause, and action is taken which is aimed
at forcing concessions through a process of confrontation and
contest. A community group in this situation may take recourse
to strategies which are intended to damage and embarrass the
power structure; for instance, the withholding of rents and
rates, public demonstration, sit-ins, muckraking campaigns,
and personalized attacks on individual power holders. These
contest strategies may involve selective law breaking and the
violation of social norms. The main community work role is
that of the 'organizer', but it is not, as Spergel and Barr
suggest,[4] a 'winner takes all' position. Conflict relations,
as will be illustrated in the case study on the anti-dampness
campaign, are intended to produce change and concessions from
a power structure and not to destroy or replace the power
structure. The ultimate conflict relationship, in which the
winner does indeed 'take all', is that of revolution or
insurrection.

Revolution or Insurrection

Although sharp distinctions can exist between these different

relationships, especially between the collaborative and the
conflictual type, each of the relationships operates within an
overall societal context which is 'taken for granted'. Even
in the conflictual relationship, which can involve abrasive
confrontations and selective rule breaking, the focus of the
conflict is limited to a specific issue or a set of related
issues. The conflict does not involve across the board confrontations which impinge on every major aspect of life and
which entail a fundamental challenge to the legitimacy and
authority of the state. Specht describes an attack upon the
very authority of the state as insurrection.

> Rebellion and insurrection differ from disruption both
> in the tactics used and the ends sought. It is not a
> call to resist the immoral acts of legitimate authority
> but the withdrawal of legitimacy from the sovereign
> authority...the entire system is viewed as impossible
> of reform.[5]

For Specht, as with many other commentators, the hallmark of
the insurrectionary or revolutionary relationship is the organized and purposeful use of violence as a means for achieving
change;

> To be revolutionary requires that one has adopted a
> belief that policy cannot be changed without replacing
> the government by force.[6]

The organized use of violence is a characteristic of several
contemporary European revolutionary or insurrectionary movements which adopt military style strategies and have a degree
of support and popular legitimacy within local communities.
The obvious British example is the Provisional I.R.A. which,
according to Griffiths,[7] has an interlocking membership with
community organizations in some Catholic areas in Northern
Ireland. Whether organized violence is an inevitable characteristic of insurrectionary or revolutionary movements might
be questioned, and it can be argued that a revolutionary challenge to established power structures is conceivable through
the means of mass non-violent civil disobedience, as occurred
in the struggle for independence in India. For the Crossroads
staff violence was not considered a legitimate strategy for
achieving change and, in Gorbals and Govanhill, the local group
power structure relatioship never moved beyond a conflict
relationship.

Goal Displacement in Community Organizations

The typology also provides a theoretical reference point for

for analysing the organizational and strategic changes which
can occur during the life history of a community group. As has
been frequently recorded in the sociological and community work
literature, community organizations often move through distinctive stages in both their collective activities and their relationships with powerful outside bodies. The 'phase theory'
of tenants associations illustrates this point.

> In the first phase, the association played mainly a
> representative role, negotiating with the local authority
> for essential services and organizing large-scale socials
> and protest meetings. In the second it became mainly a
> constructional organization, fully occupied in building
> a community centre. In the third period, the centre's
> finances were placed on a firm foundation; and in the
> fourth, popular wishes were discovered through a process
> of trial and error. In the fifth period, short-run
> equilibrium was reached; the activities of the centre
> followed a routine pattern.[8]

In terms of our typology this represents a change from a bargaining to a collaborative relationship. However, the change
can also occur in the other direction. Thus, a group might
commence its activities and representation by seeking a collaborative relationship and, following a rebuff by the authorities,
might then move on to adopt more militant and abrasive strategies. Indeed, the progression from seeking a collaborative
relationship to working on a bargaining or conflict relationship is, in our experience, as commonplace as is the move in
the opposite direction. These changes invariably occur over
lengthy time periods and the shift from one relationship to
another is rarely as smooth and rational a process as can be
suggested by the theoretical models. Indeed, one of the key
questions which often arises in community work is why local
organizations continue to operate on strategies which appear
to be inappropriate for the goals which they are pursuing and
are inconsistent with the relationship which they have with
outside power groupings. e.g. why does a tenants association
continue to adopt polite pressure group tactics - such as letter
writing - when there is a record of this tactic being ignored
by the housing authorities? In a valuable article,[9] Morris and
Rein suggest that only certain organizational forms and strategies are appropriate for change-centred initiatives and that
the employment of inappropriate forms of organizations and
strategies results in goal displacement and ritualism. Their
concept of individual rationality closely resembles what we
have described as a conflict relationship;

> Conflict is recognized as inevitable and possibly
> desirable. Persuasion, use of sanctions and any
> means compatible with democratic values are condoned.[10]

A co-operative rationality closely resembles the collaborative
relationship,

> an essential component of the strategy is the art of
> arriving at interorganizational consensus.[11]

Finally, Rein and Morris link strategies and structures with
the long term goals of the organization and attempt an explanation of goal displacement.

> An organization's structure and the major type of
> strategy it employs may be seen as critical to the
> realization of its goals. When structure and strategy
> are consistent with goals, the organization operates
> at maximum efficiency and has the greatest opportunity
> of achieving these goals. Inconsistency between struc-
> ture, strategy, and goals may lead to ineffectiveness,
> dilution, and displacement of goals. A federated
> structure and co-operative rationality strategy are
> most consistent with goals of integration. On the
> other hand, a simple structure coupled with an indi-
> vidual rationality is most congruent with achievement
> goals of change.[12]

Leadership

Rein and Morris's analysis of integration, change and ritualism
may usefully be extended to the leadership of community organizations. Goal displacement and ritualism can be directly
influenced by the character and disposition of the local leaders. Thus, groups which are committed to change-directed goals
may find themselves led by 'integrative' leaders who favour
only collaborative relationships with the authorities. Equally,
a change-directed organization might be led by a 'ritualistic
style' of leadership - a leader whose rhetoric is consistent
with the aims of the organizations but whose practice is resis-
tant to adopting anything other than the mildest form of pressure group strategies. We found it useful to classify community
leaders as 'change', 'integrative' or 'ritualistic' in their
dispositions. Community workers supporting local groups can be
classified in a similar way. In an ideal world there would be
congruence between the aims of the community organization, the
strategies which are employed, the type of local leadership and
the style of the community work support which is provided. As

the case study on Govanhill Action Group indicates, this is rarely the case, especially over the extended life of an organization. Reality is frequently more messy and complicated.

Chapter Six

DAMPNESS: ORGANIZING A MASS CAMPAIGN

Of all the issue-centred action which was supported by Cross-roads, the Gorbals Dampness Campaign was the most successful and controversial. The success of the campaign in exposing the city's 'new slums', obtaining rehousing for tenants and winning entitlements for compensation, has implications for housing policies which extend far beyond the boundaries of Glasgow. The political conflict generated by the campaign was of an unusual degree of intensity and resulted in a backlash which almost led to the closure of the Gorbals Unit (See Chapter 9).

The campaign started by seeking a collaborative relationship with the authorities – get the facts straight and the problem will be solved – and rapidly moved into a conflictual relation-ship. According to the authorities there was no dampness issue. It was a personal problem of condensation, caused by the ten-ants' living habits or 'heavy breathing' as one official sug-gested.[1] Schattschneider points out that;

> an issue does not become an issue merely because
> someone says it is. The stakes in making an issue are
> incalculably great. Millions of attempts are made but
> an issue is only produced when the battle is joined.[2]

The campaign, therefore, had not only to force the authorities to acknowledge the issue, but had also to push them to take action to alleviate the dampness – a formidable task. The strategies employed involved selective law-breaking and the violation of social norms; withholding rent; organizing demon-strations and making personalized attacks on power holders. This rule-breaking was always issue-centred. The aim was to force concession on housing policies and not to overthrow the

power structure. These reformist goals were often interpreted
by the power holders as expressions of 'revolutionary militancy'
and the campaign was, at one time or other, labelled as a front
for almost all the left-wing groups and 'tendencies' which seek
to challenge the status quo. The Gorbals tenants only wanted
'dry habitable homes'.

THE PROBLEM[3]

Dampness had proved to be a problem in many parts of the Gorbals. During the 1970s well over 1,000 individual complaints
were registered with either the Glasgow District Council or the
Scottish Special Housing Association. The majority of these
complaints were from new blocks of flats in a development officially known as the Hutchesontown-'E' estate. This estate consisted of twelve blocks of seven-storey low-rise and two
twenty-four storey high-rise blocks; in all, 1,143 flats. The
flats were constructed of prefabricated heavyweight concrete
panels, and solid precast concrete floors, walls and ceilings.
The external walls were of a sandwich construction, with a layer
of polystyrene insulation incorporated within the concrete.
This prefabricated design is known as an industrialized building
system and the proprietary name, in the case of the Gorbals
flats, was 'Tracoba'.[4] This system was developed in France and
the sole concessionaires in Britain are Gilbert Ash (Structures)
Ltd. Industrialized building systems were introduced into the
United Kingdom in the early 'sixties and they were viewed as a
cheaper and speedier response to the housing demands which pre-
vailed at the time. They also offered the prospect of increased
profitability for private contractors, especially in terms of
cutting labour costs and increasing site labour productivity.

The first tenants moved into the new flats late in 1971 and,
within months, complaints about dampness were being reported.
The term 'dampness' was used by the Gorbals tenants to describe
the conditions of their flats; wet walls, fungal growth on fur-
nishings and musty smells. Most tenants experienced considerable financial loss because of damage to furniture, clothing,
carpets, the cost of redecorating frequently, and because the
flats were extremely difficult, if not impossible, to heat to
a tolerable level. They experienced social embarrassment about
the conditions and there was the added problem of being unable
to position furniture in a way which would be considered normal.
It was not unusual for tenants to move their beds into the
living room, because the bedrooms had become uninhabitable and
had to be vacated. Most distressing of all, was the damage to
health. Local doctors stated that the dampness was a health
hazard;

This woman suffers from recurrent bronchial and urinary
infections which in my opinion are being aggravated and
caused by the dampness of her present home due to
condensation.

Professional opinion finally agreed that the cause of the dampness was excessive condensation, due to the structure of the
flats.[5] They were built of heavyweight concrete, which is a
material of high thermal capacity, and which creates extremely
cold surfaces. The sandwich of polystyrene in the concrete
panels was an insufficient form of insulation. At the edges
of the panel joints, in areas of unknown size, there was solid
uninsulated concrete, known as 'cold bridging'. Insufficient
insulation, combined with the inadequate natural ventilation
of the rooms, resulted in high humidity and excessive
condensation.

THE CAMPAIGN

Pre-Organization

It all started through Jimmy Carlin. You ought to see
his house, the wife said. So I went round and I really
was appalled at the conditions - it wasn't fit for an
animal to live in it, and his whole family were living
in one room. I reported the problem to the Hutchesontown
Tenants Association and then I went to the Information
Centre. (Chairman, Dampness Campaign)

From the earliest days of occupation the tenants had complained
about dampness. The only response from the authorities was a
visit from a housing official and advice to turn up the heating
and open the windows. The Laurieston Unit, opened in Summer
1974, had received sporadic complaints about the problem, and,
when a local resident approached the staff in February 1975, a
student was asked to explore the problem further.

As I chatted and took photographs of the conditions of
houses of people already known to the Unit, I discovered
that already the problem was fairly widespread, but very
patchy and few people knew of other people's problems.
An article in the 'View' served to publicize the issue.
I not only followed up local leads, but started to
research the causes of dampness. .A common view,
shared by many local people with experience in the
building trade, was that the dampness was caused by
a combination of pre-cast concrete and poor insulation.
Further research revealed that low cost design was

frequently the cause of such condensation, so it was
easy to argue the Corporation's responsibility to
clear it up.

Specht points out that perception determines response.[6] The
perceptions of key activists and the Unit staff were identical
and, now that the fault was seen to be with the authorities,
combined action was possible. The early moves in organization
building had been initiated and the student began to plan for
collective action.

The student unit had a discussion along the 'where do
we go from here' lines and agreed that I should encourage
enthusiasm for a public meeting and investigate ways of
getting the principal activists together, perhaps with
people from the Laurieston Tenants' Association and the
Hutchesontown Tenants' Association to discuss the tactics
and organization of such a public meeting. I also felt
it was about time to get some expert opinion on the
condition of the flats, so we contacted ASSIST - a
community-based architectural service - to see if they
could suggest anyone. This contact resulted in an
'alternative' expert report pinpointing design problems
as the cause of the dampness.

The Campaign is Launched

The informal gathering of contacts agreed to invite local
councillors and the city architect to a public meeting which
would be convened by the two tenants' associations. The Unit
organized publicity and made copies of the expert's report on
the flast available for the meeting. The public meeting, in
May 1975, marked the beginning of the campaign. The councillors attended, but the City Architect refused the invitation -
the first of many occasions when representatives of this
department would decline to meet the Gorbals tenants. Over a
hundred tenants attended the meeting and various suggestions
for action were advocated, including a call for a rent strike
and the taking of legal action under the 1897 Public Health
Act. This meeting also identified potential activists.

I'll never forget it - this chap stood up and what a
speech he made - speaking on behalf of his mother and
father, and when he finished speaking everyone just
clapped. I remember saying to the student - who is
this? I thought you knew, he said. I've never seen
him in my life, but I'll tell you one thing, he's not
getting out of here tonight until I find out who he is

because I think he would be a big asset to our
campaign. (Committee member)

The mystery man was a Gorbals resident and trainee lawyer who
was to eventually become the Secretary of the dampness campaign.
Despite militant suggestions, the public meeting only endorsed
a suggestion for a deputation to the authorities and the sponsoring of a further meeting. Battle had now commenced, even if
very quietly. The deputation to the authorities achieved
little.

> I think they thought it was some wee thing that would
> blow over - they say they'll do what they can but as
> soon as you're out the door, they've forgotten your
> name. I don't think anyone realized the severity of
> the problem and they didn't want to know. I think
> they thought if they just kept putting us off, we'd
> forget all about it. (Committee member)

The early initiatives taken by the embryonic campaign represented an attempt to establish a collaborative relationship
with Glasgow District Council. The Secretary, who joined the
organizing committee early in the autumn of 1975 recalls the
frustrations of this period.

> I got invited to a meeting after the first attempts had
> failed - the normal channels, deputations, petitions
> etc. They knew these attempts had failed in the past,
> but they tried them for 3-4 months as a final attempt.

In October a second public meeting was held. The 150 tenants
who attended instructed the organizing committee - which comprised a triumvirate of Chairman, Secretary and Treasurer - to
take more abrasive action and investigate the possibility of
initiating legal action against the District Council. Within
three weeks the first moves had been made under the provisions
of the 1897 Public Health Act. It was not surprising, with a
trainee lawyer in the triumvirate, that a legal strategy was
adopted.

> I saw it as a straightforward thing - these houses are
> defective - there is a dampness problem - let's take
> legal action or whatever we require - call in the experts,
> ascertain the problem and repair it. But then I realized
> it was not so - you had the political problem which I
> didn't know anything about. I may have read guys like
> Dahl, but that's entirely different from politics in
> Gorbals. There is no comparison between political

theory and the real life politics that goes on - just
none. (Secretary)

Fortunately, the Crossroads staff and the other committee members understood the political problem (if not the legal process)
and when, in December, a local authority 'Combat Condensation'
exhibition visited the Gorbals, the community worker saw it as
an excellent opportunity to develop the local organization and,
simultaneously, put pressure on the authorities. A two-day
counter-demonstration and picket publicized the campaign's
views on the causes of the problem, ridiculed the Council's
insistence on 'heavy breathing', and achieved press, radio and
television publicity for the campaign. The picket also convinced the Secretary of the value of direct action.

> I used to think once you took your cause to the streets
> you were defeated, but then I saw that it was important
> to the local people - they can see it and can in fact do
> something. Moreover, it brings publicity which is one
> of the most effective tactics. Mind you, the stuff on
> the streets is only successful to a point - you can't
> march every day, but you can write every day.

From then on both legal and direct action tactics were used to
pressurize the authorities.

Rent Strike[7]

In February 1976 a third public meeting attracted 300 people,
but the committee once more rejected a call for a rent strike
and work continued on the legal case. When, however, the campaign discovered that a tenant had gone on rent strike after
the February meeting, in the mistaken belief that most people
at that meeting would be doing the same, the committee not only
provided legal support, but an enthusiastic band of local tenants, complete with banners, arrived at the small debt court
when the striking tenant received a summons from the District
Council. The District Council withdrew their action and the
tenant was awarded a decree of absolviter (acquittal) with
expenses - a significant moral, if not legal, victory for the
campaign. This case occurred in June and, over the next six
months, three other tenants were taken to court for withholding
their rent. On each occasion the District Council withdrew its
action before the Sheriff could consider the cases. The rent
strike tactic, rejected for almost a year by the campaign, now
began to be considered as an effective strategy.

> We never intended it at the beginning - I didn't think

it was a good thing myself because I thought it might
get people into a mess - use their rent money and never
be able to make it up. Mr. Carlin was the first to do
it, and then another lady was taken to court and we
won - then another tenant, so then it began to seem a
good thing - maybe they'll take notice if we withhold
rent. So we put it to the people - it was entirely up
to them - if they wanted to withhold their rent and put
their money by, then by all means do so. We also started
the dampness clinic one night a week. We felt it was
very important that the people had somewhere to go where
the advice was immediate and accurate. (Committee member)

The campaign was gaining local support and was acquiring a
reputation with the media. It was also gradually absorbing
and using more militant tactics but, despite eighteen months
hard organizing, no tangible results had been achieved.

The Issue is Recognized - the Committee is Divided

In June 1976, the chief executive of Glasgow District Council
published a report admitting that 'modern building methods'
could be one of the contributory factors causing the dampness
problem. Limited recognition perhaps, but the ensuing 'commitment to take action to combat the dampness' effectively
undermined the campaign's attempt to take legal action under
the Public Health Act, yet committed the authorities to no
specific course of remedial action. A proposal by the authorities to undertake another survey, this time by the National
Building Agency, split the campaign's committee. In a period
of disillusionment, when so much action had produced so few
results, recrimination set in. Should there be a more concil-
iatory attitude to the authorities, or were more militant tactics called for? The committee threatened to split over the
issue. Angered by the suggestion, made by a local authority
official, that they did not have the full backing of the people
in Gorbals, the committee managed to patch up a compromise and
agreed to organize a major public meeting to demonstrate, once
and for all, that the campaign had the popular support of the
people in the area. The move to mass organizing had been taken.
Pressure on the authorities was to continue and the displacement
to ritualism had been avoided.

Mass Organizing

The background work undertaken for the public meeting, which
was planned for the 28 November, gives some idea of the tasks
involved in mass organizing. A student reports;

The main brunt of the responsibility for organizing for
the public meeting fell on the Action committee and a
group of about fifteen tenants, but often escalating
to forty or fifty when leafletting or postering had to
be done. No decisions were to be taken, no press statements made, no interviews given without a decision being
made by the committee first. All statements of intent,
press releases etc. were thoroughly prepared in advance.
The preparation for the meeting started in earnest about
three weeks before and the Wednesday night dampness
meetings were of vital importance. At these meetings
the Action committee delegated responsibility for making
posters, distributing leaflets, etc. Tasks included
leafletting certain blocks, fly posting at night,
arranging for volunteers to assist at the actual meeting
and the week before the meeting, arranging for people to
speak from the floor. The speakers were to raise specific
topics so as to avoid a clash of questions. In an effort
to step up activity and make people more aware, corridor
meetings were arranged. These took place on the two
Sundays previous to the meeting. Several tenants par-
aded round the area. Using loudspeakers and leaflets
they carried out door-to-door deliveries, holding a
short meeting in the corridor with those interested
enough to listen. We printed 250 posters, and some
members of the community made huge banners out of sheets.

Over 600 people attended the meeting, which was one of the
largest and stormiest in the Gorbals for many years. Television, press and radio were present and the meeting was reported on the national I.T.N. news. The elected representatives stated from the platform that they fully supported the
tenants' action and considered the flats were uninhabitable.
It was a watershed in the history of the campaign. Results
followed quickly; the local M.P. brought the Scottish Minister
for Housing to the area in December; the District Council
agreed to rehouse tenants living in damp houses - the first
tenants were moved in December - and local councillors per-
suaded the District Council not to re-let flats badly affected
by dampness.

The Use of Power

The purpose of an organization is not only to have the
power to effect a commitment, but also to make sure the
commitment is carried through.[8]

The tenants had gained considerable experience and the same

people were still the key leaders in the campaign. Theoreti-
cally, they had achieved many of their objectives, but the
fight to have these gains implemented demanded hard negotiation
and recourse, on occasions, to direct action. The leaders were
now agreed on the need to negotiate from a position of strength

> To begin with, when the Council asked for a meeting, my
> attitude was, never meet them - the others' attitude
> was that we must meet. I saw this as weakness but they
> saw it as co-operation with the Council. Eventually
> though we agreed. When the Council asked for a meeting,
> we delayed it - it was tactically good to delay, and
> eventually there was a degree of equality. There was
> a bargaining about date and time and what was to be
> discussed, instead of just being invited to an open-
> ended meeting, given a chocolate biscuit, a cup of
> coffee, a two hour lecture and you're out the door
> with nothing. (Committee member)

The campaign had also uncovered some unexpected weaknesses in
the opposition.

> I learnt in the early days, much to my surprise, that
> these guys (the politicians) don't like heckling -
> they didn't want verbal combat. There was a lack of
> verbal skills that I would have assumed they would
> have had as a natural gift. (Committee member)

The campaign was also now in a position to demand active
support from the Gorbals tenants.

> To begin with the people's attitudes was 'I won't go
> to that meeting because Mrs. So and So is going and
> she'll tell me about it' - so the woman next door did
> the same thing and nobody turned up. Eventually we
> were straight with them and wrote to them and said if
> they didn't come forward they'd be left out and nothing
> would be done for them. We wouldn't put their names
> forward for rehousing, etc. They began to realize that
> if they didn't come forward and support us, they'd be
> the ones who were left behind and that was when we
> began to get them coming forward. (Committee member)

A public meeting, held at the Citizens Theatre on 1 May, 1977,
was a further demonstration of the campaign's ability to mobilize mass support and expose the politicians to uncomfortable
public pressure. This meeting was designed to keep the pressure up on the authorities and was deliberately held on the

day before the local elections for the Glasgow District Council.
In addition to mass leafletting and door to door canvassing
several new tactics were used in the preparation and organization of the meeting; street theatre, campaign songs composed
by the '7.84 theatre company' and local residents, a pipe band,
a motor cavalcade and even disruptive interruptions of the
meeting itself.

> During the actual meeting there was a number of pre-
> arranged and rehearsed events. These interludes included
> a skit between Mr. Mould and the Housing Manager and also
> a rendering, by a local tenant, of the dampness song
> which he had composed. There was also a number of
> unrehearsed and unexpected interruptions, especially
> when impromptu fights between Mr. Fungus and Mr. Anti-
> Dampness occurred on the stage of the theatre and
> interrupted the course of the meeting. The interruptions
> caused considerable consternation amongst most of the
> speakers who were on the platform. (Job Creation Worker)

A thousand tenants attended this meeting, which proved to be
the zenith of the campaign's public events. For the politicians, the penalty of refusing to offer support was to incur
public odium and the possibility of opposition at the next
local elections. Following the meeting the rehousing of tenants
speeded up. This was a positive gain for the campaign, but the
action almost inevitably resulted in a gradual undermining of
the mass base. Most tenants were rehoused away from the Gorbals
because of the shortage of suitable local accommodation.

The Costs of Success

In our typology (see Chapter 5) the dampness campaign represents
a clearcut example of a conflict relationship. The key parties
in the relationship were polarized over their perception and
response to the issue at stake. The possibility of a collaborative agreement was minimal and the community organization had
to adopt contest strategies, in an attempt to force the power
structure into recognizing the issue and taking action. By 1977
the dampness campaign had achieved this goal. The Glasgow
District Council had, with great reluctance, accepted the building design explanation of dampness, had agreed to rehouse tenants
and had acknowledged, in principle, the tenants' entitlement to
financial compensation. These objectives were achieved only
after an intense struggle which left a legacy of bitterness,
damaged reputations and simmering tensions. Local leaders
feared that they might suffer a backlash at some later date;

> If you are a local leader, you worry that the authori-
> ties might take a chance to get back at you. Maybe they
> wouldn't dream of doing that, but it's always at the
> back of your mind. (Tenants' Leader)

The friction became most immediately apparent in the relationship with the local M.P. and some other members of the constituency Labour Party.

> Some members of the local Labour Party resented the
> style and tactics of the campaign. It was too abrasive,
> bloody minded and went over the score in the demands it
> made on the local councillors. Others alleged that it
> was really a front for a left-wing sect or a rival pol-
> itical party. It is likely that the campaign upset some
> people because it could not be disciplined or controlled
> by the established political power structure of the Gorbals.
> The campaign was an independent organization which showed
> scant respect for reputations or political orthodoxy. In
> short the campaign was seen as a threat.[9]

These tensions also surfaced in a public form when the SWSG
attempted to close the Crossroads Gorbals Unit (see Chapter 9).

THE INFLUENCE OF THE COMMUNITY WORKER

The Importance of Relationships

> When people are brought together or organized, they get
> to know each others' point of view; they reach comprom-
> ises on many of their differences, they learn that many
> opinions which they entertained solely as their own are
> shared by others and they discover that many of the prob-
> lems which they had thought of as only 'their problems'
> are common to all. Out of this social interplay emerges
> a common agreement and that is the people's programme.[10]

The organizer is an important element in the social interplay,
and it is through this interaction that influence is exerted.
Whether or not this influence is absorbed into a campaign
depends largely on the relationship which the worker has with
key local activists. These relationships can be closely
guarded. The Gorbals fieldwork teacher comments;

> The areas which were inaccessible to students were the
> very intimate relationships I had with about half-a-dozen
> leaders. These little tête-a-têtes were crucial to the
> dampness campaign, and this was an area I was not

prepared to delegate to students.

Relationships provided the cornerstone for the various and di-
verse roles which the community worker performed with the dampness campaign. In this section we have attempted to describe
the main roles which the worker played and also we consider how
these roles changed over a period of time.

Organizational Role

Prior to the local organization being formed, in what we have
described as the 'pre-organization stage', the community worker
was the organizer.

> You've got no option - the very fact of moving into the
> area and then initiating makes you a leader. It's just
> a question of deciding when, at various stages, you
> should draw back. (Committee member)

The community worker had the big advantage of time to contact
the little isolated pockets of protest, who were ineffective
on their own and rapidly becoming frustrated.

> If it hadn't been for the student putting me in touch
> with all the other tenants, I don't think the dampness
> campaign would have started. (Committee member)

The staff continued a direct organizing role by calling informal
meetings of those contacts who were concerned about the dampness
problem and used their relationship, with the two local tenants'
associations, to persuade them to sponsor the campaign and to
organize the preliminary meetings. The unit also provided
somewhere for the tenants to hold committee meetings. Once the
committee began to effectively organize itself, the organizing
role changed to one of support for the local leaders.

> It's a sort of supplementing of direct organizating. I
> help the committee to organize public meetings, committee
> meetings, the odd demonstration. It's knocking on doors;
> putting up posters; chasing up local contacts; making
> sure the people know the time of the meetings and that
> the person is well briefed to talk to the press. I also
> fill in 'gaps' when people are unavailable for work or
> domestic reasons. (Community worker)

This supplementing of the direct organizational work of the
committee continued throughout the campaign. The hard, un-
glamorous work was valued.

> The Unit did a lot of the leg work - going round doors,
> going up to the city chambers for information - we've
> got families and couldn't possibly do this all the time,
> but the Unit took some of the pressure off us. They
> also did a bit of the paper work which we couldn't have
> done. (Committee member)

At times, the community workers became more assertive;

> When to draw back is a very difficult decision which
> involves delegation, a highly skilled task. You need
> a degree of confidence to do it. The other thing is the
> ability to move back into the leadership position for
> one meeting and move back out immediately. You have to
> know which meeting - you can see the thing is going to
> collapse - they've reached a stage now that they're all
> so determined they're not going to back down, so you
> move in, solve the problem and move back out again.
>   (Committee member)

In the latter days of the campaign, when many tenants had been
rehoused, the Unit again assumed a more direct organizing role.

Tactical Role

The tactical role of the community worker involves looking at
the total situation, as far as it is possible. Tactics cannot
be transferred, without thought, from one situation to another,
and community workers must understand the organizational implications of certain tactics.

> Attempt to use a variety of simultaneous strategies when
> putting pressure on the authorities and seeking to gain
> public attention for your cause. There is nothing a
> politician or official likes less than pressure coming
> in from a variety of sources, particularly when these
> different types of pressure are sustained over a long
> period of time. To sustain different forms of action
> at the same time calls for considerable commitment and
> generates a high workload. It is not a general strategy
> which we could recommend for groups which have a very
> limited support and only a handful of regular activists.[11]

The tactical role was sustained throughout the life of the campaign. At the pre-organization stage, however, it was largely
hidden from local activists and took place, mainly, in student
supervision sessions. With the formation of the group the
tactical influence, which could now be accepted or rejected

by the local leaders, was exerted through informal discussions
with key people.

> I was involved in a sustained dialogue on a week by
> week basis, not necessarily with everyone, but with
> twelve people who were very prominent in the campaign.
> Sitting down and discussing what had gone on, what
> options were open to people, providing them with a
> sounding board to bounce ideas off, providing someone
> for local activists to talk with and test out ideas.
> It's a sort of rehearsal process and a means of clari-
> fying your thinking. (Community worker)

Obviously these discussions influenced the committee.

> One of the things that always upset me was that you
> have to spend so much time working to get support -
> it seems almost ridiculous to have to sell the dampness
> campaign - people are getting something for nothing.
> Eventually, listening to the people in the Unit, who
> have more experience in dealing with problems like
> this, I got the message - retarded possibly, but I
> got the message - that the only way is to sell the
> campaign and then you might get somewhere.
> (Committee worker)

Regardless of intent, the community worker is likely to be seen
as the expert and his advice is given more weight than the
worker may expect. Tactical advice is not only selling ideas,
but also backing these up with action, e.g. the community
worker suggested the picket of the condensation exhibition and
the staff and students joined the picket line. At times, the
'pupil' may educate the teacher. The unit 'sold' the Secretary
the value of direct action, but the staff were soon to learn
much from him about organizing techniques, fund-raising and
the tactical development of a large organization.

Mediator Role

The diversity and talents within the committee was one of the
strengths of the campaign. The Secretary comments;

> Possibly one of the reasons we succeeded was we were
> able to bring together things from various approaches
> in order to work. The Treasurer was able to attract the
> women and the Chairman called on his trade union back-
> ground and the administrative work was left to me simply
> because no one else would do it and I happened to enjoy it.

But, at times, there were acute tensions within the group. One
activist describes the community worker as a type of 'community
glue';

> The Unit was helpful in keeping the various personalities
> together because you're going to get strong personalities
> coming to the forefront in any kind of group. We didn't
> have the opportunity to get to grips with each other's
> difficulties and that's where the community worker
> helps - he bonds things together - gels things. A lot
> of my attitudes were an anathema to the rest of the
> campaign - but eventually we reached a compromise, and
> without the information centre I wouldn't have comprom-
> ised and therefore, possibly, I would have got fed up
> and moved on.

The community worker reflected on this role;

> This keeping a foot in both camps and trying to get the
> group to compromise about their tactical or, at times,
> ideological differences was very important, and one
> which depended upon you knowing the individuals very
> well indeed, helped by having been associated with the
> campaign and leaders for some time. The underlying
> tensions within the group came to a head when the group
> had done a lot of work, but, had achieved no concrete
> results. This period of disillusionment was turned in
> on the group. To illustrate how difficult this period
> was, two or three of the key people in the group became
> so antagonistic to each other that they would only meet
> together when I was present - almost as a referee - as
> an interpreter to try to keep the temperature down.
> If the split had occurred at this time, I guess the
> campaign might just have fallen apart and a lot of the
> work might have come to nothing.

Research Role

The community worker comments;

> There was a lot of legal research - checking out public
> health legislation; research of causation of dampness -
> a voluminous amount of material. Some of that work was
> done by local people - more often than not by myself or
> students who had the time to go and sit in the big
> Glasgow library all day long. A very vital if invisible
> role - very important slogging, dull work which went on
> behind the scenes to prepare the arguments which the

local activists would be using when involved in legal
debate or negotiation with the Council. That persisted
throughout the campaign.

Keeping up Morale

This role was singled out by the Community worker as being
of key importance;

> If I reflect on some of the most important work I did
> in Gorbals, it wasn't necessarily the political and
> analytical roles which some attribute to me. My main
> quality as a community worker was a capacity to develop
> a positive and emphatic relationship with local people
> and, also, almost a personality thing, of being an
> optimistic character with high expectations and a lot
> of patience. I'm in danger of saying that my most
> crucial role with the dampness campaign was almost a
> case work role, because there are certain case work
> skills which intuitively I utilize, although community
> workers are rather embarrassed talking about them! It
> is rather similar to giving tactical advice, but rather
> more emotional - keeping enthusiasm going; trying to
> stimulate local people when they feel low and depressed
> and feel their work hasn't achieved any concrete end.
> It is a role I found myself playing quite a number of
> times throughout the campaign.

The community worker also identified certain roles which he
refused to perform.

Permanent Go-Between

> At times, especially in the early days, the campaign
> needed advice from experts on architectural or legal
> matters. Often the search for the appropriate expert
> took time; frequently the community worker negotiated
> the first contact, but this contact was quickly passed
> on to local people who thereafter retained the link
> themselves. Frequently, community workers maintain
> some power by remaining the permanent go-between. This
> was a role we rejected.

Formal Leadership

> We also rejected a formal leadership role. We weren't
> involved in fronting the campaign at public meetings
> or dealing with the media, although we would often help

organize the events, and prepared information.

Negotiator Role

We deliberately kept out of the twenty or so delegations to senior officials or to the Housing Minister - we didn't even attend these meetings. It was partly a principled commitment that we should not act as a negotiator to allow residents themselves to acquire these skills; it was also partly a tactical decision because we feared, on previous experience,[12] that the politicians would use our presence to deflect the aims of the delegation.

WHY WAS THE CAMPAIGN SUCCESSFUL?

Local residents and Crossroads staff attribute the successes of the campaign to a combination of five main factors. The emphases given to these factors vary, but all stress a combination of the following ingredients; the severity of the problem; an active committee; the mass support of the tenants; the back-up of the information centre and the role of the Secretary in the campaign.

The Severity of the Problem

The sheer misery of living in a damp ridden house pushed the tenants to become involved and forced them to continue fighting. In Glasgow, where only 10% of housing is allocated to transfer cases, there is virtually no chance of easily moving to another house.

We felt like giving in so many times because we got so frustrated banging our heads against the brick wall of the authorities. And then you'd go back to your house... God no, I can't give up or I'll be here for the rest of my life. You felt you had to grit your teeth and get on with it - push and push and push to open every door. We just couldn't give up - the authorities would have loved it if we had. (Committee member)

An Active Committee

The key committee of three was supplemented by a support group of up to thirty residents, who were active on a week to week basis. It was the work of this committee, described in the text, which developed the mass support of tenants.

The Mass Support of Tenants

The sheer hard work of door to door contact gradually developed
mass support for the campaign. Apart from the 'big occasions',
described in the text, the weekly committee meetings doubled
as advice clinics for between thirty and a hundred residents.
During most weeks, over seven hundred homes were visited for
fund-raising or organizing purposes.

The Secretary

Unfortunately, the Secretary was a rarity in Gorbals; born and
bred in the area, living in a damp council house, he was also
young and an apprentice lawyer. His contribution was
outstanding;

> He was one of the greatest things that ever happened.
> He was a big asset to our campaign because he had a
> fantastic legal brain, and he opened up a lot of doors
> we could never have opened. He worked all the time –
> we'd pass the information centre at 11 p.m. and he'd be
> working. He got the services of all sorts of professional
> people who seemed pleased to work for just a nominal fee.
> (Local resident)

Most tenants attributed his capabilities to his education and
legal training. The Secretary felt that many younger people
in Gorbals would have adopted similar attitudes if they had
been suffering from the problem.

> People like me weren't involved in a Tenants' Association
> in the first place, but were willing to react strongly
> to the problem when it hit them.

He did, however, feel that his influence in threatening legal
action and bringing in other professionals was important since
'it brought a degree of fear from the Corporation'. The Staff
came to value the Secretary most as the nearest person to Saul
Alinsky, the American community organizer, that they had ever
met. He had an innate tactical sense for building large
organizations.

The Support of the Information Centre

The importance of the Unit has already been stressed, especially
in the early stages of the campaign. The presence of a fully
staffed information centre, open five days per week, prepared
to devote a considerable amount of its time to supporting,

administratively and emotionally, the efforts of the Dampness
Campaign cannot be underestimated. The practical help is most
often mentioned.

> People would have learned to live with the problem –
> people would have accepted it as they accepted everything
> in this area – they just feel they're working class folk –
> we're supposed to live like this, we're supposed to accept
> these things. But with the Information Centre at their
> back, it gives people that bit of support. They feel
> they're doing the right thing. They begin to find some
> way of fighting. (Committee member)

The staff also felt that one of their main contributions – via
the mediator role – was keeping the Secretary involved in the
campaign, without allowing him to dominate it completely.

> At times, I think the Secretary would have been quite
> happy to run the whole show himself and I don't think
> this would have been a good thing – it would have
> alienated his other committee members and other people
> if he was doing everything and they weren't doing any-
> thing. I think the Unit played an important role in
> preventing this happening without him leaving.
>   (Staff member)

The Secretary resembled Hoffman's all-purpose leader – both an
asset and a danger to the campaign.[13]

ACHIEVEMENTS

We interviewed the three formal leaders of the Dampness Committee and the chairmen of the supporting tenants' associations.
There was a large measure of agreement between the local activists and the staff over the achievements of the campaign.

Material Gains

All were agreed that the belated recognition by the authorities
that the dampness was due more to design faults than to 'living
habits' was the crucial breakthrough. In 1980, officials of
Glasgow District Council acknowledged this fact.

> For too long it would appear that officials in all
> Departments have avoided the issue by placing the
> blame almost exclusively on condensation as a result
> of tenant lifestyle; other causative factors have thus
> received scant attention. This approach has in turn

led to ad hoc responses to major problem areas,
resulting in the current chaos.[14]

Thereafter the list of successes is impressive;

(a) The rehousing of tenants living in damp houses. By the
summer of 1982 over 1,000 households have been rehoused from
the Hutchesontown 'E' estate.

(b) The granting of certain concessions in the policy and
procedures for rehousing, e.g. taking into account past as
well as current lengths of tenancies when offers were made;
the setting up of a special inquiry desk at the Housing
Management Office for dampness tenants.

(c) Following reports by the National Building Agency the
Glasgow District Council committed itself to exploring the
feasibility of a remedial programme. At 1978 prices, the
cost of a full remedial programme would have been over
£2 million. The flats cost £5 million to build. By 1982
the Council had still to decide whether to implement a
remedial programme or demolish the flats.

(d) A ban on the reletting of damp flats once they become
vacant.

(e) The non-eviction of tenants who are withholding rent
because of damp conditions. At the end of 1978, the arrears
resulting from the rent strike totalled over £50,000.

(f) The recognition of the tenants' right to compensation.
Entitlement to compensation was originally won in 1977, but
it was not until 1980 that a detailed scheme was finally
negotiated. This settlement had two major elements; firstly,
that all past and present tenants of the damp flats will
receive a back payment of one third of their rent, paid from
their date of entry into the estate and, secondly, that claims
for damage up to £300 will be met by the District Council and
that claims in excess of this figure will be subject to negotiation with the city's legal department.

(g) A reduction in rateable values for 500 tenants. This
reduction ranged from 5% - 7½%.

Political Awareness

Any attempts to assess developments in political awareness is
an infinitely more complex and speculative task than is the

evaluation of the practical gains which can be achieved through
community action. At a general level, the dampness campaign
did succeed in mobilizing and involving a large number of people
who were new to either traditional or extra-political activity
in the Gorbals. Many of these tenants, especially the women,
had no previous experience of organizing public events, lobbying politicians, running committee meetings and taking any form
of direct action. This unleashing of new leadership and the
creation of new opportunities for participation illustrated
one of the major strengths of community action – its potential
to draw into association people who do not figure as active
members of political parties and who may also have little or
no contact with the established institutions of the British
Labour Movement (e.g. the trade unions). For many residents
in Gorbals – housewives, pensioners, the unemployed – community
action represented the most immediate and accessible arena for
political involvement.

> One thing about the campaign is that the majority of
> the people who were vociferous were people who weren't
> involved in any Tenants' Association before – probably
> they were willing to react strongly to the problem when
> it hit them, but after the problem had been solved they
> just disappeared. It is important, though, particularly
> with the younger people in some other area, maybe when
> in the years to come they find themselves with a problem
> of some size, they will know what worked in the past.
> If they describe, for example, how to go on rent strike,
> or how to use professionals, such as lawyers, that many
> people have not come across before, then it will carry
> much more weight. (Committee member)

Whether this involvement will lead to a wider set of commitments and an awareness of the inequalities of society remains
an open question. Community action tends to be issue-centred
and, once the issue which precipitates action is resolved or
partially treated, the momentum needed for further developments
can be lost. Thus, in the dampness campaign the rehousing of
tenants – which was a symbol of success – served to undermine
the collective strength and future political potential of the
campaign.

> Once the dampness campaign had achieved what it set out
> to achieve, that's the end – there's no lasting effect,
> and that's reinforced by the fact that many of the
> stronger members of the campaign are spread throughout
> the city once they've successfully achieved rehousing.
>   (Committee member)

There was, however, agreement that, in the short term at least, people had lost their deference to the 'higher ups'. This was singled out as a major achivement.

> Everyone lost their fear of officials after a while.
> To begin with I felt kind of intimidated, which got me
> nowhere. As time went on I thought 'I'm not going up
> there, explaining problems to them just like a silly wee
> girl, because they're probably laughing at me anyway, so
> I went up with the direct approach – and if they were
> getting nasty, you got nasty as well. After a while
> your approach did change. I think they began to realize
> that they couldn't intimidate us and get rid of us, so
> they began to act nicer and show more respect for us –
> I think that was when I began to realize we were
> beginning to win a wee bit. (Committee member)

Wider Achievements

Both Crossroads staff and the committee valued the assistance the campaign had provided to dampness groups in other parts of Glasgow and Scotland. On the local Gorbals and Govanhill front four other tenant groups have organized around dampness complaints and, throughout the city, some thirty different local campaigns had developed by the early 1980s. The Gorbals campaign had also been frequently approach for support and assistance by groups in other parts of Scotland.

> I'd never in my life talked to the press – and it was
> a great experience to speak on television. It was one
> way of getting things across and telling other people
> about the conditions that people in Glasgow were suffer-
> ing. I think we're the only place in Britain that has
> achieved so much and through the press and media there's
> quite a lot of Tenants' Associations throughout this
> country who know of our victories and have formed their
> own associations to do the same. (Committee member)

This rather puts into question the criticism that local community action is 'parochial'.

Chapter Seven

CHANGE AND RITUALISM

In this chapter we examine the interplay between goals, organ-
azational structure and leadership through a study of the
Govanhill Action Group (GAG).

THE EXPRESSWAY ISSUE[1]

Govanhill Action Group was born out of the threat that new road
plans would destroy Govanhill. A proposed expressway would
demolish housing and a one-way traffic management system would
split up the area. This information was given to residents at
a public meeting, held in Govanhill, on 16 April 1973. The
same residents had heard the local councillor on the Planning
Committee state just four months previously, that any proposals
for a new expressway were 'just pie in the sky'. The officials
of the Planning Department explained that the plans had been
brought forward to coincide with the heightening of the Govanhill railway bridge, for the electrification of the Glasgow-
London railway line. They stressed that participation would
be encouraged through a local exhibition, when housing proposals for the area would also be on view. The week-long public
exhibition was organized and over a 1,000 residents attended.
No housing proposals, however, were on show. Worse still, it
became known that the plans had been available but had been
withdrawn from the exhibition on the order of the Director of
Planning. Neither pressure from local councillors nor an
'instant demonstration' outside the exhibition could produce
the housing plans.

At a subsequent public meeting in Govanhill, on 24 May, the
Convenor of Planning refused to discuss housing proposals and
the Director of Planning so mystified people with his historical view of planning proposals for the area that many residents

were convinced that whole streets were coming down! Although
some planning officials and local councillors were anxious to
keep local people involved, the way in which the authorities
had presented the proposals were confusing and high-handed.

On 31 May, more than 80 people attended a locally organized
meeting to hear how opposition to a road scheme had been organized in the Govan district and to consider a local councillor's
proposal for a road-widening scheme which would retain the maximum amount of land for Govanhill. The committee which was
formed, following this meeting, was angry and anxious 'to be
doing something'. Rejecting the title 'planning action group' -
'since we're here to take action, not to plan' - they rapidly
elected office-bearers, organized two petitions and a local
survey and sent a 22-point letter to all Corporation Departments
and Committees asking for their justification of the expressway
plan。 The aim of GAG was:

> To fight for real information to be supplied to the
> people of Govanhill, to discover whether the expressway
> is of any benefit to Govanhill or indeed the whole city
> and to demand that improvement of houses in Govanhill
> start immediately。[2]

GOVANHILL ACTION GROUP 1973: AN ORGANIZATION FOR CHANGE

The committee of GAG was initially composed of fourteen residents, three of whom dropped out from active participation soon
after the group's formation. The remaining committee members
were mainly young householders, who were directly affected by
the road plans. Their homes were threatened by compulsory
purchase orders and the safety of their children was endangered
by the proposed one-way traffic system. They were convinced
that the plans were 'wrong' and were prepared to adopt a conflict relationship with the authorities in their efforts to
reverse the proposals. Although nearly half the committee had
previous experience of trade union or political parties, few
of them had been involved before in community politics。 It was
only the intervention of the authorities into their lives that
had put community politics to the top of their personal priority
list. GAG displayed many of the salient characteristics which
Rein and Morris[3] identify for a change organization. It had a
simple organizational structure, focused on a specific set of
issue-centred goals and was comprised of like-minded individuals
who were prepared to 'fight the authorities'. The membership
owed their primary allegiance to GAG. They had to, since at

this time GAG was often meeting more than once a week!

Leadership

The experience of the Garbraid Action Group, in the Maryhill
district of Glasgow, suggests that crisis issues can attract
a new type of community leadership.[4] The threat of the Govanhill expressway did just that. It brought to the fore a young
leadership, with some political understanding, little deference
for those in authority and limited faith in existing organizations.

> Well the Ward committee didn't seem very effective and
> even the Residents' Association didn't seem very active -
> it dealt with housing problems but not the larger issues
> of planning. A lot of older people were brought up to
> think that officials are right and know what they're
> doing. Perhaps younger people don't always agree. We've
> seen what officials and councillors have done to other parts
> of Glasgow where it is a right mess. (Committee Member)

This style of leadership we would describe as 'change'
leadership.

Community Work Support

The basic choice facing the Govanhill Unit was whether or not
to encourage the opposition to the proposed expressway. The
fieldwork teacher and the student who was on placement with
GAG favoured different strategies. The fieldwork teacher
advocated opposition and a change-centred approach.

> As far as I was concerned, I felt we had no option but
> to fight the proposed expressway. This was the 'big
> issue' that predicted the destruction of Govanhill by
> the local authority. We had already experienced the
> destructive process of redevelopment by the authorities
> in Gorbals. The promise of a new road did not seem
> enough compensation to the residents of Govanhill, few
> of whom own a car. Moreover, the line of the road
> ruled out any possibility of new housing in the north-
> east sector of Govanhill. Even from a community service
> point of view it made little sense for us to promote
> play-groups or the Day Centre for the elderly if there
> were to be few people left in Govanhill to use these
> resources. (Community worker)

In contrast, the student argued for an integrationist
approach based upon a collaborative relationship with the
authorities.

> There had to be a better system of communication if
> local government officials are to be helped better to
> understand local issues, and if local people in the
> cities are to begin to get to grips with the possibili-
> ties for their involvement in doing something positive
> about improving their environment and living conditions.
> The most important issue is getting a meaningful planning
> presence in the area to assist general improvements.

The views of permanent staff took priority and the Unit decided
to support opposition to the road scheme, knowing that this
would bring them into conflict with the authorities.

In the initial stages the campaign started with considerable
vigour. Everyone involved felt that the issue was vital enough
to warrant a top priority in the allocation of time and energy.
Local residents spent much of their summer holidays organizing
petitions and meetings, and the Govanhill Unit made available
the fieldwork teacher, two students and considerable secretarial
resources to the group. Equally important, these energies were
harnessed in a similar direction. Rein and Morris point out
that 'when structure and strategy are consistent with goals,
the organization operates at maximum efficiency and has the
greatest opportunity of achieving these goals'.[5] We would also
suggest that it is important that the style of leadership and
community work support are also consistent with these goals.

Housing Issues

As early as August, there was a shift in emphasis away from the
expressway towards housing issues. A number of factors contributed to this process. There had been little response from the
authorities to the GAG request for a delegation or replies to
the 22-point letter, and there was a strong feeling, despite
organizing to the contrary, that the expressway scheme would
go through. There was also increased involvement of some of
the less experienced members of the group, mainly women, and
the change in emphasis reflected their primary interest in
housing. On the request of a local resident, the Govanhill
Unit had enlisted the help of the Vice-Chairman of GAG to
sponsor a public meeting on the possibilities of the house
improvement of the scheme. When this meeting was reported
back to GAG disagreements arose:

The Chairman thought this issue of house improvements
was not central to GAG concerns. He saw a danger of
losing strength to the new Residents' Associations.
Others did not agree. The Vice-Chairman explained
that he saw his involvement only at the beginning to
help get things started, and he wanted to encourage
representatives to join GAG from the Residents' Associations. He spoke also of the possibility of sponsoring
more meetings for the formation of further Residents
Associations in other improvement blocks. Soon after
the Chairman left and handed over the chair to the Vice-
Chairman, who immediately put it to the meeting that
they set up a special sub-committee to get more Residents
Associations off the ground. This was accepted.
                              (Student report)

The Chairman's formal abdication, even if only for the night,
allowed the Vice-Chairman to formalize his victory and promote
the housing strategy. During the next three months GAG spon-
sored three new Associations, two in Improvements blocks and
one in an area scheduled for redevelopment. Young members of
GAG quickly moved into key leadership positions within these
new organizations. A federated structure had begun to develop.

The Expressway Campaign

It might have been as well that energies were harnessed elsewhere because, despite a large public meeting in September 1973,
any attempts to discover or influence the progress of the highway plans seemed blocked, although unofficially GAG was told
that the one-way traffic system had been dropped. It was not
until March 1974 that GAG got a hurried telephone call from a
local councillor saying that, unknown to him, the one-way system
had been dropped but that the expressway proposals had gone
through a Special Sub-committee. This decision was to be re-
ferred back to allow the councillor and GAG to be heard. Despite GAG's ability to 'conjure up' a petition against the
expressway representing seven local organizations (in which GAG
members held key positions) and lobbying on the day, the expressway scheme went through the Sub-committee, but was successfully
blocked at the full Highways Committee. At the full Committee
a prospective Regional councillor for Govanhill, who already sat
on the Highways Committee for another area, was able to add his
voice to the protest and called upon the democratic rights of
a newly formed local Planning Working Party (see below for details) to back up his case. In a Committee room, packed with
Govanhill residents and with Press in attendance, the Convenor
of the Committee agreed to refer the issue back to the Working

Party. On 28 May, 1974, the Working Party advised 'that they
do not wish an expressway to run through the area'.[6]

The Govanhill Working Party carried no formal authority within
the decision-making structure of Glasgow Corporation. GAG's
only authority came from the support of local residents and this
support had been growing as the constituent groups developed:
the locally run Housing Association had improved a tenement
house containing twelve flats; two 'block' organizations were
undertaking backcourt improvements schemes; the rehousing group
was fighting for decent rehousing offers and was also running
a summer playscheme. By October 1974, GAG could call upon this
support to rally over 500 people to a public meeting to press
for further housing improvements and to continue the opposition
to the expressway proposals.

Despite receiving support from all the local councillors, representation from GAG to the Highways Committee was defeated by the
slender majority of 13 to 11 votes and it was only a last ditch
appeal to the Labour Group caucus that prevented the expressway
plans gaining approval. The Leader of the Labour Group was now
adding his voice to the opposition to the expressway and the
Labour Group agreed (against the wishes of two powerful Con-
venors of Committees) to refer the matter back to the Highways
Committee for further consideration. Here the matter rested.
GAG had finally defeated the expressway proposals. When, in
December 1976, officials once more mooted road plans for Govanhill, they proposed the road widening scheme suggested by the
local councillor, back in 1973. The expressway proposals had
been dropped.

GOAL DISPLACEMENT

The Federated Structure

The adoption of housing issues had resulted in the development
of a federated structure and the emergence of a broad range of
relationships between the constituent groups of GAG and the
authorities. The Rehousing Association maintained an almost
permanent conflictual relationship with the housing authorities
(see Chapter 8) but were in agreement with other local authority
departments over play provision. As Glasgow Corporation conceded the need for Housing Associations and backcourt improvements, the Govanhill Housing Association adopted a more consensual relationship with the authorities.[7]

According to Morris and Rein a federated structure is not
suitable for a change organization, yet this very structure

appeared to have enhanced the effectiveness of GAG. It could
now increase local support through the creation of new organizations and, when appropriate, could rustle up petitions and
objections to the expressway with the support of a larger number
of groupings in Govanhill. Certainly, there was little new
membership recruitment to GAG and most of the original members
now devoted most of their energy to their constituent organizations. GAG was able to remain consistent with its original
goals and strategies because the original leadership remained
active within the organization and remained united in their
opposition to the expressway. The combination of the local
leadership and community work support could maintain GAG, in
the short term at least, as a change organization despite its
federated structure. This was not, however, to be the case
after the expressway issue was resolved and the leadership
altered.

The Participation Issue

Officials within the Glasgow Planning Department were dissatis-
fied with redevelopment by means of comprehensive redevelopment
areas because, among many shortcomings, it permitted local residents no say in redevelopment plans. Impending legislation was
going to require participation in planning and the Planning
Department responded by setting up Working Parties for a number
of districts which were scheduled as Outline Comprehensive
Areas. When the authorities unveiled the housing plans to the
people of Govanhill in February 1974 they also promised a Working Party to co-ordinate consultations and the implementation
of the proposals. It was 'the most ambitious local planning
participation exercise ever attempted by Glasgow Corporation'.[8]

The Working Party meetings were held in the City Chambers and
were a replica of Glasgow Corporation Committee meetings, even
down to the tea and biscuits. Representation was strictly
limited to the leaders of local organizations and excluded
members of the public 'in the interests of space'. Such pomp
and circumstance often exemplifies the lower rungs of citizen
participation. Officials of the Planning Department had also
envisaged the setting up of local planning centres, and, as
early as April 1974, the Working Party agreed that it was desirable for an exhibition centre to be provided in Govanhill
which could serve as an office for any Corporation department
requiring a local presence in the area, and could also be used
by the various local community associations. After a lengthy
planning period the exhibition and advice centre opened, in
February 1975, from shop front premises in Cathcart Road. A
sub-committee of the Working Party, comprising four local

representatives and two officials, formed a management committee. This structure suggested, in terms of Arnstein's typology,[9] a partnership model of participation. It seemed too good
to be true.

A seemingly unimportant decision by GAG to refuse local Labour
councillors use of the centre as a surgery, for fear that it
would be seen as part of the Labour Party, angered local councillors. To discover that a former political rival - now
Chairman of the Action Group - was staffing the information
centre on a voluntary basis was the final insult. The Convenor
of Planning informed the Working Party, in April 1975, that
local groups would no longer be allowed to use the advice
centre in case incorrect information was disseminated. It had
been too good to be true! As might be expected, GAG said that
'the matter was not closed'. Proposed tactics at the Action
Group meeting ranged from a resolution against the Planning
Convenor to a call for a public meeting, which was agreed.
Yet, at the public meeting on 28 April, attended by more than
100 people, the matter was not raised by the GAG Chairman, and
it was left to a member of the audience to raise the question
of the advice centre, whereupon the Chairman counselled that;

> As it was clearly outlined in the Planning Committee
> Minutes that it was a joint community planning project,
> there was a fair measure of confidence by the local
> groups that the original aims and decisions of the
> Working Party and Planning Committee would soon be
> regularized.[10]

There the matter rested. Local residents were excluded from
the management and staffing of the information centre. The
authorities staffed the centre infrequently and in an erratic
fashion. It became used less and less by local residents.
Finally, in April 1977, the information centre and the twelve
flats above it, quite literally, fell down.

RITUALISM IN GAG.

Why did GAG, previously skilled at putting pressure on councillors and pursuing matters tenaciously, let this matter drop?
Certainly pressure from a local councillor had contributed to
the closure, but conflict with councillors had not previously
deterred GAG. There was a general agreement that the information centre was a 'good thing' from local leaders and community workers alike. It is important, therefore, to consider
the issues GAG chose to work on, at the structure and strategies
of GAG and also at the leadership and community work support

which was available.

GAG chose to work on the participation issue and this choice
had certain ramifications for the organization. This is not to
say the choice was wrong - it was very understandable. Previously in Glasgow, community groups had to organize and pressurize before the authorities would agree to meet them and it was
almost unheard of to get officials from various departments and
councillors together at any one time. It was highly unlikely
that any organization would reject the offer of regular meetings
and a local advice centre where they held management responsibilities. It is important to point out, however, the implications of such a choice. The acceptance of a structure such
as the Working Party assumed that there was 'common ground' and
a move away from a conflict relationship to a consensual relationship with the local authority. The possible result for a
change organization is that 'it is likely to go through motions
which end in inaction'.[11]

When the councillors excluded the residents from the information
centre, GAG realized it had been lulled into a false sense of
security and co-operation. By now, however, GAG was unable or
unwilling to respond aggressively. To many of the GAG members
the issue was no longer crucial. The loss of control of the
information centre was regrettable, but protest might be counter
productive and could result in the total removal of the centre.
The combination of a federated structure and a consensual relationship with the authorities made the sudden use of conflict
strategies very difficult, and, equally important, the key
leadership at this point had little appetite for conflict.

New Leadership

The original change-centred leadership remained virtually the
same from the birth of GAG, in the summer of 1973, until after
the successful appeal to the Labour Group caucus in October 1974.
Soon after, both the Chairman and the Vice-chairman left the
area. With the introduction of the Working Party and the acceptance of the federated structure for GAG, new leadership had
joined the Action Group. This new leadership was attracted to
developing their considerable potential within the Working Party
structure, and quickly gained ascendancy in the depleted Action
Group.

Older and politically far more experienced than the original
leadership the 'new men' embodied what we would describe as a
ritualistic form of leadership; a leadership whose rhetoric is
consistent with change goals but which is unwilling to adopt

strategies which are consistent with those objectives. An examination of the Chairman's action in response to the closure of
the information centre is illustrative of this leadership style.
A member of the original steering group which promoted the information centre, he was deeply committed to the idea of a locally run centre, yet his preferred tactic was one of 'wait and
see what happens'. Sometimes these leaders are dedicated
activists with years of service behind them, often to left-wing
political parties which have patently failed to fulfil their
objectives and which exist on the margins of British politics.
For these leaders ritualism has probably become an unconscious
way of life. Unlike the integrative style of leadership, they
do not disagree with the adoption of conflict strategies. The
rhetoric is appropriate, but they lack the confidence and nerve
to move from rhetoric to action. Bitter political disappoint-
ments and possible previous experiences of victimization mean,
in practice, that they caution groups away from contest strategies. But with a background of considerable expertize, this
style of leader can quickly move into key positions and may be
extremely good at developing an organization and analysing
situations. The presence of ritualistic leadership, at a time
of crisis, was one more factor contributing to the closure of
the Govanhill information centre.

Community Work Support

Changes in the community work support may well have also contributed to the goal displacement of GAG and the retreat into
ritualism when confronted with a political crisis. The fieldwork teacher who provided the initial link left her post about
the same time as the 'change leaders' left the area, and a consistent partnership was broken. When the debate over the information centre surfaced, the structure, strategy and leadership
of the group favoured co-operation with the authorities. It is
unlikely, therefore, had the original worker still been in the
post that GAG would have decided to fight the closure of the
centre. The Govanhill Unit would have supported local action
to fight for control of the information centre, but the staff
felt that it was inappropriate for a new worker to be directive
with the group. Administrative and professional reasons rend-
ered community work support ineffective during the crisis.

Following the failure of the information centre, the staff
increasingly questioned the viability of GAG as an organization
capable of promoting change. Staff allocated fewer community
work resources to the group. They neither encouraged GAG to
disband nor allocated sufficient community work resources to
influence it towards becoming a change organization once more.

A student's evaluation of staff practice might be correct;

> The main drawback of the staff's approach to community
> work is, I think, that it works best when conditions
> are very bad and authorities are blatantly unreasonable.
> In such cases, the approach of public group pressure
> backed by press coverage - rather than consultation
> and negotiation - clearly works. But the role of the
> staff is less clear in situations where authorities
> are consulting groups at an early stage or where public
> consultation is part of the statutory process.

Chapter Eight

FROM APATHY TO ACTION

Can goal displacement be reversed? Several studies of
Tenants' associations suggest a shift, over time, from change
to integration goals and the phase theory postulates a movement from conflict to collaboration. In this chapter we describe, using extracts from a student report by Mary Hemming,
how a tenant's group, the Govanhill Tenants' Rehousing Association (GTRA), reversed this process. In a week of intense
and controversial action the GTRA moved from being an in-
effectual organization to being one which had a considerable
impact upon the authorities. Once more, the presence of
ritualistic leadership had an important influence upon events.
The use of civil disobedience strategies was central to the
week of action and, during the mid-1970s, several of the
groups in Gorbals and Govanhill engaged in disruptive action;
the GTRA blocked roads to protest at poor housing conditions
(see below), the Gorbals Rehousing Association organized
physical resistance to evictions in McKinlay Street[1] and the
Dampness Campaign promoted rent strikes (see Chapter 6). In
the final part of this chapter we record some of the views of
staff, Crossroads management, local residents and politicians,
on the use of civil disobedience strategies.

GOVANHILL TENANTS REHOUSING ASSOCIATION

The Housing Survey

The GTRA was one of the housing groups which was initiated by
the Govanhill Action Group (see Chapter 7). Formed in 1973
the GTRA was concerned with representing the interests of
tenants in the north-east sector of Govanhill, who were faced
with the acute stresses and strains of living in a redevelopment area. The rehousing of tenants was the major focus of

the group's activities and local housing surveys were occasionally used as a strategy to identify problems and highlight
delays in the rehousing process. By the summer of 1976 the
group was undergoing a crisis with regards to its organizational credibility. A student reported:

> I started attending public meetings of the Rehousing
> Association though in a rather half-hearted way because
> the committee had become very depleted (there were only
> three members) and was making no headway in gaining new
> members; attendance at public meetings was dwindling
> markedly; the committee had little aim or momentum and
> people were sinking into apathy and cynicism about what
> the Association could achieve. Another student was in-
> volved in the group and attending committee meetings
> and people from the Unit were out-numbering local
> people, a fact that was remarked upon somewhat resent-
> fully by members of the committee. There seemed no
> way to become involved and yet the issue of rehousing
> was one of importance. I became involved after the
> questionnaire had been drawn up and approved by the
> committee, and when it had become apparent to the
> committee that their appeals for volunteers to carry
> out the survey had met with no response, and that they
> themselves could not undertake the exercise without
> additional help. There was a certain amount of resis-
> tance to the notion of students becoming involved, as
> some of the committee felt this should be done by
> local people.

The issue of rehousing from redevelopment areas was one of
the Govanhill Unit's top priorities. The Unit, therefore,
was prepared to undertake the housing survey as a means of
recruiting new membership and hopefully overcoming the ritualism in the committee. The student only realized this later.

> To begin with, I saw the survey as pre-eminently a
> fact-finding task, but then I perceived that it
> presented me with the opportunity for doing some
> pretty detailed and intensive development work.
> Given the numerical weakness of the committee, it was
> one way of identifying people whose anger, distress
> or determination could have strengthened the committee.

Two students worked very intensively on the survey for about
two weeks. It had a considerable impact on both of them.

> We were unprepared for the frequency with which we
> encountered very acute distress and despair, especially

among the elderly and women living alone with children.
Also predominant was fear - fear of leaving the house -
fear of what havoc vandals would cause next - fear for
the safety of children and fear of being attacked at
night.

They felt a responsibility for raising people's expectations:

My main anxiety lies in the fact that in spite of re-
peatedly impressing on these people that the Rehousing
group could not make any promises of the outcome of
the survey, their hopes have now been raised.

A local resident was arguing that the committee was ineffective and that, as community workers, the students had a
professional duty to take some action on the results of the
survey. They found it difficult to do nothing and let the
re-housing committee deal with the survey, but realized that
there should not be a divergence between accountability to
the local committee and accountability to the wider community.
They resisted the pressure to take action themselves. 'It
seemed important that the people themselves, led by the
tenants' committee, should be doing something.'

It was with considerable trepidation, however, that the student attended the public meeting which the committee had
finally arranged to discuss the survey.

PUBLIC MEETING[2]

At the public meeting the revelations of the survey seemed,
initially, to overwhelm people and requests from the chair
for ideas as to what the GTRA might do about the situation
were met with bitter comments about the pointlessness of doing
anything. A number of people felt convinced the group was
powerless, and that evidence of this was that neither it nor
any other groups had made any headway in dealings with the
Council so far. They did not see why this occasion should be
different. The meeting fell away into individuals raising
their own particular problems and complaints. The Chairman
however, clung tenaciously to the question about further
action and the fact that the committee was evidently serious
in their intent to act permeated the meeting. Suggestions
began to come in. The initial one came from a particularly
vocal and persuasive local activist who had been goaded to
fury at the conditions revealed by the survey. He formulated
ideas about blocking the traffic in Govanhill by massing
people, cars and prams at the four main entrances to the area.
He had aired these ideas in the Unit and much discussion of

them had been generated. He made the same suggestion at the meeting, a suggestion modified by the community worker, who considered it would be more feasible to block just one of those roads, preferably Cathcart Road as it bounded the Treatment area. Other suggestions were made: marching to the City Chambers and occupying The Housing Management office being the main ones. It was felt very important to get the result of the survey given wide media coverage. The cynical mood of the meeting changed and the merits of those lines of action were discussed with mounting enthusiasm. It was decided to hold a demonstration at 8.30 a.m. in Cathcart Road at a pedestrian crossing controlled by lights. As time was short it was agreed that there would be a meeting the night before (Sunday) to discuss the details and make posters, banners etc.

It is significant that tactics which had been aired in and given backing by the Unit were the ones adopted. The opportunity that the Unit affords for talking through ideas and tactics gives those activists who make use of it an advantage in situations where decisions have to be made, especially if time for discussion is limited. These activitists are largely a self-elected group.

The mechanism by which the meeting gained a sense of having some power in the situation, having started from a sense of powerlessness and cynicism, is somewhat obscure but the assurance, enthusiasm and insistence conveyed by individuals who called for direct action, was influential. There was a call during the meeting for a demonstration the very next morning. This was rejected. People felt they needed more time to organize, and a number who were working were not sure whether they could attend. Tying up the details was in fact left till the evening before the demonstration, little organizational work in fact being done during the week. A press release had been drawn up and notification of the press was to be done later in the evening by the field worker. Not discussed however, and a serious omission, was a policy line in case of police intervention: whether people would actually block the road or simply walk back and forth across it, and whether people would be prepared to be arrested.

THE WEEK OF ACTION

Monday 28 June

The Monday demonstration was attended by about 60 people. Because no line had been worked out folk were not very confident about what to do. A slow march across the road, while the lights were at green and amber, began. The marching

became slower and was still going on while the lights were at
red. Traffic was held up and police began issuing warnings
to people to cross only when the lights were green.

It became apparent because of the diminishing flow of traffic
that the police were diverting it at a point lower down Cathcart Road. The demonstration realized this and decided to
move to the still busy junction further up Cathcart Road. The
formal leadership was not greatly in evidence at this point.
The same tactics were employed. The slowness with which
people were marching across the road considerably slowed the
traffic. The majority of demonstrators were women and a number wanted to stand and block the road. This was done for
short periods and the disruption was greater, but the lack of
confidence in this tactic (arising perhaps because of lack of
leadership - the formal leaders remaining on the side of the
road) was demonstrated in the uncertainty as to what to do
when the police threatened to arrest people. The Chairman of
GTRA and the District councillor (both councillors were supporting the demonstration and the Regional councillor refused
to ask people not to block the road) conferred with the police
and agreed that the demonstrators would not block the road.
There was uncertainty among the demonstrators as to what their
rights were when the police said that crossing the road constituted an obstruction. This was however successfully challenged
by the community worker.

The demonstration lasted over two hours and got excellent press
publicity. Its effectiveness lay not so much in the number of
cars held up but in the publicity the exercise attracted and
the confidence both the publicity and the demonstration engendered in people living in the Treatment Area. GTRA was
being seen to be making an impact. At this point the Chairman was rehoused into Gorbals and left the campaign.

Tuesday 29 June

It was essential that this action should be maintained and not
simply seen as a flash in the pan. In the absence of the formal
leadership of GTRA, a group of more militant residents decided
to have another meeting the following afternoon - Tuesday - as
people were eager to repeat the direct action. The meeting
was well attended but was addressed by the formal leadership
who advocated caution, and no further action until careful and
deliberate plans had been made. The afternoon was exception-
ally hot and much discussion followed as to whether there
should be another demonstration that day or not. The formal
leadership appeared to be using the discussion as a filibuster
- to drain away the impetus to action. However, a decision to

demonstrate was made. But people were so relieved to end the
discussion and move on to the streets that once again plans
were not made. The action consisted of marching round Govanhill several times disrupting traffic and causing annoyance
to the Police and generally alerting people in the area to the
action being taken in the campaign for decent houses.

Wednesday 30 June

This poorly planned and executed follow-up could have proved
disastrous for the campaign. Although there was by now an
unmistakable groundswell against the tactics proposed by the
formal leadership, the grass-roots urge to action was un-
planned and undirected and it looked as though the impetus to
action would be lost because of the aimlessness and unproduc-
tiveness of Tuesday's demonstration. Some people felt that
all that had come out of it was sore feet. A meeting was
called for the Wednesday afternoon and was preceded by the
Secretary and Treasurer of GTRA touring the area with a loud
hailer and addressing people from the back courts. The Secretary, particularly, showed himself to be an able and fluent
public speaker. The day was, again, extremely hot and the
meeting was rather poorly attended. The police arrived before the meeting wanting to know whether or not there would
be a demonstration - they were told that that would be up to
the meeting to decide. They left.

Once again the Secretary, who had assumed leadership in the
absence of the Chairman, counselled more considered action.
An impressive speaker he argued that every day of action like
Tuesday's would dissipate the energy of the people. He argued
that what should be done was that the survey should be presented to the Housing Management Department and that the campaign should be broadened by making approaches to Trade Unions
and local political parties. He argued that it was not simply
a question of people in this area getting decent houses, but
of changing house-letting policies as they affected all treatment areas. He spoke at length about this and the meeting
became restive.

The Treasurer, who throughout the campaign had been the person
whom the membership had identified with their own militancy,
spoke for the first time, and with some anger. She said that
she felt it impossible to carry on as an office-bearer when
the other office-bearers were wanting something different from
the wishes of the membership. She said that she would resign
immediately unless more people would come forward to serve on
the committee (now numbering two). This had a strong and immediate impact and six people came or were pushed forward all of

whom had been active and vocal during the action of the past
two days.

Once again much time had been inefficiently used in the meeting and action was decided on without a clear plan. The idea
of marching that day to the Lord Provost's House (relatively
close to the area) was raised and rejected, chiefly because
it was uncertain whether he would be in and whether it was important whether he was or not. It was also felt that such
action should be more carefully considered and arranged for a
time when a larger turn-out could be ensured. Tactics were
discussed as the people attending the meeting lined up on the
road. The question of what to do about threats of arrest was
raised and the consensus seemed to be to push it as far as
possible. The demonstrators moved down on to Cathcart Road,
marched to Aikenhead Road and were directed back again.
There was some confusion about this, as people thought they
had decided to block the road at Aikenhead Road. As it was,
the marchers stopped at the pedestrian lights in Cathcart Road
(scene of Monday's demonstration) and stood in the road blocking the tea-time traffic for some time. The confidence in
doing this contrasted markedly with the trepidation evident on
Monday. The police arrived and with tantalizing slowness the
demonstrators moved to the side of the road. The police began
taking names and generally threatening people. However, they
were met with a united front and the demonstrators did not
disperse. Although it was late and had been a very long and
tiring day, there was a strong feeling among people that they
wanted to engage in further action. The idea of marching to
the Provost's house took hold of the people and the marchers
began to move south down Cathcart Road. They moved into Queen
Mary Avenue shouting slogans boisterously. The vivid contrast
between the area of squalor and dereliction where the marchers
lived less than ten minutes down the road and which we had
just left, and this quiet sedate tree-lined avenue of vast
sandstone villas standing in large and well-tended gardens,
increased the sense of urgency and the sense of justification
of the fight for the right to a decent house. Such an abrasive
and incongruous intrusion was undoubtedly extremely traumatic
to residents in this area. When we arrived at the Provost's
house, a line of police blocked the driveway and would not
allow two delegates to deliver a letter to the Provost, still
less see him. Undeterred, the demonstrators stood shouting
slogans and singing behind the line of police. In their own
time the marchers returned to Govanhill, confident and singing.

Thursday 1 July

The next day - Thursday - the police arrived at the meeting
of the GTRA with a message from the Provost inviting the GTRA
to meet him in the City Chambers. The meeting was exultant.
Earlier the Secretary had rebuked the meeting for the precipi-
tate and unproductive action of marching to the Provost's
house. He had also criticized the Unit workers for supporting
this action. The movement of the grass roots, however, was
overtaking the formal leadership. A meeting was arranged with
the Provost for the following day - Friday. The Thursday
meeting elected one of the new committee members as the new
Chairman of the committee and as spokesman in the meeting with
the Provost. The committee met later that evening to collect
data to take to the Provost. They decided that they would
demand that everyone in the area should be rehoused to their
own satisfaction by the end of August 1976 and that there
should be an end to eviction proceedings against people in
that area (something which was becoming more and more
frequent).

Friday 2 July

The committee held an open meeting on the Friday after the
meeting with the Provost. The Secretary reported that the
Provost's response had been social rather than political;
that he was interested in doing something for people in a
vulnerable position, especially the housebound and disabled,
but that he had explicitly said he would not himself be committed to demanding changes in housing policy. He promised
that there would be a stay of execution on all threatened
evictions in the area, though he warned that he was not offering policy change, that he was not guaranteeing that there
would never be any more evictions. He agreed to meet regularly with the committee and to mediate between GTRA and the
Council Departments dealing with the Treatment Area, and to
arrange a meeting between himself, the Housing Manager and
the Convenor of the Housing Committee to discuss the situation.
He indicated that he would like to visit the area that weekend,
but specified that this would not be as the 'Lord Provost' but
in a personal capacity. He also wanted a list of the names
and addresses of all the people left in the area, and of those
who were old, sick or living last in a tenement, also a list
of people threatened with eviction.

Weekend 3/4 July

The following day - Saturday - the Provost made a tour of the
area. He made a formal tour the next day (Sunday) accompanied

by committee and meeting people in the area, although he
refused to speak to the Press. All these events were given
good media coverage.

Monday 5 July

A full public meeting was held on Monday evening as a formal
report back session: this meeting was attended by the local
councillors who had been supporting the campaign. Their
message was that, in reality, the Provost had little power to
affect the situation and that direct action should probably
continue if GTRA wanted to keep attention focused on the
plight of the area. The Regional councillor explicitly said
that he would be sorry to see the demonstrations stop and
suggested picketing the next full meeting of the Council. He
also confided that the higher echelons of the bureaucracy had
in the last week become aware of Govanhill in a new way.

The new committee continued an active, if somewhat unusual,
summer of negotiations and by the end of the summer most of
the committee and the local residents had been rehoused.

REFLECTIONS ON GOVANHILL TENANTS REHOUSING ASSOCIATION

Leadership

The original leadership of GTRA had been in favour of change
but the continual turnover of leadership, common within every
rehousing area, coupled with the despair and sheer hard work
of organizing in such a situation, had contributed to the
development of a more ritualistic style of leadership from
some, but not all, of the committee. Until direct action
tactics were adopted, the Chairman and Secretary, who were
both experienced trade union and political activists, tended
to suggest the tactics for the group. They consistently
counselled 'considered action'. As direct action progressed,
however, the tactics of the leadership were over-ruled more
frequently. The Treasurer felt able to challenge, publicly,
the ritualism of the other office bearers on the committee,
and on the Wednesday, not one but six new members, all in
favour of change, were recruited on to the committee. The
Govanhill experience seems to confirm Coleman's observations
about leadership:

> New leaders tend to take over the dispute; often they
> are men who have not been community leaders in the
> past, men who face none of the constraints of maintain-
> ing a previous community position and feel none of the
> cross pressures felt by members of community organizations.

> In the literature they often emerge as marginal men
> who have never held a position of leadership before.
> The new leaders are seldom moderates – the situation
> itself calls for extremists, and such men have not
> been conditioned, through experience in handling past
> community problems, to the prevailing norms concerning
> the tactics of dispute.[3]

Most of the new committee members who emerged had no history
of previous community and trade union involvement and showed
scant regard for the niceties of 'due process'. They displayed the attributes of change leadership more effectively
than many of the more experienced leadership, who tended to
be rhetorical and ritualistic. A study in North Shields suggests that a tradition of organization within the workplace
can be an inhibiting factor in the development of change-
directed leadership in the community. Those that are relatively unorganized at the workplace 'are less likely to be
imbued with respect for bureaucratic procedures and are more
willing to translate their anger and frustration, at the community level, into direct action'.[4]

These observations and the experience of GTRA cast serious
doubts on community work practice which uncritically assumes
that previous industrial experience is a pre-requisite in the
struggle for change. It is possible to suggest that a history
of previous trade union or labour movement involvement does
not guarantee the development of change-directed leadership,
but may well lend itself, instead, to the development of a
more ritualistic form of leadership. A local leader, who
emerged during the demonstrations over rehousing, commented
upon the difference between Action Groups and Tenants' Associations and the appropriate leadership for each.

> Community groups and Tenants' Associations that have
> been going for a long time have lived with the prob-
> lems whereas Action Groups are formed to get rid of
> the problem – not in ten years but as quick as possible.
> It's the movement of individuals that makes a good
> Action Group. The person in charge says – that's not
> bad, we've done so much then somebody else comes forward
> and she's able to motivate people to come back out and
> recreate the fight. Some people go forward for the sake
> of being a leader – others are coaxed into it. Usually
> it is the ones that are coaxed into it that are the ones
> that get going in the action. There has to be a way
> of getting rid of the ones who are there for the sake
> of being there.

Community Worker Role

The Unit's most important role was prior to the week of action.
Since rehousing was an important issue to the Unit, it was
prepared, when necessary, to organize directly within the area
in order to challenge the non-activity of the committee. It
was the two weeks of intensive door-to-door development work
by students which raised people's expectations, and suggested
a collective rather than individual response to the problems
people were facing. If a decision to organize was important,
a later decision not to act was also necessary. Had the community workers succumbed to the pressure to do something themselves about the survey, the displacement of the ritualistic
leadership by the new committee members might never have taken
place. At the later stages, the community workers had once
more to discipline themselves not to control the situation,
but to remain available to offer advice when appropriate, e.g.
advice about the law relating to obstruction.

It is important that community workers not only organize to
encourage the emergence of new leadership, but that, at times,
they support the replacement of existing leadership. Often,
as is illustrated in this study, this can cause resentment
from the established leadership, who assume the support of the
community work staff. The community work literature mentions
the concept of 'supporting new leadership' more frequently
than the contentious, but associated, concept of challenging
existing leadership. In seeking to build the most appropriate
organization to achieve change, the community worker may
support the replacement of an established leadership - a
leadership which, incidentally, the community worker may have
supported at an earlier date.

Reversing Goal Displacement

In GTRA a change-directed leadership already existed within
the committee and was able to call for support from the body
of the hall in the attempt to challenge the established leadership of the committee. In GAG (see Chapter 7) the Chairman
did not face a direct challenge from a member of his committee
and was able to successfully counteract criticism of his
leadership made at public meetings. Also, in the case of GTRA,
the goals, structure and general strategies of the organization
were appropriate for a change organization, but, in the case
of GAG, a move away from ritualism required not only a change
in the leadership of the group, but also a change in objectives
and in organizational structure. GAG, therefore, faced more
formidable obstacles in its attempt to become a change-directed
organization once more.

CIVIL DISOBEDIENCE

The use of civil disobedience strategies by the community
groups in Gorbals and Govanhill always aroused controversy and
conflicting opinions. In this concluding section we note some
of the positions taken by Crossroads staff and management,
local residents and politicians.

Staff

The staff supported the use of non-violent civil disobedience
as a strategy of the last resort. Following a series of confrontations over evictions, between 1975 and 1976, a policy
statement was issued to training courses, the sponsors of the
units and local groups. Part of this statement read as
follows:

> The Crossroads staff are prepared to give physical
> support to families who, as a last resort, take direct
> action to resist evictions and other forms of harass-
> ment from either the local authority or private land-
> lords. We believe that offering physical support in
> these situations should be seen as an integral part
> of the overall commitment of the Units to support local
> action on housing problems. The students who are
> attached to the fieldwork units - and particularly
> those students who are working specifically in re-
> development areas - should not feel under any obliga-
> tion or group pressure to become involved in physical
> confrontation with the authorities. We recognize that
> for some students this form of direct action may, in
> their opinion, be politically undesirable or that it
> may place the students in situations which they could
> find extremely uncomfortable and threatening.[5]

The fieldwork teachers argued that it was educationally
valuable, although stressful, for each individual student to
make a personal decision about whether or not to become involved in civil disobedience.

> The debate and action generated by the Unit's policy was
> valuable for the student - it focussed attention in a
> very practical way, on some uncomfortable and disturbing
> questions relating to direct action, civil disobedience
> strategies, violence and non-violence and the ethics
> of professional social work/community work - which are
> either rarely discussed on courses or when discussed
> are considered in rather abstract and theoretical terms.
> The significance of the debate was especially relevant

to students who were directly involved because their
emotional involvement was, I think, an aid to learning.
(Staff member)

The views of students on this issue are reported in Chapter
Thirteen.

Local Views

Most local residents disliked direct action tactics - 'people
think you're a crank round here if you carry a poster'. Some
experienced activists saw it as an unpleasant necessity.

> Unfortunately you don't get anywhere unless you make
> a protest - the same thing happens at work. They listen
> to you and give you a lot of sympathy, but nothing's
> ever done until you go out on the street, or wave a
> banner or create a diversion. That's when you get
> promises and even then you don't just let it be, but
> have to keep the pressure on until the problem is
> solved.

To many, especially the elderly, demonstrating was hardly
respectable.

> People put up with a lot but there comes a point when
> they've had enough. There's a lot of people in Govan-
> hill, especially the old people who don't like that
> kind of action but people were getting desperate.

Civil disobedience was an act of desperation rather than an
act of principle, but people thought that it was perfectly
justified.

> I think they were very justified in taking the actions
> they did - people want to be recognized as people not
> just living in bad conditions. They knew there was
> housing, so why weren't they entitled to it. Plus the
> fact no-one seemed interested in repairing the houses
> they were living in. So people started to react
> violently because of frustration - no-one came along
> with a solution - the only solution was to give them
> better houses, so they had no other course open to
> them!

Most of the residents considered that the Crossroads staff
should be involved in supporting direct action, primarily
because the staff involvement was thought to increase the
likelihood of success.

I think they were perfectly justified in fighting the
eviction but if they had not had the Information Centre
at their back they might not have been successful.
People were evicted from closes before because there
was no-one to fight for them. But if the Information
Centre is there, and the local organization, that
gives people that bit of support to feel they're doing
the right thing. Having the Information Centre and
the group at their back brought out the councillors as
well who might otherwise have done nothing.

Politicians

The local councillors, who assisted groups like GTRA, supported civil disobedience tactics, but admitted that this
stance was unusual for councillors.

In other areas nobody bothers when an eviction notice
is sent out - very few other councillors get involved,
they either think people are anti-social or they've
had enough offers. Some councillors tend to think
you're a crank if you carry posters - some become very
respectable when they become councillors. I'm a great
believer in democracy and think people should use every
avenue to get things done. Some councillors possibly
do it successfully without people being evicted -
others don't bother their shirt. I don't go about
telling other councillors how to do their job, but at
least officials and politicians know if they put an
eviction order in my area, I won't take it lightly.

At the other extreme, the Chairman of the Housing Committee
disapproved of the use of civil disobedience tactics, not because they were unethical - 'I'm in favour of demonstrations
because I've been involved in a great many myself' - but because they were linked with objectives which the local authority was unable to fulfil.

Demonstrations are fine if you're aiming for something
which is realizable - many of the demonstrations by
local groups weren't related to realizable ends. It
seems entirely wrong to create an impression that by
making enough noise, you will get better housing offers
at the end of the day - there's no elected representative
that could allow a situation where other people's interests were sacrificed because of the noise of one particular group. All these demonstrations were doing was
maintaining the enthusiasm of people in untenable
positions in Govanhill without achieving anything for
them.

The local MP did not comment upon the ethics of the situation,
but implied that the use of civil disobedience tactics was
'unprofessional'.

> You may have done damage to social work practice - I
> don't know if I would go as far as that but you give
> the impression to a lot of people - including my
> officials and others - that the policy of confrontation
> is being encouraged. Take the evictions situation -
> students are being taught, or encouraged, confrontation
> with the police. The image of social work is being
> damaged.

CROSSROADS YOUTH AND COMMUNITY ASSOCIATION MANAGEMENT

The members of the management committee of Crossroads supported the staff policy on the use of civil disobedience.
For some members the staff involvement was a key ingredient
in improving the chances of success for local groups. Other
members felt that involvement was called for as an 'act of
solidarity'.

> Anyone who studies it and sees the reasons behind the
> evictions should be involved for that reason - not
> because they are staff but it should be an act of
> solidarity. The trouble with many officials is that
> they are so busy remembering what the official above
> them will think, they forget about being human beings.

There was, however, a recognition that staff involvement
could result in a sponsorship backlash. What is 'good' for
the local groups might prove uncomfortable for the community
worker.

> I don't know if it is really advisable for a social
> worker. Certainly people are going to ask advice of
> a social worker and a social worker is going to tell
> them how to protest to get what they want, but to be
> tarred with the label of organizing people into
> protesting groups isn't good for the social worker
> himself. Even if you don't actually go on the protest
> with people, you can be seen as possibly inciting them
> to protest on their own. It's good for the local people
> and possibly what social work is all about, but the
> powers that be might decide that instead of being a
> social worker you're a troublemaker. Yet housing is
> the basic issue in Glasgow and it would be very dif-
> ficult not to touch it.

It was precisely this type of backlash which created, between 1977 and 1978, a major threat to the future of the Crossroads units.

Chapter Nine

THE POLITICS OF SPONSORSHIP

During the period covered by this study Crossroads was subject to a series of reviews by its outside sponsoring bodies. Between 1974 and 1975 the then Glasgow Corporation reviewed its grants to voluntary organizations which employed community workers, a review which was sparked off by senior councillors expressing concern over the political content of voluntary sector activities. Due to the pending re-organization of local government this review resulted in no cutbacks in the allocation of existing grants, although it had the effect of placing a moratorium on the making of any new awards during the year-long course of the investigation. From 1976 to 1978 annual reviews of Crossroads social work and youth work grants were undertaken by the Strathclyde Region. This was a Region-wide review, affecting all types of non-statutory organizations, and it was a direct response to the cutbacks in public expenditure introduced by the Labour Government from 1975 and 1976 onwards. Compared with some organizations Crossroads emerged comparatively unscathed from these reviews.[1] The social work and youth work grants were pegged to the level of previous awards (with no allowance made for inflation costs), whereas some other voluntary organizations had their grants reduced by as much as 75% or, as in a handful of cases, were completely cut.

The third review which was experienced by Crossroads was undertaken by the Social Work Services Group (SWSG) and it differed in two major aspects from either the Glasgow Corporation or the Strathclyde Region reviews. Firstly, the SWSG reviews of the fieldwork units were specific to the work of Crossroads, which was singled out as a 'special case' for close and sustained scrutiny. Secondly, the reviews were geared to directly questioning the community work content of the Associations

work in Gorbals and Govanhill. What was at stake, in these
reviews, was the possible closure and transfer of one or both
of the fieldwork units. This case study is concerned with the
SWSG reviews between 1977 and 1978. The key events are described and, in the concluding section, an analysis is made of
the strategies which Crossroads adopted in its campaign for
survival.

THE 1977 REVIEW

The first SWSG review started as a direct result of the public
meeting held by the Gorbals Dampness Campaign on 1 May, 1977
(see Chapter 6). When the public meeting finished, at 10 p.m.,
some members of the local Labour party, including the local MP,
held an impromptu post mortem on the events of the evening.
At 11.30 p.m. the fieldwork teacher for the Gorbals unit received a telephone call from the MP, who accused the Crossroads
staff and students of masterminding an attack on the local
Labour Party. The MP also reminded the staff member that, as
a Junior Minister at the Scottish office, with a brief which
included social work, he had a direct responsibility for the
funding and sponsorship of the Crossroads fieldwork units.

Ministerial Visit

Early in June Crossroads received an official 'Ministerial'
visit. The official party comprised the local MP in his
capacity as a Junior Minister at the Scottish office, senior
SWSG civil servants and social work advisors, public relations
staff from the Scottish office, the Director of Social Work
for the Strathclyde Region and the Convenor (Chairman) of the
Strathclyde Region Social Work Committee. The senior local
government presence in this party was explained on the grounds
that Crossroads received a grant from the Strathclyde Region
to employ a community worker, who was employed as a back-up
resource for the fieldwork units. The official party met with
staff, students and Crossroads management representatives.
During the course of three hours of tense discussion the Minister, who dominated the questioning of the Crossroads representatives, outlined four major criticisms of the fieldwork units.
These were:

(a) That the staff and students of the Units had devoted too
much time to housing issues and had not concentrated enough
on other social problems in the local area, such as work with
the elderly and alcoholics.

(b) That the students with the Units had been encouraged to
take irresponsible action in support of local community groups.

It was alleged that the students acted as 'cheer leaders' at
demonstrations and generally 'stirred things up'. The support
for the Dampness Campaign and a previous local campaign against
evictions were cited as examples of this disorderly behaviour.

(c)   That the staff of the Units had given incorrect advice to
local residents on the respective responsibilities and roles
of local political representatives. The MP complained that he
was being held accountable for problems, such as the dampness
issue, which were not his responsibility.

(d)   Finally, it was stated that the Units represented too
great a concentration of community work resources in the Gorbals and Govanhill areas and that it might be of value, in
educational terms, if one or both of the Units was transferred
to a different locality.

This last point was reinforced by the SWSG social work advisors
who suggested that the Crossroads Units only provided a limited
fieldwork experience in a narrow range of community work settings. The meeting ended with the Crossroads staff and representatives having the distinct impression that one or both of
the Units might be moved. The tension at this meeting was
best summed up by a local management representative who commented 'So that was what the Spanish Inquisition was like!'
By the beginning of August, following further meetings with
the SWSG social work advisers, a stalemate had been reached.
Crossroads refused to accept the educational rationale for the
transfer of one or both of the fieldwork units, arguing that
this was merely an academic smokescreen for a political attack
on the Units. The stalemate was broken when SWSG notified
Crossroads that there was a 'possibility' of redundancies
occurring amongst the fieldwork unit staff.

Save the Units Campaign

The choice, as described by one staff member, was between
'action or prayer'. Invoking the gods was ruled out as a
viable strategy. Crossroads decided to go on the offensive
and fight back. At a management meeting on 18 August, a
pressure group campaign was devised. The key ingredients were:

(a)   To organize a broad-based lobby of the local MP by representatives of community groups in the Gorbals and Govanhill
areas.

(b)   To appeal for support from those colleges and universities
which used the Units for fieldwork placements. Also, to appeal
for support from other community workers and professional

bodies associated with community work in Scotland and south
of the border.

(c) To mobilize support through the voluntary workers' branch
of the TGWU, the union which represented the staff.

(d) To attempt to gain some support from those local Labour
party members and representatives who were known to be either
sympathetic to the Units or embarrassed by the actions of the
local MP. Although, it was apparent that the hard line taken
by the MP was supported by a majority of the active members
of the local Labour Party, it was known that certain influential Labour Party members had not been consulted about the
attack on Crossroads. Prominent amongst this minority group
was the Regional Councillor for Govanhill, who was also the
Convenor of the Strathclyde Regional Council, and a founder
member of Crossroads.

(e) To circulate information about the threat to the Units
to all MPs and councillors in the Glasgow area, in order to
draw their attention to the possible loss of social resources
in two 'deprived' inner city areas.

Less than twenty-four hours after this strategy was devised,
the appeals for support and letters of information were being
sent out. Within this overall strategy the lobby and representation by local residents was given the major priority.
They represented the local management structure of Crossroads,
were consumers of the community work service and were voters
in the Queen's Park constituency. A number of other tactics
were not included, at this stage, on the agenda for action.
These tactics - such as press publicity and demonstrations -
were to be held in reserve and used only if the more orthodox
pressure group tactics failed to produce any results. Despite
the news about possible redundancies, the Crossroads management still had some faith in the feasibility of a negotiated
settlement.

An Unexpected Success

When Crossroads drew up its 'fight back' campaign it was
anticipated that matters would not be resolved for a considerable period of time. Events were to prove this expectation wrong. Within three weeks, the immediate threat to
the future of the Units was to be lifted. On Friday 26 August
a delegation from Crossroads met the local MP at the Labour
Party Office in Gorbals. This delegation was twenty-strong
and comprised representatives from ten local community organizations who were involved with the day-to-day work of the

fieldwork units. The delegation covered a wide spectrum of
groups, including leaders from tenants' associations, action
groups and representatives from community service and self-
help groups. Politically, the composition of the delegation
embraced Scottish Nationalist and Communist Party activities
as well as Labour Party supporters. The full time staff of
Crossroads were not included in the delegation. The exclusion
of the staff was a conscious decision, taken in order to avoid
the meeting concentrating only on the role and alleged mis-
demeanours of the staff.

The meeting with the MP lasted an hour. It was a tense and,
at times, very emotional encounter. The MP denied that there
was any threat to the unit and argued that the review was only
part of a normal process of ensuring accountability for the
expenditure of public funds. The news about possible redundancies came, apparently, as a surprise to him and he denied any
knowledge of this development. At the end of the meeting the
MP agreed that he would put in writing a statement to the
effect that there would be no closure of either of the units.
This positive commitment came as a quick and unexpected success
for Crossroads. The MP's action was mainly attributed to the
strength of the local delegation and the demonstration of
broad-based popular support for the units. The feeling that
the tide was moving Crossroads way was confirmed, over the
following weekend, when it became clear that behind the scenes
moves were under way within the local Labour Party which were
aimed at 'cooling out' the conflict between Crossroads and the
MP. These moves were mainly initiated by those Labour Party
members who had not been consulted about the attack on the
fieldwork units and they were influenced, in part, by the
feeling that the closure of one or both of the Units could
damage the image and reputation of the Labour Party in Gorbals
and Govanhill.

A Bizarre Event

On Monday 29 August Crossroads received a letter from the MP
which stated, in very vague and general terms, that neither
of the Units would be removed from Gorbals or Govanhill. A
further meeting between Crossroads' representatives and the
MP had been arranged for the following Friday and, despite
the apparent assurances about the future of the units, it was
decided to go ahead with this meeting. At 4.30 p.m. on Friday 2 September, the delegation gathered at the Gorbals Unit
for their meeting with the MP. Just as the delegation was
leaving for the meeting a hand-delivered letter arrived from
the Social Work Services Group in Edinburgh. This letter had
a traumatic effect. The key sentence read:

We have not yet completed our review, but I think it
is only right that I should inform you at this stage
that our provisional view is that there is a sound
case for moving one of the existing units to a new
location where students would obtain experience of
different aspects of community work in another kind
of area. You will appreciate that the final decision
will be for the Minister.

The content of the letter changed the attitude and organization
of the delegation. Because of the clear implication of redundancies, resulting from the moving of one of the Units, it was
decided to include staff members in the delegation. It was
also decided to confront the MP, at the start of the meeting,
with the content of the letter. Following an impromptu tactical talk, the delegation left for the meeting in an angry mood.

The meeting started with the Secretary of Crossroads reading
out, in full, the contents of the SWSG letter and demanding an
explanation. The MP claimed to know nothing about the letter
and, after reading the letter himself, he announced that he
intended to over-rule the recommendation of his civil servants –
the units would stay in Gorbals and Govanhill. He then went on
to talk, at considerable length, about the need for accountability in the management of public expenditure and also
repeated many of his previous criticisms about the 'irresponsible' behaviour of staff members. No satisfactory explanation
was given for either the content or the timing of the SWSG
letter. The first review of the Units was over.

THE 1978 REVIEW

The 1977 review was called off abruptly on 2 September and the
next confrontation between Crossroads and SWSG did not occur
until the summer of 1978. The event which sparked off the
second review was the resignation of the fieldwork teacher with
the Gorbals Unit. In June Crossroads notified SWSG and requested permission to advertize for a replacement. There then
followed a period of delays until, on 16 August, a Crossroads
delegation met with SWSG civil servants in Edinburgh. The outcome of this meeting was an agreement by civil servants to
replace the Gorbals post, providing that positive reports were
received from the Scottish based social work courses which
used the Unit for placements. By early in September these
reports, which were positive about the value of the Units'
student work, had been received by SWSG, but no action was
forthcoming. Further delays occurred and, following representation by Crossroads, the SWSG wrote indicating that no decision
had been made and that 'some misunderstanding' had occurred

about the content of the meeting held in Edinburgh in August.
The SWSG minute of this meeting contained no reference to the
agreement to base the decision about replacing the Gorbals
post on the feedback received from the Scottish social work
courses. A Crossroads management member, who had attended the
disputed meeting, commented 'They've re-written history'.
Around the same period, Crossroads heard, via contacts in the
academic world, that the Minister was holding private discussions about the future of the units. By the autumn the Gorbals
fieldwork unit was unable to plan any long term work. Student
placements were being cancelled and the process of local community work was being adversely affected.

Action Plans

Early in October the staff and management began again to draw
up plans for action. Compared with the 1977 'Save the Units'
campaign, the options which were open to Crossroads in 1978
were more complex and unpredictable. A number of new factors
had to be taken account of in the planning of action. These
included:

(a) The 'non-decision making'[2] strategy adopted by the SWSG
and the local MP had successfully thrown Crossroads on the
defensive and had created uncertainty in the minds of local
people in Gorbals and Govanhill. Whereas in 1977 the 'review'
had been a relatively public and open affair - symbolized by
the Ministerial visit to the Units - in 1978 the issue appeared
less clear-cut and definite. Crossroads was faced with a
situation in which they knew, full well, the seriousness of the
threat but could not, apart from odd items of correspondence,
produce much detailed evidence.

(b) The MP and SWSG had developed new tactics out of the experience of the 1977 review and they had also gained an insight
into the tactics of Crossroads. The surprise and shock value
of a 'Save the Units campaign' was likely to be considerably
reduced in the 1978 review.

(c) In May 1978 the Govanhill councillor, who had acted as a
peacemaker in 1977, died of a heart attack. As a consequence
of his death the ability of Crossroads to bring pressure to
bear on the local MP, from within the Labour Party, became a
far more difficult task. Apart from the local MP there were
six councillors covering the Gorbals and Govanhill areas -
three Labour Party, two Scottish Nationalist Party (SNP) and
one Conservative. Of the Labour Party councillors, only one
was regarded as being positively pro-Crossroads and having the
necessary commitment to promote the case of the fieldwork units

within the Labour Party. The only other enthusiastic support
came from a SNP councillor, whose ability to influence the
local MP was obviously very limited.

Despite these new factors, the second 'Save the Units' campaign
differed little from the programme devised for the 1977 review.
Appeals for support were to be sent to courses, professional
associations, other community projects, the local social work
teams and politicians in the West of Scotland. Action was to
be taken by the staff, through the Voluntary Workers branch of
the TGWU. On the local front, which was again the key arena
for the campaign, strenuous efforts were to be made to inform
local groups about the situation and to mobilize a broad based
lobby of the MP. The role of the behind the scenes 'negotiator'
and 'peacemaker' was taken over by the one Labour party councillor who was known to be committed to the work of the Units.

The overall strategy of the campaign was to implement action
quickly and attempt to bring out into the open the behind the
scenes debate about the future of the units. Three valuable
months had already been lost and further delays could be fatal.
A lobby and meeting with the local MP was organized for 17
October.

Meeting with the Minister

The meeting was held in a community room at the Stirlingfauld
Flats. This room had a seating capacity of forty. At 7.30 p.m.
over a hundred residents were packed into the small room. In
all, some twenty-one local groups were represented. The meeting was dominated by a forty-minute-long speech by the MP,
speaking in his capacity as a government Minister. This speech
was a tour de force of criticism and polemic against Crossroads.
The main points were:

(a) That Crossroads had manufactured the 'crisis' about the
future of the Gorbals unit. Information about that situation
had been distorted and falsified.

(b) The units existed to provide student training and not to
promote militant action. Much of local community action supported by Crossroads was unnecessary, damaging to the image of
Glasgow and directed against the Labour Party.

(c) Crossroads received generous grants from the government
and the staff were well paid. Many other organizations in
Gorbals and Govanhill — including the Labour Party — did
invaluable voluntary work without receiving a penny of public
money. It was also alleged that insufficient public information

was ever revealed about the management of Crossroads.

(d) Acting against the advice of his civil servants, the
Minister had decided that the Gorbals post could be advertized
providing, and this point was stressed at great length, that
there was consultation with the elected representatives and
other interested parties about the job remit and guidelines.

At the end of his speech the Minister announced that the meeting was over as far as he was concerned. After a stunned
silence, an uproar of reaction broke out. With the Minister
poised to leave the meeting a Crossroads management representative demanded that the pledge about the Gorbals post should
be put into writing and signed, by the Minister, before the
people at the meeting. After an initial hesitation and amidst
cries of 'Sign!', 'Sign!' from the audience, the Minister
agreed to put his signature to a short statement. This statement read as follows:

> Permission to advertize forthwith the position and
> appointment of a fieldwork teacher for Crossroads is
> hereby given on condition that agreement is reached in
> guidelines and policy involving consultations with the
> elected representatives for the area and selected mem-
> bers of Crossroads and a representative of SWSG.

The sting in the tail was the reference to consultation on
'guidelines and policy'. Crossroads went ahead with advertiz-
ing the vacancy with the Gorbals Unit. This was a gesture of
hope rather than confidence, because no appointment could be
made until the 'guidelines' had been settled. The concern
over how the guidelines would be formulated was confirmed when
the Minister's ad hoc committee on the Gorbals appointment was
set up and held its first meeting.

Policy and Job Description

The Minister insisted on selecting the Committee which was to
decide on the policy and job description for the Gorbals post.
Those invited, in addition to the Minister and two senior
civil servants, were four councillors from Gorbals and Govanhill (three Labour representatives and the SNP district
councillor for Gorbals), one management committee member of
Crossroads and three 'community' representatives chosen by the
Minister. Of the councillors, two were known to be sympathetic
and supportive of Crossroads, one was defined as hostile and
the fourth was likely to sit on the fence in any serious controversy. All the three selected community representatives
had, either in the present or the past, been associated with

the affairs of Crossroads; two were very sympathetic, but the third was felt to put his loyalty to the Minister and the Labour Party above any commitment to local organizations. Attempts by Crossroads to influence the composition of the Committee failed.

After two meetings, both of which were dominated by the Minister, Crossroads were presented with three proposals.

(a) That one of the Units should be transferred after a two year period and that during this period Crossroads should come up with plans about which Unit should move and also make suggestions about new locations.

(b) A revised job description for the fieldwork teacher's post which sought to define more narrowly the student training role of the Units and included, most significantly, a clause which sought to prohibit 'militant activities' by fieldwork teachers and students.

> The fieldwork units are funded solely for educational purposes. Teachers and students shall require to see their relationship with local groups is one of enabling and not initiating or promoting activities. In particular students and teachers shall not be personally involved in militant activities in the training area.

(c) A selection committee which could vet applications for the Gorbals post and appoint the new fieldwork teacher. The composition of this selection committee would be the Minister, two Labour Party Regional councillors, three Crossroads management representatives and one academic representative. These persons would have voting rights. A Crossroads staff member and an SWSG social work advisor would attend in a non-voting capacity.

When asked what he defined as militant activities the Minister replied 'staff and students leading demonstrations'. He considered it legitimate for staff to undertake background work for local groups, but drew the line at them figuring prominently in collective forms of action. The Minister would not permit any changes in the procedures for interviewing candidates. He refused to accept a Crossroads proposal that the Association's management committee representatives should be in a majority on the selection committee, as they had always been in previous selection committees for fieldwork teaching posts. Indeed, the Minister stated that he had the authority, if he cared to exercise it, to make the appointment himself and that participation by Crossroads was not a right. Even more

remarkably, the Minister went on to outline the qualities
which he valued in community workers and named a Glasgow-based
community worker who, in his opinion, had the necessary experience and attributes for the fieldwork teaching post. Amongst
the desirable qualities, singled out by the Minister, was this
person's 'loyalty to the party'.

Crossroads Decides

Crossroads were presented with a stark choice – either they
accepted the Minister's proposals on the Gorbals post (including the two year transfer period for one of the Units) or they
faced a further very uncertain struggle over the future of one
or both of the Units. The staff decided to recommend to the
Crossroads management that the proposals should be rejected,
on the grounds that they imposed unacceptable restrictions on
the role of staff and undermined the independence of Crossroads
as a non-statutory community work agency. It was clearly recognized by the staff that rejection of the proposals would lead,
almost inevitably, to the closure of one or both of the Units
and staff redundancies.

The last act in the 1978 review was played out, very appro-
priately, by the Crossroads management committee and local
community groups. An emergency meeting was convened for 26
November, at which a decision would be taken over whether or
not to accept the Minister's proposals. This meeting was
thrown open to all those local organizations which had supported the Crossroads campaign and it drew representatives
from ten of the major community organizations in Gorbals and
Govanhill. Prior to this meeting it had become apparent that
local opinion was divided over the proposals. On one side was
the view that no compromises should be made. The proposal
should be rejected even if, as seemed likely, this would result in the closure of the Gorbals Unit. One advocate of this
position summed it up by saying: 'I'd prefer not to have a
Unit in Gorbals than one controlled by the Labour Party'. On
the other side, was a view which proposed that the Unit should
be kept open, even at the cost of compromise and the erosion
of Crossroads' independent status. This school of thought
argued that Gorbals and Govanhill could ill afford to lose any
community work resources and its advocates also raised practical
questions about how effective the monitoring and implementation
of the new controls might be. It was argued that 'militancy'
was open to various and differing interpretations; that the
contract did not impose constraints on the fieldwork teachers
in their non-educational roles; that the Minister would find it
difficult to keep detailed checks on staff activities and that,
indeed, his powers and responsibilities might change at the

next general election: (a prophetic argument in the light of the 1979 election results). One tenant activist in Gorbals stated:

> The Gorbals Unit must be kept open – we need it. Agree to the proposals and let them do the worrying. Go on working normally and we'll fight the controls when they arise.

These competing views were clearly expressed at the meeting on 26 November. The first part of the meeting was a general debate on the situation. Everyone present, including the staff, had the opportunity to put forward their opinions and recommendations. After this debate the staff left the meeting. The final policy decision was left to the Crossroads committee members and the representatives of the local groups. During the period when the staff were absent the meeting considered and voted on three separate motions. There was a maximum of fifteen votes available for each motion. Each local group represented at the meeting had one vote (10 in all) and the remaining five votes were exercised by Crossroads office holders and individual members of the management committee. It was agreed that if a motion did not have an overall majority, then the motion with the least votes would fall and a further vote would be taken on the remaining motions. The three motions put before the meeting were as follows:

(a) *'That the management accept the contract under protest but reject the interviewing committee.'*

This motion received two votes in the first ballot.

(b) *'That the management reject the contract.'*

This motion received six votes in the first ballot.

(c) *'That the management accept the contract but reserve the right to veto anyone chosen by the interviewing committee.'*

This motion received seven votes in the first ballot. With no motion having an overall majority in the first ballot motion (a) was deleted and a further vote was taken on the remaining two motions. The voting was:

Motion (b): 7 votes
Motion (c): 8 votes

Thus Crossroads accepted, by the narrowest of majorities, the Minister's proposals, with a qualification over the right to

veto candidates. When they returned to the meeting the staff
were informed of the decision. Only one staff member commented
on the decision. He expressed his disagreement with the decision, but said that he respected the open and democratic manner in which the meeting had reached its decision. He might
also have added that the meeting had been a clear demonstration
of the process of community self-determination which the staff
had attempted to stimulate in Gorbals and Govanhill. The Minister accepted the Crossroads policy decision and, on 23 December,
the selection committee interviewed candidates and made an
appointment which was acceptable to Crossroads. The second
review of the units was over.

Postscript

In the 1979 General Election the MP comfortably retained his
seat, but lost his ministerial position at the Scottish Office.
The future of the Crossroads units passed into the hands of a
new Conservative Minister. Early in 1980 Crossroads were informed that the SWSG were no longer interested in moving
either of the two fieldwork units. The restrictive clauses in
the fieldwork teacher's contract still remained in force, but,
in the absence of political pressure from the top, these restrictions have had little effect on the pattern and style of
the local community work. The pragmatists amongst the Crossroads management were proved correct. It is ironic to note
that Crossroads might have been one of the few community work
agencies in Scotland to have positively benefited from the
return of a Conservative government.

STRATEGIES FOR SURVIVAL

The 1977 and 1978 reviews forced Crossroads to make many
compromises and concessions in order to survive. The conflict
with the Minister resulted in Crossroads temporarily losing
its independence as an employer of staff, reluctantly agreeing
to the insertion of a political clause in staff contracts and
being forced to accept a two-year period of closure for one of
its Units. Against these major concessions must be balanced
the fact that the campaigns fought by Crossroads defeated in
1977 and delayed in 1978 moves for an immediate closure of one
of the Units. How we judge the outcome of the reviews depends,
very much, on the price one is prepared to pay for survival -
the very criteria upon which the Crossroads management had to
decide at its crucial meeting on 26 November. The same actions
can be interpreted as either a 'sell-out' or a 'shrewd tactical
move'. Strongly-held principles can also be modified in the
light of subsequent experience. Thus, the staff vigorously
opposed the Minister's proposals, but no staff member resigned

in protest over the narrow acceptance of these proposals by
the management. In contrast, the then Secretary of Crossroads
did resign over the decision, on the grounds that Crossroads
had 'sold out to the MP'.

Whatever judgement is made, the ability of Crossroads to sustain itself through the two reviews, which in total added up
to twelve months of sustained conflict spaced over a two-year
period, is worthy of comment. Many voluntary organizations
have folded and collapsed in the face of far less pressure
from their sponsors. The strategies adopted by Crossroads
rested on the interplay of three main factors: the role played
by local residents and community organizations in exerting
pressure on the Minister; the capacity of Crossroads to mobilize broad-based external support in the 'Save the Units' campaigns and the collective discipline of the management and
staff in the face of sustained pressure and adversity.

Local Involvement

In political terms the local community-based support for Crossroads was crucial during both the reviews. In 1977 the local
pressure on the Minister played a decisive part in abruptly
ending the first review and, in 1978, the turnout at the 17
October public meeting may well have helped to swing the scales
away from an immediate closure or transfer of the Gorbals Unit.
While it would be naive to say that this local support represented a direct threat to the Minister in voting terms, it did
represent the threat of growing discontent and criticism within
the parliamentary constituency. No MP, however safe his seat,
views with complacency the prospect of local groups constantly
snapping at his heels and making life difficult in terms of the
management of constituency and party affairs. It was this
threat of disruptive action at the grass roots level, carried
out by groups and individuals who were largely beyond the
direct control of the Minister, which comprised the crucial
sanction exercised by the local support for Crossroads.

The ability of Crossroads to mobilize this support was due to
a combination of factors. Crossroads had been active in Gorbals and Govanhill since the late 1960s; its staff had been
closely identified with a number of popular and broad-based
community campaigns, and, very significantly, Crossroads had
opened its management structure to include representatives of
local groups. By the time of the reviews the management 'council' was dominated by local representatives who were resident
in either Gorbals or Govanhill. Many of the local activists
who figured prominently in the 'Save the Units' campaigns were
also management committee members of Crossroads. They were the

employers of the community work staff and, as a consequence of
this, they were directly involved in the sponsorship disputes
from the start. Thus, when the disputes surfaced in 1977 and
1978 the conflict was between, on the one hand, the Crossroads
staff and local management, and, on the other, the Minister, a
majority of the local Labour Party and the SWSG civil servants.
The conflicts were not, as has happened in some community work
projects, confined to a sectional struggle between professional
workers and politicians or between professional workers and the
administrators for the sponsors. In the case of Crossroads,
the local management members defined the attacks on the staff
as attacks on themselves and a threat to resources over which
they legitimately exercised control. The local people were not
passive spectators on the side-lines, or, as sometimes happens,
called in at the last moment for assistance when other strategies have failed in sponsorship disputes.

A commitment to developing local influence over the management
of community work resources should be a basic ingredient in
any community work process. It also provides, for professional
staff, a valuable source of legitimacy and support in times of
conflict with sponsors. This local involvement is not, as
Corrigan and Leonard argue, a diversion from the primary aims
of community work, or, for staff involved in job security
struggles, a diversion from taking trade union action.[3]

External Support

Although, during the reviews, much of the energy of Crossroads
was devoted to organizing local support a considerable emphasis
was also placed on mobilizing external support for the 'Save
the Units' campaign. Pressure from the staff's trade union,
the sympathetic letters of support received from Colleges and
Universities and the personal lobbying undertaken by individuals,
all functioned to exert pressure on the Minister and imposed
limits on the degree to which it could be argued that the Units
had a deserved reputation for either irresponsibility or for
failure to fulfil student-training tasks. Equally vital was
the support received from those members of the Labour Party who
dissented from the hard line taken by the Minister and the
majority of the local Party. The role of the Govanhill councillor as a peacemaker in the 1977 review was influential in
speeding up a settlement and, in the 1978 review, the support
of a sympathetic Labour Party councillor served to put a further
brake on the Minister taking hurried and precipitous action over
the future of the units. One should not also discount the impact of the support received from the SNP district councillor
in Gorbals, whose party stood to gain considerable propaganda
value from any cutback in Crossroads resources. The fear of

the SNP capitalizing on the conflict between the Labour party
and Crossroads, especially in the run-up to a general election,
may well have also influenced the Minister's decision to concentrate on the job description rather than immediately closing
or moving one of the Units.

In tactical terms, the approach to the mobilization of external
support was similar to the methods adopted in many of the local
community action campaigns in Gorbals and Govanhill. The
Crossroads staff and management used and applied this experience in their own struggle for survival. The basic tactic was
that of 'organizing on many fronts' (see Chapter 6) and, within
this strategy, a priority was given to developing trade union
support and gaining the sympathetic backing of Colleges and
Universities. These sources of external support were viewed as
complementary activities and not as alternative tactics or competing reference groups.

Collective Discipline

Reports on sponsorship conflicts invariably mention the debili-
tating effect these can have on staff and organizational morale.
Work can no longer be planned on a long term basis: worries
grow about job prospects and the stresses and strains begin to
have adverse effects on personal and professional relationships.
To survive a long-term dispute, especially within the context
of small 'shoe string' agencies, requires a high level of trust,
solidarity and mutual respect between staff members and, as in
the case of Crossroads, the local management members. Compared
with some community work agencies, Crossroads was well placed
to survive the experience of a lengthy sponsorship dispute.
Some of the staff had worked together for a number of years and
had previously resolved any serious disagreements over political
opinions and work style. Similarly, a number of the local
management committee had been associated with Crossroads for a
number of years. In some cases, their involvement started with
the setting up of the first unit in the early 1970s. Also, the
experience of community work in Gorbals and Govanhill had, on
many previous occasions, exposed the staff and local management to the tensions of operating in conflict situations and
coming into confrontation with the authorities.

The value of this shared experience was most apparent in the
collective discipline which existed during the reviews.
Policy decisions once taken were adhered to: disagreements
rarely carried over into personal friction; no-one broke ranks
and went off on a personal 'ego' trip or attempted to try out
tactics which had not been previously debated or discussed.
This collective discipline not only helped to sustain morale,

it also prevented the internal organization of Crossroads from being seriously disrupted by the pressures of the review and was a safeguard against 'divide and rule' situations developing. This is not to imply that the pressure of the review did not take its toll. During the 1978 review, one of the youth-work staff left because of his understandable concern about future job prospects. Such casualties have to be weighed against the capacity of Crossroads to sustain itself through twelve months of attack, uncertainty and tension.

Chapter Ten

LESSONS FROM EXPERIENCE

> Successful community work practice is still very much
> an art and an accident with improvisation a frequent
> manoeuvre.[1]

In this chapter we draw upon the case study material and interviews with Crossroads staff to offer some reflections on the
theory and practice of community work, with particular reference to the debate about 'directiveness and non-directiveness'
and the organizational processes involved in the development
of community groups. These reflections provide a backcloth to
the more detailed evaluation which is presented in Part Three,
when staff views on community work practice, training and local
organizations are compared with those of community activists,
students, politicians and informed outsiders.

COMMUNITY WORK METHODS

In Chapter Four we noted how the contexts in which the community
worker operated - the employing body, the funders, the local
setting - shaped the practice of community work. We suggested
that the worker was neither independent of these influences nor
imprisoned by them. Within a shifting set of boundaries the
worker's own value-dispositions did influence the selection of
issues and the methods of work which were adopted. The Crossroads staff were sympathetic to the Friere[2] prescription that
the way to work, for both structural and personal change, was
though a process of 'dialogue'. However, in the actual practice of community work it became painfully apparent that deciding upon the appropriate means to achieve those objectives
presented a constant source of tension for the workers.
Ideally, a local project would achieve success through a process which expanded the abilities and power of the participants

and contributed to wider structural change in society. In real
life, however, a choice had often to be made between these
variables, and the emphasis the worker placed upon each factor
would influence the method of work which was adopted.

In the British community work literature this debate has tended
to be couched in the language of 'task goals' versus 'process
goals' and the emphasis, which the worker places on each, is
defined along a directive/non-directive continuum.[3] Rothman
has usefully clarified the use and misuse of these concepts.

> The goal of enhanced functional capacity (loosely what
> we have described as process goals) has become synony-
> mous with non-directive role performance. On the other
> hand goals related to delimited functional problems
> (what we have loosely described as task goals) become
> tightly linked with a directive role stance. When one
> analyses the problem it becomes obvious that hypo-
> thetically either goal category may be approached from
> either a directive or non-directive practice standpoint.[4]

The emphasis on the directive and non-directive dichotomy has
served to conceal an important value variable, which relates
to whether action flows from a decision of the client system
or from a decision of the practitioner. A recognition of this
variable prompts us to seriously question some of the stereotyped classifications which have developed around the different
conceptual models for community work. Thus, the community
development model, with its emphasis upon process goals, is
usually categorized as non-directive when it can be either
democratic or manipulative according to who makes the final
decision. The community action model, which is frequently
labelled as directive by its critics, can also be democratic
or manipulative depending upon the primary source of decision-
making. Similarly, a caricature of the 'organizer'[5] has
developed because this value-dimension has not been fully taken
into account.

Rothman suggests that it is more appropriate to categorize projects on the basis of this value dimension. The Crossroads
approach to community work predisposed the staff to adopt
'organizer' roles in relation to local groups and to favour
'bargaining or conflict' relationships with the authorities.
Staff sought to avoid covert forms of manipulation and operated
on the premise that the open articulation of preferences for
action was not incompatible with a respect for the principles
of client self-determination.

> The Crossroads staff had never operated on a simplistic
> non-directive approach and had always been prepared –
> when local circumstances required it – to become heavily
> involved in exposing needs, direct organizing and arguing
> for certain lines of action to be taken. For the staff
> the acid test of success or failure in community work
> was whether, over a period of time, the local groups
> developed a capacity for self-determination and a collec-
> tive ability to decide, whether the community worker
> agreed with them or not, on their own action policies.
> (Staff member)

This approach would be classified as directive according to
conventional typologies of community work, but the crucial
factor, according to Rothman, is that the citizen group has
the final decision.

> It is not the act of giving goal direction that may be
> questionable, but rather the way it is given. Within
> this logic, the practitioner it would seem may validly
> suggest, advocate and stimulate as long as the approach
> is factual and a rational one, conveyed without enter-
> ing into personalities or invective, without expressing
> primarily personal motives or desires, without bringing
> overbearing pressure and most important of all, as long
> as the final decision is left with the citizen group in
> which ultimate authority resides and this lay preroga-
> tive is manifestly conveyed. There is no theoretical
> or ethical difficulty encountered in the practitioners
> offering a suggested plan and supporting fact. The
> community representative group may make of it what he
> likes.[6]

On this basis, the Crossroads position would be contrasted
with some of the Marxist prescriptions for community work practice, which place a central emphasis upon the political educational role of the worker.[7] Corrigan and Leonard outline this
perspective:

> The whole experience of community politics is not one
> with a long historic tradition within the English
> Working Class and consequently it is essential for the
> full-time worker to take a directly political role
> rather than simply following the wishes of the meeting.
> This latter role of being the non-directive instrument
> of others' intentions is essentially wrong because the
> mass meeting will not have any spontaneous feeling for
> the best strategy.[8]

While we would not disagree with the necessity of workers
declaring their political preferences, we would dispute that
the workers' views have an enhanced value over those articulated by local activists, either in mass or individually.
The argument that the worker is more likely to have the correct
political analysis - to 'know best' - is a recipe for political
paternalism and it is dubious to claim the backing of history
to legitimize this vanguard thesis. To suggest that working
people have no history of 'community politics' is more a
reflection of the orthodox Marxist obsession with work place
struggles than it is an accurate comment on historical experience.[9]

Implications of Client Self-Determination

Client self-determination does not absolve the community
worker from making ethical decisions. Crossroads staff refused
to organize against squatters in redevelopment areas or to campaign to remove a hostel for alcoholics from the Gorbals area.
At times, the community workers considered withdrawing support
from a long-standing group:

> At one time I had to consider whether I would continue
> to work with the Tenants' Association. Certain tenants
> were suggesting that they would not support a woman's
> stand against eviction because of her personal back-
> ground - mainly allegations that she was an unfit mother
> and possibly a prostitute. The Tenants' Association
> members were going against policy, not because there
> was a new analysis of the situation, or as a new tactic,
> but simply because of their personal views of the person
> facing eviction. Fortunately, these views didn't pre-
> vail, and I could continue to work with the Tenants'
> Association. (Staff member)

Community workers must also accept that independent local
organizations may not always agree with their views. When the
staff refused to allow one of their colleagues to fill a
leadership position in a local group, the local organizations
boycotted the Unit (see Chapter 3) and, in the sponsorship
disputes, the staff had to accept that the Crossroads management committee could reject their tactical suggestions (see
Chapter 9). As Harry Salmon argues, this form of rejection
can be a source of satisfaction as well as frustration.

> Residents, having gained some understanding of the role
> of community workers, are very quick to spot any tend-
> ency on the part of a professional to manipulate or
> dominate a situation. They are rightly jealous of

their independence and freedom to make their own decisions. We take it as a measure of success that even
some of our more directive comments are ignored.[10]

For the Crossroads staff, the benefits of self-determination
far outweighed the personal or political disadvantages. Unlike
Corrigan and Leonard, their practical experience indicated
that local residents had a 'feeling for the best strategy' as
often as did the community workers.

Management of Community Work Agencies

Specht[11] has noted that client involvement in the management
of projects has rarely been given a priority in British community work, and, in our experience, many community workers
argue forcibly against this policy. This opposition tends to
be a mixture of serious ideological objection and, far less
edifying, an expression of cynical self-interest by community
workers who are threatened by the prospect of local people
'telling them what to do'. Local management is far more
likely to develop in projects which place a central emphasis
on client self-determination than in projects, like some of
the Home Office Community Development experiments,[12] where the
parent organization maintains control over the purse strings
while supposedly passing over management responsibilities to
local residents. For Crossroads, local management involved a
redistribution of power and control over financial resources.

> Participation and power should go together. Redistri-
> bution of power needs to accompany any scheme to obtain
> the involvement of local people in the life of their
> neighbourhood. If people are to be encouraged to
> engage in self-help then they must be given control
> over the necessary resources.[13]

The ideological objections tend to view local involvement in
community work management as a diversion from wider struggles
and as a political cul-de-sac which saps local energies in the
minutiae of administration. Fears along these lines were
expressed about the Crossroads developments, but the reality
was somewhat different. Local activists tended to retain their
wider commitments and work on management affairs. The inevitable involvement with detailed administration had to be
balanced against the experience gained in negotiating for funds
and active participation in the various struggles over sponsorship. These later experiences widened rather than narrowed the
political horizons of the local residents.

In the early days there weren't the big decisions to
be made, but now it's changed, and there have been some
decisions to be made - not very pleasant decisions -
and it was better these were not made by the staff. My
outlook has changed. I used to feel politicians were
bound to support us because we were doing a good job.
They're not bound to support us. I find it horrible
but now I realize that some politicians support local
projects for what they can get out of it. (Local
resident)

An involvement in community work management - like an involvement in the running of self-help groups and community-based
housing associations - provides small scale opportunities to
test out alternative forms of organization and management
which are, hopefully, rehearsals for larger things to come.
To postpone these experiments until wider societal changes
have occurred is to reinforce and perpetuate the conditions
for rule by professionals and political elites.

INSIGHTS INTO COMMUNITY ORGANIZATIONS

The successes and failures of community action provide valuable
insights into the organization and functioning of local community groups. Organizing in low income areas presents particular
problems of motivating people to become involved in collective
action and several factors can be crucial in determining
whether collective action will be successful. These factors
include the nature of the political representation for the
area, the presence of a 'political entrepreneur', the internal
structure and leadership qualities of the group and the
organizational support which is available. Apart from the
significant omission of the politicians, these factors are
similar to those identified by local activists when they pin-
pointed the reasons for the success of the Dampness Campaign
(see Chapter 6). In this discussion we will not elaborate upon
the question of organizational support - the resources provided
by community work agencies and other professionals - as this
factor is more fully examined elsewhere (see Chapters 11 and 12).

Organizing in Low Income Areas

One of the major problems, for nearly every organization in
Gorbals and Govanhill, was overcoming the apparent apathy of
low income residents. An extensive literature on poverty and
political participation suggests that this apathy can be a
rational response to the vicissitudes of living in a hostile
world, rather than being a symptom of deviant, pathological
behaviour.[14] The very struggle for daily survival makes the

poor less likely to engage in political action which only
promises relief at an uncertain, future date. The poor, moreover, are especially vulnerable to sanctions from public agencies and the police. The movement out of apathy will only
occur over issues which directly affect self-interest and are
amenable to producing tangible improvements in the life situation of residents.

> The first problem which the protest organizer faces is
> finding an issue which will interest the poor enough to
> induce them to support a boycott, demonstration or some
> other kinds of protest tactic. That is, he is seeking
> to clarify the structural sources of their discontent
> and to convince them that they can ameliorate their
> life situation through collective action.[15]

In Gorbals and Govanhill dampness, rehousing and redevelopment
proved to be such issues, but for many residents planning
issues were not such a direct and effective stimulus for collective action. Established political elites can function to
suppress and cool-out potentially controversial issues and
prevent them from getting on to the agenda for public debate.[16]
Community workers can act in a similar manner and, by refusing
to support an issue, they may well limit a local group's
chances of success.

> In one area in Glasgow the community workers, who were
> in the Labour Party, actually got together, to block a
> local issue which would embarrass the Party. (Local
> authority planner)

In contrast, the political philosophy of the Crossroads staff
predisposed them to highlight issues which directly affected
the poor, and brought them into conflict with the authorities.

> On the one hand in Govanhill there are those with the
> power - the Council and officials. On the other hand
> there were the people - those without power - those
> were the ones we worked with. (Staff member)

Political Representation

> Love them or hate them you cannot ignore the councillors.
> (Staff member)

Politicians can make or break community groups. We have
divided the elected members - councillors and MPs - into
integrationist politicians and change politicians, since we
find this classification a useful simplification for the

purpose of analysis. Integrationist politicians are in line
with the Party and, in Glasgow, are frequently members of the
ruling administration. They have little inclination to 'rock
the boat' since this would not, normally, be politically
advantageous to them. Integrationist politicians, who represent the Labour Party, find consistency between rhetoric and
practice by blaming the ills of society on structural inequalities and by blaming many of the ills of their local areas on
the social pathology or undeserving nature of some of their
constituents.

> I think you have to draw a line. Are you helping the
> real people, the deserving people, or helping those
> who are just using you as a body to further their own
> purposes. This is where the knowledge of the local
> councillor comes in. (Councillor)

Integrationist politicians are more likely to favour limited
participation in politics and to give a top priority to the
needs of the Party organization. Paternalism and patronage
are common.

> Each person has a problem but it's their own private
> problem – you hold public meetings – you may get a few
> who do the bawling and shouting, but each one has
> their own private individual problem and can't give
> it to you because it's public and they're too
> embarrassed. So naturally they've got to have one
> person they can go to and they expect to be able to
> go to their councillors. If the councillors were
> doing their work there would be no need for organ-
> izations in the area. (Councillor)

In contrast, change politicians are often, in our experience,
fairly junior within the administration and are, at least in
this early stage of their political careers, in favour of
change – both in the wider society and within the Party organization. They may also be less personally threatened by certain forms of challenge to established politics, because their
formal administrative responsibilities do not embrace a direct
managerial role. e.g. the backbench councillor who is not a
Convenor (Chairperson) of a major Committee or the Regional
councillor who has no formal responsibilities for Council house
policies (a District Council responsibility).

> The real reason, I think, Regional Councillors are
> prepared to go along with community action is because
> we don't have much to lose – we don't control housing.
> (Regional councillor)

The ills of society are blamed largely on structural inequalities, and, more occasionally, on the shortcomings of the
Labour Party's organization and policies. They, therefore,
have less need to scapegoat the undeserving poor in order to
find consistency in their political beliefs, and are more
likely to favour a broader form of participation in politics.
Indeed, the advocacy of grass roots activism may be an alternative, if less predictable, way of climbing the career ladder
within the Labour Party, as compared with the more orthodox
route of 'faithful' service to the needs of the party.

> I believe that everyone should be involved in politics -
> there's no such thing as a 'gifted few' who should be
> involved in it. I'm in favour of local organizations -
> they put pressure on me and that makes me put that bit
> more pressure on the authorities. It also makes it
> slightly easier for me because you feel you've someone
> at your back supporting your stand. (Councillor)

Political Entrepreneur

Olsen's public goods theory of interest groups suggests that
rational appeals to self-interest may not be sufficient
grounds to sustain collective action.

> Individuals in a large aggregate will not <u>voluntarily</u>
> pay for the costs of collective goods even if they are
> all rational men and aware that they will receive
> individual benefits from these goods. In order to
> persuade individuals to pay for collective goods, an
> interest group must either provide a device with which
> members can coerce themselves into paying for the costs
> of the goods or provide in addition to the collective
> goods, some kind of selective individual benefit.[17]

O'Brien identifies the presence of a 'political entrepreneur'
as a key factor if collective action is to be sustained.

> The political entrepreneur was successful in developing
> social and political organization because they were
> able to provide selective individual benefits to
> individuals supporting collective organization.
> Political entrepreneurs saw to it that appeals to
> altruism were heavily intermingled with concrete
> inducements to the individual self-interest.[18]

The Secretary of the Dampness Campaign understood the need for
personal inducements to encourage collective organization and
this might have been one reason for the campaign's success.

> The campaign provided extensive individual benefits to
> members - information, advocacy services, legal advice -
> and was also prepared to exercise sanctions over the
> residents who failed to contribute to the Dampness
> Campaign. Lacking the hard organizational sanctions
> which can be exercised by trade unions - such as black-
> listing and 'sending to Coventry' - the campaign exer-
> cised control by threatening to withdraw from non par-
> ticipants the individual services which were organized
> by the campaign. e.g. before residents could collect
> their forms for making a compensation claim they had to
> attend a collective event (a public or committee meeting)
> at which the forms would be handed out. (Staff member)

Exercising sanctions and excluding non-participants can be
essential in the building of community organizations, especially those which, like the Dampness Campaign, are involved
in a protracted power struggle with the authorities. But, as
O'Brien notes, this exercising of sanctions can pose serious
dilemmas for community workers.

> The neighbourhood organizer is faced with the difficult
> choice between maintaining the 'purity' of his ideology
> and accepting a principle that may be distasteful but
> does offer some hope of truly giving power to the poor.
> We are   to find, for example, among idealistic
> community development workers a resistance to the need
> to go beyond voluntary participation and to use some
> form of coercion in order to ensure a solution to the
> public goods dilemma.[19]

A local Gorbals resident highlighted just such a resistance
amongst the Crossroads staff.

> I'll tell you one thing, the community workers should
> have done that which they didn't do - they should have
> charged every member a fee to join the organization.
> Local people, then, if they're charged a fee they want
> some service for that fee, and they'll work to get that
> service, but the community worker didn't see it that way.

The staff frequently discouraged formal membership and the
payment of dues in Tenants' groups because, they argued, such
a policy would exclude those residents who were most in need
of support. Gradually and, in some instances reluctantly, the
staff came to accept that membership conditions and the exercising of sanctions over non-participants, were vital to the
organization of some community groups. A balance had to be
struck between lofty idealism and hard headed realism.

Leadership and Organization

Crossroads staff were committed to change and the most effective structure for a community organization was a 'simple
structure of like-minded individuals owing sole or primary
allegiance to each other over goals'.[20] Some of the groups
supported by the staff had such a structure - the Redevelopment groups, the Dampness Campaign and, in its early days, the
Govanhill Action Group. Federated groups, such as the Govanhill Working Party and Community Councils, were viewed with
suspicion by staff. We have also suggested (see Chapter 7)
that leadership and community work support should reflect the
major objectives of the organization and should encourage
tactics consistent with these objectives. Consistency of goals,
structures, strategy, leadership and community work support
offers the best chances for a successful attainment of goals,
and an inappropriate structure or inappropriate tactics can
result in goal displacement and ritualism. As the case studies
illustrate, the presence of ritualistic leadership can be a
common cause of goal displacement in community organizations.
Support from ritualistic community workers could have a similar
effect. The suggestion that ritualistic leadership may often
be found within the more experienced local leadership (see
Chapters 7 and 8) casts doubts on community work practice which,
uncritically, assumes that previous industrial or political
experience is a pre-requisite in the struggle for change. Some
of the evidence from Gorbals and Govanhill supports the suggestion that residents with little or no previous political
experience might be less inhibited and restrained in their
willingness to adopt and support militant strategies. This
observation echoes some of the experiences reported in the
Women's Movement literature, which suggests that women, after
they have finally been drawn into organizations, prove themselves very committed and change-oriented.[21] The majority of
newcomers to collective action in Gorbals and Govanhill were
women.

On the thorny question of the internal organization of groups,
the Crossroads staff tried to find an uncomfortable balance
between open groups, which could encourage the maximum participation of residents, and a structured organization which
could present a disciplined challenge to the authorities.
There was an awareness that completely open organizations,
which deliberately lacked formal leadership positions and explicit rules for procedure, could generate informal norms
which excluded and mystified new participants. This experience
reflects criticisms made in the literature.

Contrary to what we would like to believe, there is no
such thing as a 'structureless' group because the idea
of 'structurelessness' does not prevent the formation
of informal structures but only formal ones. The rules
of how decisions are made are known only to a few and
awareness of power is curtailed to those who know the
rules, as long as the structure of the group is informal.
Those who do not know the rules and are not chosen for
initiation must remain in confusion, or suffer from
paranoid delusions that something is happening of which
they are not quite aware.[22]

The most telling criticism of unstructured groups is that 'they
may be very effective in getting women to talk about their
lives; they aren't very good for getting things done'.[23]   The
Crossroads staff were primarily concerned with achieving practical results and not organizing therapy groups. They, therefore, accepted the need for a formal organizational structure,
but attempted to make this structure as open and democratic as
possible. A former staff member, Colin Kirkwood, has defined
the ideal model.

> Open democratic Tenants Associations, Residents Asso-
> ciations, Action groups and other similar organizations –
> these are the growth points for participative democracy.
> This is in spite of their reactionary features, the
> tendency for the platform to dominate the floor; men
> to dominate women, the old to dominate the young; the
> danger of a subservient or client relationship with
> the local authority. It is romantic to imagine that
> the self organization of people at the bottom of the
> heap in capitalist society will not reproduce many of
> the features of that society. We should recognize and
> work to encourage their democratic co-operative features
> – sharing out decision-making; encouraging people to
> express themselves sometimes at the expense of the
> orderliness of the agenda; trying new suggestions by
> new people, a conscious attempt by the key experienced
> activists to see their job as facilitating the develop-
> ment of younger newer less confident people rather
> than hogging the interesting jobs and so on.[24]

Staff felt that this type of organization could extend the
skills and experience of local people:

> It's when you get a chance to compare some of the key
> members of the committee with similar people from dif-
> ferent areas who are starting to do the same job that
> you really see the difference in skills – the folk who

stuck with the project through thick and thin have
gained fantastic experience - they have great skill
in obtaining and managing resources. The skills are
not only practical but also personal - two years ago
they found it difficult to criticize each other or the
worker, to say the things they feel. Now folks are
much more able to say 'I don't like the way things are
going' or 'I think you're better at it'. The skill of
relating to each other in groups is much better.
(Staff Member)

Community work is essentially about the building, maintaining
and changing of organizations. A curiosity about how organizations 'tick' and an awareness of the tensions between theory
and practice are indispensable ingredients in the art of doing
community work. For the Crossroads staff the experience of
seven years of daily organizing confirmed some past experiences
and also exposed them to new insights, some of which were not
particularly palatable. The conservatism of some experienced
local leaders came as a surprise and the need, on occasions,
to enforce sanctions was a jolt to idealism. While the staff
helped to shape many of the community organizations in Gorbals
and Govanhill, the local situation also prompted the staff to
revise and rethink some of their previously held views.

PART THREE

EVALUATION

Chapter Eleven

WHAT MAKES A GOOD COMMUNITY WORKER?

How did local community leaders and other significant figures
in the social and political life of the area view the Crossroads community staff work? How did the staff view themselves
and other community workers? What qualities and skills did
they rate as being of a positive or negative value? What did
they consider to be good community work practice? In this
chapter we look at these questions through the eyes of staff,
local activists, politicians and a small group of informed
observers. Finally, we relate our findings and experiences to
the broader context of the community work literature. The
related concepts of skills and qualities assumes an importance
in this chapter and a dictionary definition might be helpful.
Skills relate to 'expertness', 'practised ability', and 'facili-
ty in doing', whereas qualities relate to 'mental or moral
attributes' and 'traits of character'.[1] Implied in this distinction is the suggestion that skills can be acquired as a
result of work experience, education or training, whereas qualities are more personalised and essentially reflect the social
and psychological make-up of individuals.

STAFF VIEWS

Although in the training of students the Crossroads staff
stressed the skills of community work (see Chapter 4), when
questioned about what made a good community worker, most staff
members mentioned qualities as frequently as skills. It should
be stressed that the qualities noted below are an ideal list
and are those considered significant for the workers with one
particular organization. We have divided our assessment into
political, personal and survival qualities.

Political Qualities

A Collective Perspective. The political perspective of the
Unit emphasized the ability of workers to link the private
troubles of individuals to wider public issues;

> The ability to link up individual grievances and try to
> encourage people to link these up into collective action
> should be a major stance of a community worker.

An ability to work with conflict. Staff acknowledged conflicts
of interest within the community as well as conflicts of interest with the authorities;

> You're committing yourself to all sorts of confrontations -
> between yourself and community members; between community
> groups and their tactics; between the agency and the
> delivery of services and between the community group
> and the authorities.

Personal Qualities

High Expectations

> You don't need to be radical to work for Crossroads -
> you just need to expect people to get a fair deal. If
> folks are middle class they know it's an awful deal
> people are getting - Crossroads is an organization
> which encourages staff to express their indignation
> instead of suppressing it.

Non-judgemental attitudes

> Crossroads staff are unusual in not categorizing the
> lowest grouping as undeserving yet they're able to cope
> with the more articulate deserving poor. I've yet to
> meet a worker in Crossroads who takes a deserving-
> undeserving poor attitude - the two groups don't meet
> that often but they are treated equally by staff.

Imagination

> I disagree with Alinsky's free and open mind - that's
> an academic statement and an impossibility. In a
> political sense you've already made up your mind about
> the manner and type of society you wish to see. You
> don't get objective community workers because they're
> concerned and interested and the political parameters

have already been set. Within these parameters,
however, I wouldn't close my mind to new developments
and new policies and testing out ideas to the full -
you need to be inventive and imaginative.

Staff also stressed the importance of working in one area for
a reasonable period of time, because a rapid turnover of staff
was detrimental to the development of local organizations. We
have, therefore, listed survival qualities, since staff felt
that it was important not only to work for a period of time
but 'to survive intact as a consistent personality'.

Survival Qualities

Patience is a virtue, a sense of humour important, and
commitment is vital;

A community worker has to be totally committed to the
work he's involved in - not only what the agency is
trying to do, but perhaps more important, committed to
the organization in the community which he's working
with, because the success rate in community work is
pretty low, and unless you are capable of looking in
the long-term, and also attracting some meagre amount
of success, then it's quite easy to fall by the wayside.
It's quite easy to give up.

Skills

Qualities alone were not sufficient and the staff also put a
strong emphasis on the skills of community work.

Relationship skills. These were the backbone of community
work; 'the credibility on which our work was founded'.

The community worker has got to be able to make contact
with all sorts of people - to be able to work with the
material he's given. Ideally you want a strong community
organization, but you never really get the ideal, so you
have to try and bring out the best in people - search for
people in the first place, then having got them involved,
work on their plus-points, bring out the strongest factors
and try to co-ordinate these with other plus-points that
other members of a group may have.

Communication skills. Skills in verbal communication are
closely linked with relationship skills. Written skills were
also rated as an asset and skills in the use of the mass media
were considered to demand more specialized knowledge and to

be linked with tactical acumen.

Organizational skills

> Our main work was setting up associations, committee
> structures and then supporting these in their work. This
> support took many forms - helping draw up and distribute
> leaflets; helping to draw up posters, draw up press re-
> leases, writing letters to various officials, helping
> tenants formulate demands based upon knowledge of the
> housing acts; set up delegations, demonstrations, and,
> where appropriate, participating in demonstration, and
> showing where our loyalty lay.

There was not a standard kit for developing organizations;

> I think there has to be a major concern about organization
> building and maintenance and a curiosity about different
> forms of organization, because the danger of community
> work is that we just reproduce the same institutional
> structures as the ones we're attacking.

Mediating skills. Generally, the perspectives of staff predisposed them to have a distrust of the 'honest broker' role
with the authorities. In contrast, they frequently fulfilled
a mediating role between opposing factions within a local group
(see Chapter 6). At times, the community worker may reject this
mediating role within groups. For example, in the case of the
GTRA (see Chapter 8) the community worker decided not to mediate
between an established and an emerging leadership but, instead,
supported the emerging leadership on the grounds that they
were more inclined to pursue change-directed goals.

Negotiating skills. Although staff quite frequently acted as
an advocate on behalf of individuals, they generally shunned
the role of negotiator with the authority. This was partly a
principled commitment to allow residents themselves to acquire
negotiting skills, but it also represented a tactical decision,
based on the fear that politicians could use the presence of
community workers to deflect the process of negotiation. The
experience of the Govanhill Action Group (see Chapter 7) however, suggests that the negotiator role with the authorities
might be appropriate at certain times. The skills of negotiation tend to be foreign to many local residents, and, especially
in a structured series of negotiations (such as a Working Party),
it might be more helpful to include the community worker in
the initial stages.

Entrepreneurial skills. Community work staff had to be

enterprising in attracting resources to the areas, and skilled
in locating sources of finance. The staff helped several local
groups to obtain funding from local and central government
sources (e.g. urban aid) and also from charities, such as the
Gulbenkian Foundation.

Research skills. All staff accepted the need to provide back-up
data for local organizations and to work on the time-consuming
task of the collation and analysis of survey material (see
Chapter 8).

Political and analytical skills

> I fail to see how we are going to change the world without
> analysis and curiosity of how things fit together and
> ability to enquire into our own personal experiences.
> I want to encourage people to view themselves in relation-
> ship to the wider totality of Society which is the first
> step in that tortuous road towards political sophistication.

Staff, continually, stressed the difference in their role when
compared with politicians;

> Politicians are tied to one party, philosophy and programme
> whereas a community worker is tied to the felt needs and
> stated objectives of the community. How the community
> defines its needs and objectives is what the worker deals
> with. But, although the issues and problems are self-
> defined by the community, the community worker tries to
> channel the grievances in a political manner.

Tactical skills

> The community worker's always got to be that one step
> ahead - he can't afford to lag behind the organization or
> if he does, there isn't a role for him because they can do
> it on their own. He has to plan ahead, be aware of possible
> outcomes and alternatives facing the community. He doesn't
> develop the community group in a certain direction, but he
> is aware of the likely results of certain actions.

Obviously, to fulfil this role, the community worker must have
a good grasp of the politics of local government, and the
particular circumstances which exist within the local community.

Knowledge in Community Work

Staff felt they needed knowledge of how local government and

the political system operated in practice and how these institutions affected the local area. They also required knowledge
of how to get resources for local groups and of the statutory
responsibilities of government, especially in respect of
housing legislation. Most important of all, they felt that it
was essential to have expertise and experience of how to bring
pressure to bear on the authorities. This was rated as the
most important type of knowledge needed for community work.

> The worker has to be politically astute (not in a Party
> sense), and to understand the mechanics of institutions,
> bureaucracy and the formal political structure.

LOCAL VIEWS

Before attempting to discuss how local activists assessed and
evaluated community workers, it is important to understand, at
least superficially, their view of the world. The values and
perspectives which they bring from their life experiences shape
the criteria by which the community worker is judged as being
helpful or unhelpful. We interviewed sixteen local activists.
All were residents who had been involved, some for many years,
with local community organizations and, in most cases, they had
been intimately involved with the work of Crossroads. Their
main concern was the development of effective local organizations, and there were several barriers to collective action
which were identified in the interviews.

Barriers to Collective Action

A personal view of the world. Although many of the activists
had a collective and class-based view of society, these perspectives were not shared by other residents.

> Most people see things personally: if it doesn't hurt me
> then it must be all right, but if it hurts me, it must
> be wrong.

Even those who were trade unionists at work became individually
orientated at home.

> When people leave work they become individual and
> conservative-minded; they don't want to know their
> brother next door.

To counteract this, residents must become involved outside of
the home.

> The most difficult thing is getting people out of their

houses - that's the only way people will realize the
house is only part of the place you stay - it's the
environment as much as the house. People have to
realize that if the world outside your home improves,
then what happens inside must improve too.

Political conservatism was by no means the only barrier to
collective action which was identified. Cultural barriers, the
product of adaptations to the vicissitudes of working-class
life, were considered equally important.

Deference

It's only since I got involved in the Tenants' Associations
and Crossroads that I've got to realize that officials and
councillors are only everyday folk like myself

Low Expectations

People would have learned to live with the problem - they
would have accepted it as they accepted everything else
in this area, they just feel they are working-class folk
and we are supposed to live like this. It's only when
you have a back-up group you begin to find some way of
fighting.

Fear

There's a universal fear - I mustn't oppose authority
because of retaliation - it's fear of 'big brother' and
the only way to fight this is by getting people organized.

Apathy

When people are forced to live as sub-humans in dilapidated run-down areas where vandalism is rife and the
housing conditions intolerable, they often become apa-
thetic. This apathy does not stem from an acceptance of
the conditions in which they are living, but is an extension of the apathy of the powers that be towards the
conditions and the people who have to live in them. When
you have tapped all the obvious and available sources of
help without success - councillors, officials, etc., where
do you go next? - you just give up.

Isolation

Someone like myself had lived in that house in that area

for three years and I was fully convinced that it was
only myself and the man next door who had a dampness
problem, and that we shared a defective wall. There
was no way I knew about anyone else. I'm the sort of
person who could live in an area all my life and not
even know the person living next door.

Domestic constraints. Many residents felt a split between
family and community responsibilities and some, especially the
women, experienced constraints which were imposed by the disa-
proval of their partner.

The majority of local activists are women, who often get
involved when their children start school and they start
having a little time. But it does take up a lot of time,
and sometimes you feel there's not enough hours in the day
and that you are neglecting the family. If you are a
woman you have more problems than a man. It does cause
problems at home, even if your husband is quite sympathetic.
Either you give up everything altogether and stay at home -
which to my mind is stupid - or else you just tell him
that you won't stay at home every night.

Qualities

Local residents stressed that the qualities of the community
worker were more significant than his skills or knowledge. To
overcome the barriers to collective action the community worker
should display the opposite characteristics. Often, these positive qualities are found as cultural adaptations in individuals
coming from more favoured social and economic backgrounds.

Funnily enough the real good community workers do not often
come from people who were actually brought up in the poor
conditions. If you live poorly you don't need to imagine
what it is to be poor - you get used to being poor and
not knowing where the next meal is coming from. Sometimes
a middle class person imagines it is even worse - it's not
as bad as they imagine, but it is bad enough.

The possession of these qualities is not enough. The community
worker must also be 'a catalyst in a process which transforms
failure into success'. Local people recognized that the community work role in this process demanded reliability, dedi-
cation and determination.

I think they're a special sort of people - dedicated -
they've got to be involved with the people more than their
own family - listen to people's troubles and do something

to help them.

The community worker is an individual who starts out losing
but he has to hold on in the face of adversity and then
eventually lie back once the organization is successful.
Most people can ride success - how a person reacts when
he's losing tells you the calibre of the community worker.
When something is successful is the day the community
worker should be moving on to his next project.

The most significant quality of all was the ability to change,
how local people perceived themselves - 'We need you to make
us feel important'. This plethora of qualities is rarely going
to be found in one individual!

Skills

Relationship skills. The above qualities are only of value if
the worker has the relationship skills to make himself acceptable to the local community. These skills are especially
important in community work, where relationships are not, as
in some branches of social work, authorized by the state. To
make good relationships with local people, the worker must be
approachable and accessible.

You've got to be approachable first. I should be able to
come and talk to you - you should be interested, not just
appear interested and you should then become involved.

Accessibility was not confused with proximity; it implied
having time for people.

Having time for local folk when they come in is
important - local people like to know that .... is in
charge and he's got time for them. If they were coming
into the Unit and getting brushed off they would stop
using the Unit.

Superiority was immediately sensed and was fatal to forming
relationships.

The thing I like about the professional staff is that
there is no feeling of superiority. If you go to one of
the Corporation officials, they speak down to you. The
staff here are well educated, but they speak to you on
the same level, person to person, not somebody above,
looking down.

Trust, the aim of the relationship, will only become possible when you have proved to the people that 'you're on their side'.

> They cannae trust officials and they cannae trust
> councillors - you've first to prove to people that
> you're on their side and then you can be trusted.

It is relevant to mention here the special importance of the
secretarial staff of the student units. To many residents,
they were the 'public face' of Crossroads, and it was crucial
that they too possessed the appropriate qualities in making
positive relationships. Many local residents would only return
to meet the community work staff if their initial contact with
the secretarial staff had been sympathetic.

Communication skills. The community worker must have skills
in communication, especially in the written word. 'People talk
a lot of sense but if you ask them to write it down, they find
it very difficult'. He must also develop these skills in local
people.

> A community worker must be able to put over his ideas
> and to write things down - to put in writing what local
> people are trying to say because a lot of local people
> don't have writing skills. A community worker has to
> be able to write a letter, write a report and then help
> local people develop these skills - it's not enough for
> him to do it all the time. He has to try to help local
> people develop that skill.

Organizational skills. Many regarded the 'creation of an issue'
as the crucial organizational skill. The ability to high-light
a common problem, was as important to the established leadership
as it was to newcomers to an area. An experienced tenants'
leader commented:

> You don't know some of the problems exist. A tenant
> comes with a problem about an individual house and you
> cannae generalise. If the student unit does a survey
> then we know what the general problem is, but we just
> don't have the time.

Organizational support was valued, especially in the early
days of an initiative. The secretarial and administrative
resources of the Unit were an essential part of this support.

> In the initial stages the support of the Unit was vital -
> they were supplying the secretarial services; supplying
> a degree of organization, for example, they organized the

initial meetings; the Unit was a base where people
could go and meet.

Mediating skills. The community worker was seen, by some, as
a type of 'community glue' (see Chapter 6).

Negotiating skills. The community worker should help local
people negotiate with outside authorities.

> A community worker has to help people speak and get
> their case over. It's different to arguing in the
> workplace with the foreman, getting your points over
> when you know all the pros and cons of it. We're working
> class and we don't meet people in authority - that's the
> first thing. All of a sudden you're asked to go to a
> committee meeting - that's an unknown quantity and you
> only learn through experience. The person going for the
> first or second time stutters and makes an idiot of
> themselves. It's all unknown and you've never done it
> before, so you go trying to look your best because your
> mother always told you to look your best. I think it's
> the Scottish heritage we've had battered into us!

Research skills. These were highly prized by all groups.

> I think this is one of the places where the Unit comes
> into its own. They seem to know where to go to get
> information and are very helpful in getting information
> when it's needed. It certainly saves a terrific amount
> of time for people not engaged in community work full
> time. Ability to get information - that's a must for
> a community worker - digging in archives, getting briefs
> for local groups.

Analytical skills. These were valued because they broaden
the perspectives of the local group.

> A community worker seems to be able to look further
> ahead and see where you are going, whereas being
> involved in the local group and working on the par-
> ticular issue, you don't see the wider aspects. Put
> differently, a community worker tends not to take what
> officials say at face value but questions the impli-
> cations behind it.

Political skills. Local residents stressed the need for
political action as well as political analysis, with the
ability to work with conflict as a necessary attribute.

A successful community worker is going to be at odds
with authority, particularly in rough areas where there
is a degree of deprivation. Most community workers are
going to work in deprived areas - you're not going to
get them in the suburbs where the problems are solved
by the psychiatrist and the coffee mornings - they're
not solved by opening up a social work unit in the
bungalow at the end of the garden. Most social workers
are going to end up in deprived areas and attempt to
get more from the local Council - so they're going to
be at loggerheads with someone. They must be able to
work in an area of combat.

Knowledge

The knowledge which local residents felt was important was
similar to that cited by community work staff. 'The Unit
was able to explain the Local Authority set-up which we didn't
understand.' Many activists did not expect the community
worker to be a 'know-all'.

They must recognize their lack of knowledge· the
community worker is not going to be a lawyer, doctor,
architect or any of these things. What he's got to
recognize is who to go to when the need arises.

Methods of Work

Local residents were concerned that community workers should
possess the appropriate qualities, skills and knowledge, and
they were even more concerned with how these attributes would
be used. Some felt that the community workers should use
their skills in whatever way would be most beneficial to the
local area.

I don't see why community workers shouldn't take the
chairman position or any other position offered. They've
got all the advantages of their training - local people
can go and talk to officials and it's the layman against
the professionals. If we've got a trained community
worker then the balance is better - he can talk the
officials' language. The community worker shouldn't
be frightened to be at delegations and stand up and
say we're right. Yet they're always looking over their
shoulders to see whether there will be any come-back
from the authorities. This shouldn't happen.

Others considered that this was impractical, because the

authorities would not permit the workers to accept leadership roles.

> I used to think that community workers should accept leadership positions but I've changed my mind on it... I feel if the community worker did this, no matter what your politics, somebody would say it was inappropriate, somebody would complain because you can't please all parties. So you should help people - give them as much help, support as possible, but encourage them to do it themselves.

The majority felt that community workers should encourage the development of independent groups, so that local residents could themselves acquire the skills and, even more important, the confidence, to run activities for themselves.

> I've always thought the Unit tries to put the community worker in to establish groups, and then let the groups try and carry on themselves with advice and help. That's quite good in a lot of ways because if it's just ordinary people who have formed themselves into a group, it gives ordinary people a better chance to develop than if someone is running it for them. Certainly they'll make mistakes, but how else will they learn? I've seen a number of people you never would have thought who have become involved, gone to meetings and gradually improved and improved.

This was seen as an important distinction between Crossroads and the normal local authority practice.

> I think Crossroads is a pretty good organization because they don't think for people - they may advise but they don't say to people - do this or do that. The ordinary social worker in the local authority would just take over the case. In practice, this is the main difference between Crossroads and the local authority - Crossroads helps people to help themselves.

One activist felt it was inevitable that community workers would impose their own judgements on local groups.

> I suppose you have to make a political judgement and then you force this judgement on other people. You have to say, I am a socialist or a capitalist or something else and then say that's the best system and I'll push in the direction of that system.

Most residents did not feel this way at all. They felt able
to make decisions independently of the community worker, and
regarded it as part of the community work role to foster this
independence. 'The sole purpose of having a community worker
in an area is in fact to get people to do it themselves'.

Political Action

It was in discussion about party politics that local residents
most clearly articulated how the values of the community workers affected them. Community workers, it seemed, were very
unlikely to directly influence political behaviour - a view
which is consistent with reports from other areas.[2]

> I don't see you're going to make anyone vote a different
> way by anything you say to them.

Nor could community workers persuade local groups to adopt
'militant' strategies against their will.

> If they got someone in the Unit trying to spout rhetoric -
> some left wing radical, say at the Citizens Theatre or
> trying to get people to throw tomatoes at the M.P., they
> wouldn't get a hearing. I think the control is imposed
> by the tenants - they may be apathetic but they're not
> daft. You can only go so far - say a march on the
> streets, they're not the type of person that would go
> outside the City Chambers and throw bricks and any
> student trying to advocate that wouldn't get a hearing.
> So despite the fears of the politicians I think they're
> unfounded.

Most residents felt that community workers should be evaluated
on the local work they did, rather than on their personal and
political values.

> Although your political ideals may affect the kind of
> work you do and your attitude to officialdom, when it
> comes to the community you don't walk about airing your
> political views all the time. I'm a member of the Com-
> munist Party but because of the work I do they forget
> what my political affiliations are and ignore the fact -
> they evaluate you on the work you do locally, not your
> political ideals.

This feeling was not shared by everyone.

> If you fight for people, right away you're marked as a

Communist, a Red somebody that's terrible. I think every
one of our tenants' committee has been branded a 'red
under the bed' - a monster - your own working class does
that to you. I think if you were a member of a political
party and a social worker you'd have to keep it quiet -
people would automatically think you were fighting for
the aims of the Party; the political tones come over and
people say 'He's a Red - they're all Reds there'. That
can break up a Tenants' group if they're known to have
political leanings, particularly to a Tenants' group in
a Catholic area like this.

Most residents felt that it could be disfunctional for a local
organization to have a community worker who was an active
supporter of one political party. 'Once you're labelled either
religiously or politically then you invariably alienate people'.
The communtiy worker's primary loyalty might no longer be to
the local residents, and this could contribute to community
organizations becoming less effective. It was considered
inappropriate for community workers to move from the enabling
role to that of preacher or advocate for the cause of a political party.

To what extent they (the community workers) can be
involved in the more general political questions, I've
got some reservations about, you know, because I don't
think outsiders can come in and foist political views
or attitudes about political questions which the people
may not be responding to. So I think the attitudes to
political questions have very much got to come from the
organizations themselves.[3]

POLITICIANS' VIEWS

We interviewed six politicians, all but one of whom were based
in the Queen's Park constituency. As in Chapter 10 we have
classified the elected members as either 'integrationist politicians' or 'change politicians'. The perspectives of the
'change politicians' were much more in line with the views of
the staff, and it is hardly surprising therefore, that they
were much more favourably disposed to community work and
Crossroads than were the integrationist politicians.

The Integrationist Politicians

As long as the councillor sees himself in the paternalism
and the Mafia game - I've got the goodies and you'll

come to me — the community worker will have problems.
(Councillor)

Most integrationist politicians expected the community worker
to develop a 'special' relationship with them.

The failure of Crossroads was not to take advantage of
myself sitting as Minister for Social Work for the last
three years — a Minister who dictated to his officials
what he wanted. Crossroads didn't revolutionize social
and community work practice as a partnership — that's a
deep sense of regret.

They were critical or angry when the community worker disagreed
with them.

I think the councillor and community worker, working
together can get things done, understand one another's
problems and get a better understanding of the reasons
things can't be done. The community workers don't want
a co-operative approach — they regard the elected representative as someone they are basically in conflict with.
Instead of going to the elected representatives and
saying can't we do a, b and c, they come to a conclusion
that they want a, b and c done, whether it's practicable
to do or not and whether the legislation allows it or not.

They did not expect the community worker to raise expectations
unrealistically.

Your aims must be realistic — you can't afford to adopt
a blinkered approach and say the interests of my area
are paramount and must be looked at and to hell with
everybody else — this is basically what you are doing.
You have to understand that in overcoming the problems
of the group in your area you must be concerned with
the problems of other areas as well. It's not an
isolated situation — the problems are repeated throughout the city. It seemed to me that people were kept
unnecessarily in deplorable situations because their
aspirations were unrealisable. I don't think the
interests of individuals in these situations were
being served.

Change Politicians

Generally, the change concillors expected a less intimate
relationship with the community worker.

Since the community workers have become an established
part of the area, their efforts should be combined to
work for the good of the area and they should travel the
one road if they can. They should be open about their
criticism and tell the councillor where they think he
can do better than he's doing. There is not necessarily
a conflict between them, because they both might feel the
same, but the elected member is tied by the Party vote.
Of course, they won't always be chummy chummy.

Indeed, one councillor was critical when the community workers
sought a close relationship.

I think I'm quite close to quite a few community workers –
maybe too close for their good although I think I'm O.K.
There's one community worker who is almost the touchstone
against which I measure other community workers, and the
relationship, there, is a distant relationship. Very
occasionally he's phoned me up when he's really got a
problem – maybe twice a year. I respect that relationship.

Methods of Work

Integrationist and change politicians clashed over the appropriate method of work. Most integrationist politicians did not
believe that local organizations were, or could be, independent
of the community worker. To them the enabling role was an
impossibility. In reality they felt that the community worker
manipulated a largely passive and ignorant population. Self-
determination was a myth.

The community workers don't so much represent the view
of people in the area, as the views and attitudes
which they themselves come to accept. In other words,
they're not serving the interests of that community, but
using the community. Take the Gorbals View, it's really
written by the community workers – local people think
they're writing it, but they're not really – the main
features are written under the guidance of the community
workers and reflect the views which have been instilled
into the local organizations largely by the community
workers.

Change politicians felt that the community worker should play
a broadly educational role:

There is an important role for political education, not
Party Politics. A community worker can't be a good

community worker unless he makes people aware of where
the source of their problem is - if they trace the
problems back to their source they usually lie with
the local or national authorities - with those who take
the decisions. I feel the community worker should be
forced to make people aware of this, even if it proved
unfortunate for the politicians.

All the politicians were adamant that the community workers
should avoid Party politics.

I certainly don't believe in them setting themselves up
as another political group - I think that would stulfify
what they are really trying to do because then they would
be blinded by the Party side of things. It's a very
difficult thing to stay clear of, I know that myself,
but in their job they must be above all that.

Community work and party politics were different:

Well, it's two different jobs - a community worker
can't be a social worker, politician and everything
else.

The community worker was seen either as a threat to the established position and authority of the councillor or was perceived as a potential ally in the 'job to be done'.

It's very difficult for a councillor to look after an
electorate of 15,000 without assistance and especially
in a deprived area where there aren't the facilities
available in some suburbs. The best thing to do is work
with the Unit rather than against it, although many
councillors do feel community work is something moving
in on top of them. Rather than work against the Unit,
I used it and all the resources they had.

All the politicians expected as harmonious a relationship with
the community worker as was possible, but the integrationist
politicians expected agreement. All politicians agreed that
the community worker should raise expectations, but the integrationist politicians expected to decide what expectations
were realistic. What is seen as political education by one
is regarded as manipulative by the other. Basically, the
response depended on whether the politicians agreed with the
political perspectives and priorities of the community worker.

Skills and Qualities

The elected members were more concerned about political beliefs and the role of the community worker than with the skills and qualities which were required. All agreed, however, that personal skills were important. 'Definitely you've got to be skilled in handling people'. Communication skills were envied and considered important. 'You people have all the gift of the gab'. Organizational and political skills, however, were valued mainly by the change councillors.

> A community worker needs certain organizational skills - he needs to know about groups and he needs to know about politicians. Indeed, I don't think a community worker was ever successful unless he knew something about politics and how politicians work.

The quality most often mentioned was hard work.

> If it wasn't for the Unit climbing the stairs, getting names and addresses of people left, where they would like to go - doing the work of the Housing Department - no one else would have done it.

All councillors were united in their criticism of community workers where, regardless of rhetoric, self interest or personal needs determined the work which was undertaken.

> When the community worker started, however, he had to prove himself and he did this by organizing against the councillor. If the councillor could do it all there was no need for him.

There was a fear that community workers would seek personal power.

> They can certainly influence groups because of their professionalism. There's a danger they can become king-makers, and I would be afraid that they might see that should be their role. You are hopeful when you do employ someone that he is a responsible person who is more aware of the task of training local people to become leaders in their own community than he is involved in looking for personal power.

There was also an awareness of the careerism within community work.

> After all, there is no guarantee the length of time a
> professional person will be in the area - if promotion
> or anything else comes up he will leave.

THE OUTSIDERS' VIEWS

We interviewed a number of people who had been closely con-
nected with the work of Crossroads over a period of time; two
community workers, a former SWSG advisor, a former non-resident
secretary of Crossroads, two planners employed by the Local
Authority and a community-based architect. All were people
who had close experience of Crossroads, and considerable experience of other community work projects within Glasgow and elsewhere. It was an opportunity of viewing Crossroads from a
wider perspective. These people tended to stress the qualities
of the workers. Self-knowledge was highly rated.

> They need a professional understanding of themselves and
> their work - what they are able to offer and what skills
> they have - an awareness of their own limitations.

Survival qualities were mentioned;

> Balance and stability are important if the angry young
> men are not to be quickly picked off, and if longer term
> community work is to become possible.

Imagination, openness of mind, awareness of other people's needs
and honesty were desirable. 'Never be dishonest - you can let
things ride for a bit but never be dishonest'. It was the
stricter virtues, however, - discipline and efficiency - which
were commended.

> The Unit gets things done on time - it produces the goods.
> People deserve an efficient organization.

> Staff not only have the confidence to say what they think,
> but they have professional discipline to carry this out.

It was this professional discipline which allowed the political
perspective to be carried into practice.

> The student units have the ability to apply ideology -
> you work with and from the local power base of local
> organizations - local people legitimize your work. Some
> other people don't have the professional discipline to
> wait and build a legitimate local power base because
> very few people stick with it as long as Crossroads

staff - Crossroads staff are prepared to commit themselves for a long period of time and so this local
cohesion can develop.

Knowledge was also required:

> They need an understanding of how individuals function,
> how groups function, and knowledge of community struc-
> tures and political structures, e.g. how Church, Labour
> Party, Trade Unions affect an area. They need a thorough
> understanding of how local government operates.

Once again, an awareness of the worker's own limitations is
stressed.

> It's as much to do with an awareness of what you need
> to find out as hard knowledge about duplicators, or
> how to organize a meeting.

There was general agreement that a combination of skills,
qualities and knowledge was required from the worker, but the
most important factor was 'personal competence as a human
being'.

> The critical thing is whether people want to be involved
> with you as a person. If you haven't got that skill, no
> matter how clever or talented or intellectual you are,
> you won't be able to function as a community worker.

The role of the community worker was 'motivating people' or
'raising consciousness' or 'stimulating, educating and supporting'. Compared to some other projects, the Crossroads
worker was 'much more prepared to speak his mind'. One worker
was concerned that, before the debate over the sacking of the
Govanhill Unit's secretary (see Chapter 3) the Units had
'drifted into being directive'. This, she felt was now less
likely, because 'local people seem to have thought through
much more clearly the role community workers should play'.
Generally, the outsiders were very concerned that the residents
made the decisions about priorities and policies:

> Community workers must be patient and find out what
> the residents' point of view is, and support that and
> not their own preoccupations about what the struggle
> is about.

WHAT MAKES A GOOD COMMUNITY WORKER?

The local activists stressed personal qualities as the

foundation for good community work; the 'kind of person' who
would help them overcome their feelings of inferiority and
their grudging acceptance of the status quo. The worker must
be optimistic with high expectations and little deference for
those in authority. Skills and specialist knowledge were rated
as important, but were ranked as a secondary criteria in the
assessment. The informed outsiders also stressed qualities,
especially the virtues of efficiency, professional discipline
and self-knowledge. The politicians, whether of a change or
integrationist orientation, were less concerned with skills
and qualities. These attributes took a secondary priority, in
their assessment, to the political beliefs of the workers and
the roles which they performed. The favourable quality most
mentioned by the politicians was a capacity for 'hard work'.

How do these assessments and criteria compare with the reflections of the Crossroads staff? The staff's assessment of good
community work overlaps with the criteria identified by the
locals, politicians and informed outsiders, but there are also
some significant areas of difference. The personal qualities
rated highly by the staff - high expectations, non judgemental
attitudes, imagination - are shared by the local residents,
but the staff concern with political qualities, - a 'collectivist world view' - received less priority and attention from
the local leaders. There was total agreement that the essence
of community work was the relationship with local residents.
Staff, however, define this as more than a skill in personal
relationships. Their community work was effective because of
what Friere[4] describes as 'dialogue' with local people; community worker and local residents, on the same side, learning
from each other how to deal with the basic inequalities in
society. Local residents agreed that the worker must 'be on
our side' but stressed that this relationship depended upon
the worker being approachable, accessible and not superior in
his attitudes. The ideological dimension of the relationship
is played down by residents, and in this respect the staff
shared more in common with the change-oriented politicians who
also placed a central emphasis upon political beliefs, rather
than on personal qualities, in forming relationships. Some of
the qualities stressed by staff were not even rated a mention
by the local activists. Thus survival skills, which were also
singled out as a priority by the informed outsiders, were not
recognized by local residents who quite rightly thought that,
if they could survive twenty-four hours a day in a deprived
environment, favoured professionals should easily cope!

Community work skills and specialist knowledge were an important but secondary priority in all the interviews. There is

considerable overlap and consensus between the staff and local activists. Both groups placed an emphasis upon the value of communication, organizational, research and information-gathering skills. The local activists, however, mentioned the practical skills related to fact-gathering - 'paper work' and research - more frequently than they did the more qualitative skills of planning and tactical insights. This mirrors other research findings into consumer views, which emphasize the value of workers being seen to 'do things' rather than 'sitting around', listening and talking about problems.[5] The politicians also highlighted some of these active skills - especially those of research and information gathering - although, for obvious reasons, the integrationist politicians were suspicious of organization skills which involved issue-raising and which were directed at encouraging collective action.

We have already discussed (see Chapter 10) how Crossroads staff were prepared to be forthright in their advice to local groups, but accepted, indeed fostered, the local organization's right to determine its own objectives and strategy. To most local people this was one of the policies which was 'good' about Crossroads and it contrasted with their experience of local government administration. Most of the informed outsiders and change politicians agreed with the emphasis on self-determin-ation, but the integrationist politicians strongly dissented. They believed that community workers directed and instructed the local organizations and that the local activists were manipulated by the community workers. This was one of their major criticisms of Crossroads.

Skill and Qualities: An Appropriate Balance?

The distinction between qualities and skills can become very blurred and muddled. In both the textbook literature and in everyday usage the terms are often used to describe and denote the same attribute. Thus, for example, 'self-awareness' and 'self-knowledge' is described in some textbooks as a skill and in others as a quality. Where the distinction becomes more apparent is when we compare skills which obviously require some training and experience to perform - such as research skills and report-writing - with qualities which cannot be easily acquired through training or even work experience and which are more likely to be the product of the individual's social and personality make-up; qualities such as imagination, an open mind, hard work, perseverance, sense of humour and use of initiative. Blurred and muddled as the distinction is, it is apparent from both our own experiences and the existing com-munity work literature, that a combination of qualities and

skills is required in community work. What the blend of qualities and skills should be will obviously be influenced by value
perspectives on the nature of community work goals and it is
likely that different combinations will be appropriate for
different types of community work, e.g. a quality of irreverence towards authority, combined with political skills, is
unlikely to be welcomed by an agency which is committed, in
its community work philosophy, to consensus and integration
goals.

Irrespective of the approach to community work, a balance will
need to be struck between skills and qualities when it comes
to make any assessment of the performance of students and workers. It is a balance which will also be relevant to staff
recruitment and the design of educational programmes. For the
authors of this report the feedback from the Crossroads staff
raised some very critical questions about the balance - or more
accurately, the lack of it - in the student training work
undertaken by the units. Crossroads staff, including the
authors, rated qualities of prime importance in the assessment
of community workers, an emphasis which also was shared by the
local residents and the informed outsiders. Practice skills
were given an important but secondary rating in the assessment.
Yet, in the student evaluations which were undertaken in the
Units, a skill-based set of criteria provided the reference
point for assessment and qualities were not mentioned (see
Chapter 4). This paradoxical situation reflected a reluctance
by the fieldwork teaching staff to engage in the personality
assessment of students. This reluctance was based, in part,
upon a distaste for making judgements of this nature and was
reinforced by the view that the student's work rather than the
student's personality should be the foundation for any placement assessment. While the emphasis upon skills was itself
shot through with value judgements, it was felt to provide,
especially in the areas relating to practical skills and knowledge of the social services, a more objective set of criteria
for assessment.

On reflection, the fieldworkers' emphasis on students' work and
the practical skills of community work pushed into the background the more problematic and personalized assessments about
whether students had the appropriate qualities required of community workers. Students who performed competently on their
practical work passed the placement although, at times, the
staff may have had private reservations about the ability of
the individual to cope in situations which tested their qualities of patience, initiative or their capacity to handle political conflict. (For further discussion see Chapters 13.)

Wider Debates

This lack of balance between qualities and skills is also a characteristic of much of the recent British community work literature. Yet, as early as 1959, a UN Report on Community Development was stressing that:

> the personality of the worker is likely to be more important for deciding his or her suitability than any particular qualification by experience or training.[6]

In contrast, the British textbook literature[7] is strong on descriptions of methods, skills and techniques but rarely mentions the personal qualities required in different types of community work settings. The first Gulbenkian report[8] stresses qualities such as diagnostic thinking, the ability to create confidence and establish relations, flexibility and patience, but later publications - such as the CCETSW report[9] and second Gulbenkian report[10] - give comparatively little weighting to qualities when compared to the formidable check lists of skills which are suggested for community work practice. Even the Association of Community Workers publications, which tend to reflect more accurately practitioners' viewpoints, relegate discussions about qualities to a minor position when compared with the attention devoted to skills and sources of knowledge for community workers. An ACW booklet[11] briefly mentions the qualities which 'workers need in order to live with the reality of community work' These include patience, perseverance, imagination, caring about people, curiosity, energy and the ability to relax. The significance of some of these qualities were also stressed by the Crossroads staff and, considering their importance as a foundation upon which community workers can build their practice skills, it is rather remarkable that so little attention has been devoted to the 'kind of person' criteria. For more thought-provoking material on this debate we need to turn to Alinsky,[12] who defines the talents of his ideal organizer purely in terms of qualities - curiosity, irreverence, imagination, a sense of humour, a free and open mind, a blurred vision of a better world, an organized personality and a well integrated political schizoid! He is frank enough to admit something which many community workers, especially those in the educational field, would be reluctant to articulate openly - that it may not be possible to train and educate people in some of the qualities which are thought to be desirable for community work.

> The qualities we were trying to develop in organizers in the years of attempting to train them included some

qualities that in all probability cannot be taught.
They either had them, or could get them only through
a miracle from above or below.[13]

Even if we reject the notion that the good community worker is
made in heaven (or hell as the case might be) it is not un-
reasonable to suggest that the qualities of the individual
worker will be vital in influencing practice. Workers who had
little appetite for challenging authority or, in the words of
one Gorbals' resident, working in the 'area of combat', would
not have survived long with Crossroads during the period covered by this study. The question naturally arises whether
workers with these qualities and dispositions are being attracted into community and social work or whether current recruitment policies and broader political trends are attracting
recruits of a more conformist stance? A lecturer at Glasgow
University, who had a long association with the Crossroads
units, felt that the radical zeal and independent spirit, which
had once spurred students to undertake community work placements, was on the wane.

I think it has a lot to do with the students. The
students now don't seem to take an independent line.
They take their image of social work from what goes
on in local authority departments.

Some of the personal qualities required of workers who are
committed to integrationist policies and servicing the established social service system are likely to be similar to the
qualities which are required by workers operating in the more
radical or change-centred forms of social and community work.
e.g. the virtues of patience and hard work are likely to be
important in any setting, but, as we indicated earlier, other
qualities are likely to be less valued and legitimized within
agencies which are committed to a consensus approach. Qualities of irreverence, a collectivist world view and independence
of mind could be positively threatening and some research evidence suggests that it these very traits and qualities which
are 'cooled out' in the more orthodox fieldwork and social
work training settings.[14] It is precisely these non-conforming
qualities which, we would suggest, are required for workers who
are committed to change-centred social and community work.

Chapter Twelve

WHAT IS A SUCCESSFUL COMMUNITY WORK PROJECT?

In this chapter we examine how local residents, politicians and informed outsiders evaluated success for a community work project. Their reflections are then compared with the staff views which were outlined in Chapter 10. On the basis of the interviews we have identified six major criteria which the participants used to denote success. These are;

(a)   material gains of money or services for individual residents and for the local area.

(b)   some redistribution of power or greater local control over services.

(c)   policy changes or changes in the practice of policy.

(d)   the personl development of residents.

(e)   therapeutic support for residents.

(f)   the political development of residents.

In addition to these factors the participants also commented on criteria which related to the organizational style and form of community work projects; the issues which staff worked on; the action processes which were favoured and promoted; the emphasis placed upon the independence of local groups and the type of local leadership which was encouraged and supported.

LOCAL VIEWS

Most residents agreed that the major function of a community work project was to deal with the collective and organizational needs of the area and to increase the chances of local groups being successful in the achievement of their goals. This

emphasis on collective and organizational needs was not shared
by everyone. Some residents considered that the personal needs
of residents should be a priority and the emphasis, which
everyone who was interviewed, placed on the value of advice
work indicates that - irrespective of the weighting given to
collective or personal approaches - the provision of an advice
service was considered an important ingredient in a successful
project.

> The shop's important in a whole lot of ways. The normal
> householder would hesitate to go up to Clive House but
> they'd come round the corner to the information centre
> and speak to staff and they'd speak more openly there.

What Constitutes Success?

<u>Material gains</u>. This was the primary reason for collective
action and the achievement of material objectives took priority
over the process or style of organization. Indeed, a process
was evaluated primarily by whether it was a means towards
achieving a material gain.

> The one success of the working party was getting the
> route of the road changed. As far as anything else is
> concerned, I'm now beginning to think the working party
> was just a big time-wasting game. At first I thought it
> was a very good thing because we could put our views but
> when you think of what has happened - we've all put our
> views and now the planners say they can't build houses
> because the whole area is undermined. Unless there's
> to be new housing the working party has all been a
> waste of time.

Material gains could be of an individual nature - such as a
better offer of housing and financial compensation for home-
loss - or for the 'common good'; a new playgroup, old people's
centre, local information shop or youth club.

<u>Local control of services</u>. Residents frequently become in-
volved in running their own services, because the local authority failed to provide adequate facilities for the local area.
Many of the residents who, out of necessity, became involved
in resource administration, came to value the process very
positively:

We had the chance of handing the youth centre back to
the authorities when the worker left. We just felt that
we had made a choice that it would be run by local people
and that we would have another go. We try to cater for
local people and provide what people want at the moment,
not what is laid down by the Corporation.

When the demand for local control involved the risk of resources being removed from the community the residents usually
opted for keeping the services, and relinquishing or watering-
down their management powers. It was over this question that
staff and residents frequently disagreed, as in the case of
tactics which the Crossroads management adopted in the sponsorship dispute (see Chapter 9).

Policy changes. Several of the local community organizations
vigorously campaigned for policy changes, especially in the
field of housing. The redevelopment groups protested, with
limited success, against eviction policies and the 'grading'
of council tenants. More positively the Dampness Campaign
achieved policy 'spin offs' which affected council tenants
throughout the city (see Chapter 6). Changes in national legislation and citywide policies were rarely mentioned, however,
as a major priority and the residents mainly defined their commitments in terms of changing local conditions. This limitation
has been critically commented upon by one local activist;

> The difficulty about activities in the political field
> is that the Tenants' Associations have not had many
> successes, despite the fact that we have had stacks of
> successes in many other fields. It's not any problem
> to get a new bus shelter, to get a new telephone, to
> get a piece of waste land landscaped, or argue about a
> new community centre and maybe one day get it. This is
> all encouraging, helping to establish the authority of
> the organization, and allowing this to be seen in
> people's eyes. But only when we start getting some
> successes in the political field will people be con-
> scious of their ability to control political affairs
> which at the end of the day, is really what is going
> to count.[1]

Personal development. Generally, the residents believed that
participation in community organizations enabled people to
develop their potential.

> I think there's talent and brains in the community.
> They need to develop certainly but the only way to

develop them is for people to take an active part in
the organization and develop the skills - lots of people
have surprised themselves at what they can do.

Therapeutic support. This was particularly mentioned in relation to the redevelopment groups - 'providing support when
your home area is falling apart at the seams' - and in the
context of self-help groups.

One of the successes of the Day Centre is the companion-
ship. You meet people you haven't seen for years and
there is an immediate kinship, and friendship. Those
recently bereaved and distraught with grief - the
majority within about six months make new friends and
come here. Most members live alone and make friends
with people they haven't known. If it wasn't for the
Centre many would be sitting at home moping.

One resident criticized her neighbours for concentrating upon
therapeutic support instead of attacking officialdom:

I don't think there's an area in the city with finer
people - but they don't help each other in the way they
should help each other... They should teach each other
about what's going on, and fight that way. It's all
very well to chap (knock) someone's door, someone who's
elderly, and do what you can for them, but the real
fight is with officialdom - for a better way of life
and better amenities. In that sense, this area is a
disgrace.

Political awareness. The political effect of participating in
community action was rarely expressed in the language of class
consciousness and socialism. More commonly it was described
in populistic terms - the awareness that 'you can fight the
higher ups and win'. Some established community leaders combined an active local involvement with membership of a political party, usually either the Labour or the Communist Party.

People grow up and would like to see the world changed
so they join a political party. It's difficult to be
a member of the Labour Party and attack it but the
point is the Labour Party isn't perfect, not even 50%.
I personally do more outside the Labour Party - and
attack them, although on many things I support them.

Other residents did mention that their involvement in community
action had prompted a greater interest in trade union affairs -

an interesting reversal of the usual connection - while, in
more general terms, the Crossroads staff did have knowledge of
residents (numbering no more than a dozen) who joined various
political parties after first becoming involved in community
groups. But, for many residents, membership of a political
party was not a natural development from their local involvement. Some explained their non-participation in party politics
on the grounds of a lack of interest and knowledge:

> I'm not in the least bit interested in party politics.
> I feel if you don't really understand it you should leave
> it alone. When we're in the Tenants' Association we're
> there as tenants fighting for our rights. When I look
> at things locally, I try not to let politics come into
> it.

Others, however, felt they understood the situation only too
well. It was disillusionment, not ignorance, which accounted
for their non-participation:

> I don't know if I believe in the Labour Party but I
> believe very strongly in socialism. The Labour Party
> was the best vehicle you could see towards socialism.
> I say it was the best. You accepted what they said -
> maybe you didn't agree with it entirely but the alterna-
> tive was capitalism so you simply accepted their type of
> socialism - certainly not the kind you're getting now.
> You invite councillors from two different parties and
> invariably they are both trying to get their wee bit in
> and that sickens me. The feelings of the people are put
> behind getting a wee boost for the Party. In my type of
> socialism people are first. I don't believe in Party
> politics at a local level - it would be my delight if
> there was some way in which they could be abolished,
> which they can't.

For many residents their political commitment, whether newly
formed or of long standing, were more likely to be expressed
in community activism rather than through any variety of party
politics.

Organizational Forms

Process. During the 1970s there was a proliferation of community groups in Gorbals and Govanhill. Most of the activists
agreed with this development, primarily because it was an
effective means for getting people involved in collective
action.

> I think you need the separate groups because that's the
> way you get people interested in their particular thing.
> Each group likes to be responsible for doing their own
> things and they don't want anyone to interfere.

This view was not, however, accepted by everyone. An experienced community leader and political activist was highly
critical and blamed Crossroads staff for encouraging the
proliferation of groups.

> It gets them into their own set narrow question - divorces
> them from issues affecting everyone else. If the issues
> get settled that's them quiet again whereas if you get
> them into one body you give them permanent interest in
> coming.[2]

This debate and conflict over centralized versus autonomous
group structures also surfaced when government supported and
financed Community Councils were set up in Glasgow in the mid
1970s.[3] During the period covered by this study the Community
Councils in Govanhill and Gorbals, which numbered three in
all, were relatively inactive bodies when compared with the
action groups and issue-centred campaigns. There was a tendency for the advocates of centralized, broad-based organizations to favour and actively support the formation of Community Councils, whereas the activists from the issue-centred
campaigns or neighbourhood groups were often suspicious of
area-wide organizations.

> I never liked the idea of Community Council because I
> think it's an attempt to cut down local animosity and
> local action.

This debate was more than an issue about size and structure
or relations with the local authority. It also reflected,
we suspect, differing political ideals about participatory
and representative models of democracy.

Leadership. There was no consensus over the style of leadership which was most appropriate for community organizations.
Some local groups and activists did attempt to evolve forms
of organizational representation which placed an emphasis upon
the accountability of leadership:

> I think a weekly committee meeting is important. Mail
> would come in and it was up to the committee to give the
> secretary the answers to this mail, otherwise the secre-
> tary could answer totally different to what the rest of

the committee wanted.

Others recognized the difficulties involving in promoting collective leadership:

> It's vitally important that people should become involved and in many cases it might be for the first time in their lives. This is one of the difficulties about it, because it is often for the first time in their life. Even here there are problems, because the leading committee members take on the responsibility of doing things for them, to the point where the tenants themselves won't be too involved.

For some leaders, achieving material results was more important than gaining popular involvement in the running of local groups;

> You don't need to be all that democractic if you produce the goods. If people are happy they're not really interested in throwing you out at some vote - the only reason you have democracy in, say, politics, is that they're making policy and some people are going to disagree because of the various interests of one street and the interests of another. If you're successful they're not worried - they don't want to take minutes, read documents; they're quite happy to go along.

The paternalistic style of leadership felt that people needed guidance;

> The folk on the floor of the meeting don't know how local government works - they're looking for advice.

Others disagreed;

> There's too much of them sitting up on the platform and talking down to people. They must play a greater role in encouraging people that it is right for the people to make their own area a better place.

Many, sadly, felt that this was very difficult;

> People don't want to do things for themselves - they want it done for them. You will only get a handful coming to meetings.

Despite some sharp differences over preferred leadership styles all the residents who were interviewed were adamant that local

organizations should be independent and self-supporting. There
was a common concern expressed about control being imposed from
outside, either from community workers, local authority officials or political parties.

Issues, Some of the residents who lived in the 'better' type
of housing resented the priority Crossroads placed on working
with the 'worst' housing areas. They felt, rightly, that their
organizations had been neglected in terms of community work
support.

> I was very jealous that you never worked with us, although
> to your eyes we may have been in front and the problem
> lay in the older type of housing.

Others felt that Crossroads concentrated too much on working
with the less respectable residents in Gorbals and Govanhill.

> I think the Unit came into the area and took I presume
> what they saw as the worst area. The people in Govanhill
> in my area who are living in conditions a bit better
> because they look after their property - do their stairs,
> their windows etc. and don't allow their property to
> become a slum - have been forgotten; I think you're
> forgotten。

However, most of those interviewed felt that the priority given
to the worst areas was justified.

> Bad housing is the basic issue in Glasgow and it would
> be very difficult not to touch it.

THE POLITICIANS

The politicians viewed community organizations mainly in terms
of how their activities related to their personal values; how
activities affected their constituency work and whether or not
the organizations were sympathetic to the politician's party。
The most direct and honest answer from the politicians about
a successful community work projects was 'a good community work
project is one that's supporting me'. We examine their responses by considering whether they pursued integrationist or
change goals, although it is important to point out that few of
the politicians were completely consistent - 'in politics, consistency is neither a vice nor a virtue, it is an impossibility'.[4]

Integrationist Politicians

The integrationist politicians tended to differentiate very

clearly between different issues and types of organizations
when evaluating success or failure. In an extreme form, the
integrationist perspective suggested that local action would
be unnecessary if the present political system functioned
'properly'. 'There's no need for organizations in the area
if councillors are doing the work'.

In an imperfect world local groups might be needed, but only
those which focused on 'personal service' were welcomed.

> The good things were the pensioners' club, the detailed
> surveys of conditions, the advice provided from the
> Information Centre.

Action groups were criticized for undermining personal
initiative.

> The Action group has taken away people's individuality
> and the people simply rest on the Action group as a
> crutch. I don't want to sound like a Tory on this but
> it takes away their sense of independence that they can
> do something for themselves.

Consistent with this view was an emphasis upon the 'social'
rather than the 'political' role of community work.

> At the time I think the students were moving away from
> the social side and getting involved in the political
> things which they shouldn't have been doing. There was
> enough work for them on the social side - looking after
> the senior citizens, helping them fill in forms. That
> would have been a lot more appropriate than the public
> meetings with a lot of heckling.

Integrationist politicians rarely relished any redistribution
of resources and even personal service projects which required
finance were liable to receive criticism:

> The street warden scheme is good but the big criticism
> of it of course is that it cost several thousand pounds,
> whereas the Church of Scotland does it for nothing.

Pressure on the established power structure also drew a critical
reaction, especially when it directly affected party loyalty.

> I'm not saying you shouldn't campaign against authority
> but Crossroads has been intensely political against the
> Labour Party - there's no record of groups criticising
> or demonstrating against the Tories.

On the question of organizational form and leadership the integrationist politicians generally favoured one centralized group
for an area and a 'mature' leadership.

> We did the rehousing in Gorbals and we did it because I
> insisted we had one group to deal with - namely Hutcheson-
> town Tenants' Association in Hutchesontown and Gorbals
> Group in Laurieston. We fought with officials and we
> fought with the Council and even against my own party
> but we worked with one group. Of course, there was a
> big difference between young students and people of the
> maturity of Gorbals Group members, who were understanding
> people although they campaigned ferociously.

Underpinning this approach was the assumption that the community worker and the politicians should work together.
'Maturity' was measured in terms of consensus;

> In the Gorbals Group days, politicians and local
> organizations could sit down together and work it out.

The proliferation of action groups was not welcomed;

> The philosophy of street groups or action groups has
> created antipathy with authority and caused confron-
> tation with the councillors.

Integrationist politicians favoured Community Councils and
criticized Crossroads for being partly responsible for the
failure of Community councils to get off the ground in Gorbals
and Govanhill.

> There's one main failure of Crossroads that they've
> never set up a strong group like a Community Council.
> You should go in and try to create a sense of community
> and a Community Council is an obvious vehicle. It's the
> street action groups that have stopped a Community Council
> getting off the ground in any viable form in Govanhill
> and Gorbals because people don't see any need for it.

Change Politicians

Change-directed politicians adopted a more relaxed and liberal
view of successful community work practice. They generally
favoured collective action within their area;

> A lot of people don't recognized their needs and it's
> part of the community workers' job to make people aware

of them. They should organize people within the area
and teach them that unity is where their strength lies.

It was recognized that community workers would deal with
political as well as social issues;

> Social work is political - social work relies on the
> policies of Parties and can be altered by a change of
> administration.

Redistribution of resources was one measure of a successful
community work project;

> The project has been very successful as far as I'm
> concerned - it's made the local authority, both
> regional and district, face up to their responsibilities.

On the issue of organizational form, change politicians, by
and large, favoured small action groups;

> I'm in favour of small groups - I think you've got to
> break them down into smaller groups - the idea is sound.
> You don't want one group to look after back courts,
> playgroups, housing, vandalism - you must have different
> groups。

In the interests of time (and possibly for other reasons)
change politicians also favoured a forum of small groups;

> The structure of the groups was right but a Working
> Party is needed - a federation of different groups.
> It is a good idea for the councillor because every
> group wants a meeting with the local representative
> to exchange views and press for facilities. If they
> all have individual meetings, the councillor is out
> every night of the week.

They did not expect that local leaders and community workers
would always agree with them.

> Ultimately, the priorities of the elected Member will
> be to his Party, whereas the community worker is
> primarily responsible to the local organizations
> who sometimes need to remind the councillors that
> they should represent the people's interests.

OUTSIDERS' VIEW

A number of the outsiders stressed, as important criteria for

assessment, the ability of a project to attract resources to
an area, the active participation of local residents in the
project, and the personal development of the participants.

> It's the anarchist in me - the sharing of skills. One
> measure of success is how much learning is accomplished -
> for me and other participants.

The outsiders, more than the other groups interviewed, also
placed a greater emphasis on projects having well defined
organizational and administrative structures; objectives which
were clearly stated; mechanisms for reviewing work progress and
a system of accountability for the professional workers. Accountability was needed as a safeguard against workers abusing
their freedom and, also, to ensure that they actually 'did some
work'!

> I certainly think the community worker should be account-
> able to someone - some community workers are just playing
> at community work. It's not what they're doing that I
> disagree with, it's just that they're doing nothing.
> The authorities never close you down just for being
> inefficient.

Generally, Crossroads was commended for the issues it worked
upon;

> The Unit works on the hard-hitting and critical issues -
> dampness, road systems, poor housing - real immediate
> issues which demand sophisticated responses from local
> government, and which local government doesn't seem
> capable of providing.

Most supported the political actions of the staff, but one
observer speculated that the Crossroads functioned 'to take
the heat our of Party Politics'.

> The very interesting thing from a political point of
> view is that I suspect that community workers could
> have supported the status quo - people have been able
> to identify that all remedies don't lie in the Party
> political structure - so the politics of community
> groups may have taken the heat out of Party Politics.
> Some of the activists have had some of their political
> aspirations satisfied in community politics, but if
> this aspiration hadn't been satisfied, it might have
> flowed over into Party Politics. There may be a danger
> that community work dissipates anger.

WHAT IS A SUCCESSFUL COMMUNITY WORK PROJECT?

The creation of local groups, which fulfil some or all of their
objectives and organizational needs, is a basic measure for
evaluating the work of a community work project. Amongst the
people we interviewed there was considerable agreement over
what constituted organizational needs although one set of re-
spondents, the integrationist politicians, dissented from including political criteria in the assessment of successful
local groups and stressed, instead, personal service criteria.
Differences also occurred over the ranking and weighting which
was allocated to different goals. The Crossroads staff tended
to emphasize long-term political goals - redistribution of
power and resources, the development politically conscious
groups - more overtly than did the local residents. The residents stressed immediate material rewards and benefits as a
primary criterion for assessing success and this distinction
might well reflect the degree of economic security or deprivation experienced by the two groups. Long term visions of
the 'good' society can be a luxury for the less well off.

Differences in priority and interpretation also emerge when we
consider questions relating to the qualitative aspects of community organizing; the issues projects should work on, and the
types of groups and leadership which should be supported and
encouraged. At the heart of the disagreements over these concerns lies the question 'what is open for change'? How broad
or narrow are the political boundaries within which established
social habits, power structures and organizational procedures
are defined as being legitimate targets for change? Responses
to those questions are intimately related to conflicting con-
ceptions of politics and, many of the people interviewed,
implied that a successful community project is one which supports their concept of politics and their view of what required
to be changed or preserved in the existing social order. The
staff tended to articulate and practice a broad concept of
politics, which transcended the narrow confines of party politics and questioned the distinction between social and political behaviour. Some of the residents shared this perspective,
but others drew a clear distinction between political action,
which was exclusively identified with party politics, and their
work in the community. The most narrow definition of 'what is
open for change' came from the integrationist councillors, who
clearly separated out personal troubles from public issues and
social from political action.

These contrasting definitions influenced the assessment of the
issues, types of leadership and organizational processes which

it was considered appropriate for a project to work on. Thus,
the advocates of the narrow concept of politics were more likely
to define certain issues and action strategies as being outside
of the legitimate remit for a community work project - such as
organizing demonstrations over housing problems. They were
also more likely to favour a limited form of participation from
the more respectable and 'mature' leaders in the local community and to exclude participation from less respectable groups
(the 'undeserving poor'). Finally, they were more inclined to
support organizational structures and processes which repro-
duced the formal administrative characteristics of established
political parties and local authorities - Community Councils
rather than street or action groups. On the other hand, the
advocates of the broader model of politics were more likely to
embrace wider definitions of what issues were open to collective action and tended to be reluctant to reproduce, within
their own groups, paternalistic forms of leadership, organization and participation. This broader approach also had its
limitations, because the activists and professional workers
were selective over which issues became a target for collective
action. e.g. despite their adherence to the 'everything is
political' viewpoint, the Crossroads staff were only marginally
involved in attempting to challenge the key issue of unemployment in Gorbals and Govanhill. They emphasized housing as the
major issue in their work and this selection was reinforced by
the priorities which were defined by many of the local residents. In private, the staff often expressed frustration and
a sense of powerlessness about the economic situation and their
failure to work on this issue.

Evaluation in Practice

The mixture of political self-interest and dispassionate criteria which characterize assessments about community work projects naturally assumes a significance when we consider the
politics of sponsorship - the process whereby projects receive,
maintain and lose grants. When conflict occurs between the
policy makers and projects, political self-interest can become
the primary criterion for assessment, as happened in the SWSG
reviews of the student units (see Chapter 9). The formulation
of evaluative guidelines for grant allocation will not necessarily resolve this dilemma. During the mid-1970s the Strathclyde Region devoted considerable energy to identifying criteria
for assessing the work of voluntary organizations[5] but, when
it came to making decisions, the personal interests of councillors still held sway.

When faced with hard choices about which branches of

social work to fund councillors become very subjective.
I doubt whether they've really worked out the basis on
which they give grant aid - a lot is still what they feel
about the organizations and the personalities running
these organizations, rather than the quality and competence
of the work done. In one case a personality conflict between the director of a project and a councillor, who had
been hassling within the Labour Party for years, resulted
in closure of the project even though the officials
recommended continuation. (ex. SWSG Advisor)

A senior councillor confirmed these impressions and added that
the vested interests of officials could also be very
influential.

What counts in evaluation is the prejudices of individual
officers and individual councillors in a particular
situation and obviously if a particular organization
has got by some process a label, the Committee does
emphasize the individual councillor's view. It is
therefore very easy for a particular organization to
fall foul of the system simply because it arouses the
ire of one particular councillor and maybe one particular
official - two people can really screw the whole thing up.

Community workers who receive public funds must expect that
local politicians will be a party to the process of evaluation
and assessment. Rather than fighting this democratic convention, it is more appropriate to devise policies which are
capable of responding to both the political and the dispassionate criteria which might figure in any reviews. A Crossroads
management representative rated this ability as being crucial
to the survival of projects:

We survived the cuts because Crossroads had a greater
awareness of the spoken and unspoken questions we were
meant to be answering and we had a greater willingness
than a lot of people to show our ability to meet these
tests.

Whenever possible the politically astute project attempts to
win sponsorship-support from elected representatives:

You've got to get inside him and find out what's
troubling him.

However, when conflict arises, personal contact is no substi-
tute for a power relationship. In situations of conflict a

project has to mobilize popular pressure and, as was illustrated in Chapter 9, even the most hostile of reviews can be
challenged if this local pressure threatens the credibility
of a politician in the eyes of his electorate.

I've been a politician for twenty-four years, and I
don't take on battles with my own people lightly.

Chapter Thirteen

WHAT DO STUDENTS GAIN FROM
COMMUNITY WORK PLACEMENTS?

In this chapter we examine the education and training programme
of the fieldwork units. What was the value of a community work
placement for a social work student? What expectations and
experiences did social work courses have of the Crossroads
units? What did the local activists - whose groups provided
the practical focus for much of the student fieldwork - feel
about the student involvement? These and other questions are
discussed from the perspectives of local residents, a group of
twenty seven students who completed placements with the units
and thirteen tutors who were employed on Scottish social work
courses. Their reflections are briefly compared with the aims
and expectations which the Crossroads staff defined for
students' placements (see below and Chapter 4). In the final
section of the chapter, we relate our findings to some of the
recent British research into social work education and training.

THE STUDENT UNIT AS AN EDUCATIONAL SETTING

The staff considered that the major educational value of their
work was providing 'alternative styles of thinking and working'.
An assumption was made that the units offered a corrective to
individualistic or social pathology perspectives on social
problems and provided a work setting which, in its democratic
ethos and comparatively unstructured organization, presented
an alternative to the norms of conventional social work agencies. For a model of conventional social work most of the
staff used, as their reference point, local authority social
work departments and, more specifically, the structure for
statutory social work which existed in Glasgow. Linked with
this critical perspective on social work was the view that an
experience of community work could encourage students, especially those who were going into local authority employment

(the majority of students), to utilize a broader approach in
their work.

> Social work is very myopic and doesn't tend to look at
> social work in a local and national government setting.
> But you can't work in a social work department and ·
> understand fully its role without understanding generally
> what is going on within the Local Authority. We expose
> students to contact with councillors·- to the formal as
> well as informal political processes and this is very
> important and likely to equip the student a little bit
> better for his understanding of local government.
> (Staff member)

Staff felt that the most important element in the educational
process was the student being part of the Unit's work and
directly experiencing the process of local action. This exposed the students to the emotional feeling of 'doing' community
work and gave them the opportunity to test out whether community work was 'for them'. Certain learning experiences were
considered common to all placements, especially the clients'
view of the world, the direct working with local residents on
a collective basis and the gaining of some insight into the
political context of community work and the interaction between
local groups and formal power structures. Other experiences,
insights and specialist knowledge depended more on the specific
nature of the placement task. Thus, for example, staff felt
that students working with community service projects (e.g.
playgroups, senior citizen clubs, youth clubs) were more likely
to gain experience and insights into the problems associated
with the community management of resources and the mechanics
of obtaining funds, while students working on the various
housing projects - such as the Dampness Campaign or redevelopment issues - were more likely to acquire a specialist knowledge of housing legislation. Some placement tasks were considered to be more demanding and stressful than others. Work
in redevelopment areas was usually singled out for particular
mention; the relevant housing legislation was very complex;
the social pressures on residents were acute, and the political
conflicts were potentially explosive. At the same time as
emphasizing these difficulties, some staff also singled out
redevelopment work as providing students with the most direct
and testing experience of the 'politics of community action'.

> I can't think of any situation at college that can match
> attending a public meeting of the tenants where a housing
> official blatantly lies about rehousing. Learning about
> conflict is a big advantage of the student unit. The

style of work demands both informality and coping with
conflict, and this is something you have to come to
terms with, but not all students can cope with it. To
get the balance right - especially early on in placement -
is difficult.

THE STUDENTS

Of the twenty-seven students who returned the questionnaire
(see Appendix 1), over a third were ex-students of the Glasgow
University Social Work Course (11). The remainder had been on
social work, youth work or specialist community work courses
at Moray House (7), Aberdeen University (3), Edinburgh University (3), Sussex University (1) and Surrey University (1). The
majority of the students were in their mid-20s when they undertook their placements and over two thirds had previous social
work experience (e,g, as trainees) before starting their
courses. All but one of the students' group had specifically
requested a community work placement as part of their course,
and nine out of the twenty-seven had asked for a placement with
Crossroads in preference to other community work agencies.
Over half of the students' group had placements which focused
on work with issue-centred groups or campaigns. e.g. working
with Tenants' Associations, Redevelopment groups or the Dampness Campaign. The remainder of the students worked with
service-delivery projects, such as playgroups, old people's
clubs, summer play-schemes or on the development of information
services linked with the resource role of the units.

Knowledge

In terms of the new knowledge which was acquired during a
placement the majority of students cited information and insights concerning working with groups, housing problems and
legislation and an improved grasp of the processes of local
government policies, organization and politics. A number of
students also mentioned gaining new insights into the workings
of the mass media and the development of a consumer or client
view of public and social services. The importance of the
linking of 'personal troubles' to 'public issues' was frequently
mentioned in this context.

Practice Skills

On the question of whether the placement had enabled the
students to develop and test out practice skills, the majority
of the students singled out organizational skills (e.g. working
with committees, helping to organize public meetings) and self

organization (e.g. planning use of time, use of initiative) for
special mention. Engagement skills, developing working relationships with colleagues and local activists, and fact-
finding were also frequently mentioned. Political skills,
related to decision-making processes and the interaction between
local groups and power structures, were cited less frequently.
Thus, the bread and butter skills of developing local organizations and using time more effectively were rated as more
significant areas of learning than were political skills. This
was a rather surprising feedback, especially in the light of the
students' comments on the importance of the new insights and
knowledge they had gained in relation to the working of local
government and politics.

When asked what they considered to be the most important skills
for the practice of community work - as opposed to the skills
which they had developed in the placements - the students cited,
in a ranking order, engagement, communication, political, organizational and self-organizational skills. The difference
between this ranking order and the skills which were cited as
having been developed during the placement reflected an appreciation by the students of the skills which they were familiar
with and were confident about before the placement started.
This related especially to engagement skills, which figured as
the top priority for the practice of community work, but which
was ranked below organizational and self organization in the
skills which had been developed during the placement. Only a
handful of the students mentioned personal qualities, as opposed to skills, as being the foundation for good community
work practice. This response may well have reflected the fact
that the student assessment procedure in the units was based
on a skill-centred evaluation. (See Chapters 4 and 11.)

Values

The extent to which the placement prompted the students to consider their value perspectives on social work obviously depended
on a complex range of factors, including the students' existing
perspectives; the fit or conflict between these values and
those of the agency; the nature of the placement experience and
the relative rigidity or openness of mind with which the student
approached the placement. For many of the students, the placement experience reinforced, rather than conflicted with, their
value perspectives;

> For me the placement reinforced my belief that a wider
> perspective that includes political and economic factors
> has to be taken before we can tackle social problems.

For a small number of the students the Unit's emphasis upon
collective action was a challenge - a 'radical change' - which
prompted some reflection.

> My placement challenged me to examine the importance
> which I attached to working with individuals and how
> this related to tackling problems that many people
> in the same area share.

While the Unit's political perspective on community work may
not have been shared by all students (although no student who
returned the questionnaire openly dissented from this view)
the need to move, in social work, from an individualistic to
a collective approach was accepted by all the students in the
survey. It was positively welcomed by many, but confronted a
few with varying degrees of difficulty and heart-searching.
The fact that a number of the students had opted for a placement with Crossroads may help account for this value-fit and
the staff often felt that they attracted the more political
type of social work student. Indeed, it was not unknown for
some courses to place certain students with Crossroads because
they considered the students' political views might cause problems in more orthodox social work agencies!

For the majority of students it was the practice of a community
action approach, rather than the political rhetoric or theory
which informed this approach, which proved to be the challenge
on a placement. For those arriving with high hopes that community work held 'the solution' it was an exercise in realism.
For others, it opened their eyes to conflicts of interests in
social work, and, for most of the students, it removed the
mystique of community work and opened it up for questioning.

> My reason for doing social work was to help those in
> need - this placement made me realize that I must be
> prepared to challenge authorities and Government to
> do this.

> I dislike the tunnel vision of most social workers.
> On the other hand the overt political commitment of
> many community workers made their professionalism
> suspect.

All the students agreed that they should not be protected from
making choices of an ethical nature during placements, as, for
instance, in deciding whether to support the use of civil disobedience strategies (see Chapter 8). The majority agreed with
the view expressed by one student; 'In social work that's the

name of the game'. Most students preferred to make ethical
decisions in a real life situation where the local activists
injected realism into the debates about action strategies.

> Local people had a realistic grasp of what was happening
> in the area not a theoretical grasp and therefore the
> presenting problem did not get lost in theoretical
> discussion, e.g. civil disobedience over evictions
> became a real not rarified discussion.

The very realism implied, however, that certain safeguards
must be built in:

> Before exercising personal choice the participants,
> local people and students, must appreciate the
> potential consequence of action.

So must the training agency;

> the agency must be prepared to accept a decision
> against its own stance and avoid branding a student
> as naive, immature or whatever.

Working with Local Groups

A number of the students commented that contact with local
groups had prompted them to re-think their attitudes towards
'clients'. Working with talented and able local leaders undermined stereotypes about expert-client relationships and challenged the social pathology perspective of deprived working-
class areas.

> It changed my view of the potential of local people;
> it made me realize clients are more capable than social
> workers give them credit for.

> It told me that I don't know what's best for my clients.

> Hopefully it will make me more able to allow people to
> decide for themselves.

It also challenged the traditional community education approach
of 'leading from the front'. An experienced youth and community
worker commented;

> This is my first experience of community education where
> staff don't organize events themselves but local people
> share the workload.

In addition to these experiences, some students found the local
residents the most informed sources of information on the sociology and political structure of the area.

It was a large part of what education was all about –
the residents provided invaluable knowledge about the
area; helped me understand local attitudes to the Local
Authority, the place of political parties and councillors
and sort out my own values in relation to the local people
and groups.

Others commented that the support and friendship of local people
was important as they settled into the placement and established a role for themselves.

The Student Contribution

Most students felt that their contribution to the development
of local groups was limited by the short-term duration of
placements. There was a recognition, especially from those
students who were involved with long-term interventions (e.g.
work in a redevelopment area), that their participation was
restricted to only an episode in a group's history. A sense
of practical achievement was more marked amongst those students
who were directly involved in the completion of a concrete task,
such as the carrying out of a housing survey or the setting-up
of a local service. Students who had clear-cut concrete tasks
to perform tended to report more positively than those students
whose placements were focused on more generalized 'enabling'
roles, such as supporting a local tenants' committee or working
with an established group.

Most students thought that their enthusiasm and hard work were
positive assets to local groups; 'a captive labour force for
people to use as they wish'. Some also suggested that 'new
faces' brought new enthusiasm, new ideas and helped to avoid
stagnation in local groups. However, for a majority of the
students, this introduction of 'new faces' was cited as one of
the major disadvantages of student placements for local groups.
The rapid turnover of students, together with the change in
personalities and work styles, presented groups with problems
of adjustment. Another possible disadvantage was the inexper-
ience, lack of local knowledge and 'tendency to pursue pet
theories' of students. Some of the students felt that these
shortcomings were minimized if full-time staff were available
to provide continuity in the work with local groups, and ensured that students followed local priorities rather than their
own.

With the Crossroads Units local residents were only informally
involved in the administration and assessment of placements.
They did not, for instance, have a role in the selection of
students or the final evaluation of student performance. The
students were divided over the question of the degree to which
local residents should be formally involved, as opposed to
being informally consulted, in the placement process. Some
would tend to limit the involvement of residents because the
work of the local groups took priority over student activities.
Others would limit involvement because of capability; 'Local
residents should not be involved unless really interested and
capable'. Others felt strongly that the residents should be
involved in the management of placements.

> Local people should be more involved in the mysterious
> process of training and supervision. A situation where
> student and supervisor exclusively exchange ideas and
> attitudes about working with a third party is inherently
> patronizing in its structure. Local activists should be
> given a recognized formal place in training.

Community Work and Social Work

Most of the students felt that there was a link between community and social work. For some the objectives were the same;

> It should be emphasized that there is no fundamental
> contradiction in the values held by caseworkers and
> community workers: rectifying political and social
> injustices should be the concern of all types of social
> worker. Casework and community work are not separate
> elements at opposite ends of a social work continuum.
> These two forms of social work can be conceived as
> operating under the same principles, which can be
> applied with equal facility to individuals and to
> individuals in communities and with the same end in
> view.

Others identified a common base in skills.

> Relationships are an integral part of maturity both for
> the individual and groups in the community, the only
> difference being in the setting which defines the type
> of relationship required. They are the focus on which
> caseworker and community worker must concentrate as a
> means of attaining maturity, and the goals of social,
> political or personal development.

Some dissenters argued that there were no automatic links between social work and community work.

It would depend on the type of ideology of either social work or community work.

Others agreed that the emphasis in practice, if not in theory, was different.

Although in theory social work intervention can help people develop as individuals, in practice, in my experience, it is normally used to control them.

All the students felt that a community work placement was of value to someone working in another setting, mainly because it gave a broader experience of social work and provided alternative ways of working with people. Social workers could now value self-help groups and appreciate the social supports available within the community. Although the students identified with this broader perspective, the translation of the perspective into practical work was a source of difficulty and frustration. A number of the students reflected, critically, on their post-course experience of attempting to link social and community work within the setting of local authority departments.

I tried in vain for a community orientation in the team.

I doubt if my experience of battling with housing and local politicians can be put to good use in the present situation, apart from my feeling of cynicism.

The most positive response came from a student who now worked with an area team which had a community worker post.

I was sympathetic to the community worker in my team. I was able to identify groups of clients whose needs were broader than those dealt with by case work skills.

From the feedback we received it would appear that students experienced considerable difficulties and obstacles in linking community and social work in their employment situations, an impression which is confirmed by other research reports.[1] There were two different interpretations made of this situation. Some felt that the placement had provided a stimulus for radical practice;

It gave me considerable enthusiasm and the courage to say what I thought. It helped me expose 'unsound' value

> systems and the judgements of the social work
> department and officials in it.

Others made a plea for social work education to concentrate
on the 'art of the possible'.

> The training course was very detached from how things
> actually are in Glasgow. Doing social work in a local
> authority setting in the West of Scotland is bloody
> hard work and often depressing. They should help you
> evaluate the things social work can do something about,
> as opposed to things it can do nothing about. Too much
> energy is drained away coping with this in practice.

Placements in Specialist Student Units

The most commonly cited advantage was the opportunity of learning in a group and sharing wider experiences. Many valued the
support and opportunities of learning from other students. The
high priority accorded to student training was also appreciated;

> There was time for supervision and for informal discussion –
> this was part of the structure of the Unit and not some-
> thing to be wrested from other more urgent commitments.

There were some practical advantages too, such as better links
with educational establishments and access to community work
literature, which apparently was sadly lacking on some courses.
On the negative side it was noted that student units had a
tendency to be 'artificial settings' which trained students
in isolation from clients and the local community. This criticism was not levelled against the Crossroads units and the
response indicated that this dilemma had been avoided by combining the student unit with a local resource and information
role and by the staff combining the fieldwork teaching function
with a substantial commitment to 'doing community work' themselves. The students were enthusiastic about this dual role
and several mentioned the advantage of learning by example.
The apprentice-journeyman analogy was cited to illustrate this
point. Several students also emphasized that the dual role
encouraged the linking of theory and practice. The local involvement of staff was linked with theoretical discussion with
students and encouraged them to make connections of their own.
Also, it helped to dispel criticisms and negative feelings
about fieldwork teachers.

> He become a campaigner, not just an armchair theorist.

Some frustration was expressed about the lack of student control over the allocation of tasks and projects. This is a
common source of dissatisfaction with placements and, in the
case of the Crossroads units, it may well have been reinforced
by the close and intimate involvement of staff in the local
work. It was a frustration which was largely accepted by the
students as being inevitable 'given the time in placement and
the students' place in the hierarchy'. As this comment reveals,
even small, relatively unstructured agencies, which pride themselves on having an egalitarian ethos, do have hierarchies of
status and power! The dual role of the staff may well have
resulted in a frustratingly tight control being exercised over
the allocation of tasks, and it could create role confusion.
Also, the ever present twin demands of fieldwork teaching and
local community work could result in neither role being properly
fulfilled by the staff.

Links with Courses

The most effective links were with Glasgow University, largely
because of its proximity to the units and its long-term associ-
ating with Crossroads. The employment of a specialist community
work lecturer on the Glasgow course, who was responsible for
community work teaching and acted as a link during placements,
also proved helpful to students. Most courses attracted a fair
amount of criticism from the students, and the dissatisfaction
stemmed largely from the conviction that community work had a
marginal status within courses and that this resulted in limited
theoretical teaching and poor links with the field. Many of the
students felt that there was little time within the course curriculum to improve the community work teaching, unless a system
of options or electives was adopted.

Was the Placement Satisfactory?

All but three of the students found the placement a satisfactory
experience. The reasons given for this were varied. For some
students, the very fact of doing a community work placement and
gaining new experience was the major criterion - 'any community
work experience would have been satisfactory'. Others cited
more specific reasons; being part of local work which was
'relevant' to the residents; being actively involved in local
groups which moved from 'apathy to action'; having the opportunity to pursue a wide range of activities spread over two
different areas, and having experienced 'good supervision' on
the placements. The placement experience was less than satisfactory for one student because his placement was during the
early days of the Gorbals Unit, and the limited range of local
work had not 'stretched' his experience of social work. Another

student was critical of part-time fieldwork teachers.[2] The
limitation of time, combined with the dual fieldwork teacher
and community worker roles, resulted in less than rigorous
supervision and a failure to respond quickly to any 'lack of
fit' between the students' expectations and the work in the
agency. Inevitably, the students' experiences tended to reflect the staff regimes and employment arrangements which were
dominant during different periods in the history of the units.

Apart from almost universal complaints about the spartan and
primitive work conditions which existed in both units - 'better
heating systems and new toilets would have been appreciated' -
the suggestion for improving the placements included 'longer
placements', 'more discussion of theory', 'the employment of
full-time fieldwork teachers' and 'more detailed and regular
supervision of students'. The majority of the students agreed
that the Crossroads placements offered experiences and insights
which were 'not usual' in social work education. Especially
cited in this context was the emphasis upon political debates
and perspectives, the consumer view of the social services,
the opportunity to work with local residents 'as equals' and
the student involvement with collective forms of action.

TUTORS' VIEWS

The thirteen tutors who provided comments and reflections on
the Crossroads units were employed on the following social work
courses; Edinburgh University (6), Glasgow University (4),
Moray House (2) and Robert Gordon's College (1). The main value
of the Units for the training courses was providing a standard
of practice and supervision which was, especially during the
early 1970s, unusual for community work in Scotland.

It's a good placement in the terms that I would apply to
any placement - the students have an adequate amount of
time, attention and interest from the supervisor for
their needs; supervision and discussion has engaged them
and made them consider more their own practical work and
also theoretical considerations; and in most instances
they've been able to get involved in a project and 'do
work' which they can do, they can discuss their practice
as well as observe other things.

The structure of the unit enabled both the practitioner and
the teaching role to be fulfilled;

The ideal in a teaching unit is having people who are
good community workers and good teachers, I think this
is the ideal, but, provided you have the right kinds of

structure and routine you can make it easier for someone,
primarily a practitioner, to fulfil the teaching role.
What I mean is that I appreciated the structure of
supervision that students received, and the structure
for evaluation and other tools of the trade that the Unit
evolved, that make it less likely that an individual
fieldwork teacher or community worker fulfilling that
role, or individual student will come to grief in that
placement.

It was clearly recognized that the Units offered a particular
approach to community work and, with the exception of one tutor,
who felt that the Units should teach comparative approaches to
community work, the orientation was accepted by the courses.

The Unit operates on a particular dimension but so do
many casework agencies. It is our view that it is the
responsibility of the course to provide forums for discussion and to enable the students to examine their
practice in a wider context.

In terms of the acquisition of skills and knowledge, many of
the remarks made by the course tutors mirror those of the
students. New insights into the functioning of groups and increased knowledge of housing policy were cited, and the course
representatives also singled out, more so than the students,
the opportunities to develop research skills through the carrying out of local surveys and undertaking background fact-gathering for campaigns. Given this emphasis, one tutor felt that
'more attention to survey methods would have been appropriate'.
Some tutors, but by no means all, considered that the placements
provided an opportunity to explore the 'political dimension of
social work' and to develop skills which are relevant to radical
forms of practice. Others stressed the value of the placements
in helping students to establish non-paternalistic relationships
with clients.

Community work takes away a lot of the defences between
the worker and client. You can't hide behind a desk in
a way I think you can sometimes in casework. So in terms
of enabling a person to be themselves in a helping situation, a community work placement can achieve quite a lot.

In this context, the value of the non-statutory status of the
Units was stressed and comments were also made about the
'optimistic' assumptions which inform community work. Indeed,
for some of the tutors, this optimism about 'what people can
do and achieve' was a key distinction between community work

and casework.

> You are always trying to build up self-respect in the
> casework situation, and one way of doing this is to
> take someone capable, which you do in community work.
> In most casework situations, the task is very tied up
> with the person's inability to cope with their personal
> lives - which means we don't help them build up their
> self-respect.

All the tutors considered community work placements as being
relevant to social work;

> Community workers are often trying to tackle problems
> like bad housing, lack of facilities, which social workers
> are meeting, and dealing with on an individual or family
> basis. Social service teams could deal with these
> problems on a collective basis.

Criticisms

Criticisms mainly focused on how the organization of the units
affected students and the reservations, which some tutors had,
about the assessment of fieldwork performance. The comparatively unstructured and non-hierarchical organization of the
units was cited as a potential source of difficulty for students,
especially during the early stages of a placement.

> Students starting at the Unit are often surprised there
> is so little structure - they've been used to social work
> units where everyone had a desk; procedures laid down;
> regular weekly timetables, and the thing is much less
> informal. They arrive at the Unit and find people
> sitting around reading newspapers, there is an attempt
> to develop some kind of social cohesion amongst the
> students at any one time. Sometimes this had been
> remarkably successful. I think the first reaction of
> the students is to wonder what it is all about and not
> be able to see what the job really is. Their later
> reaction is, I think, a very favourable one in that
> they feel that what is being undertaken is the creation
> of a viable working team within the Unit, which is dif-
> ficult given the rapid turnover of students and the small
> number of permanent staff.

The pressures to conform to this unusual ethos could result in
students adopting attitudes which were 'out of character' for
them.

I notice some students who don't normally express
certain attitudes and opinions about authority who
during the placement fell into the orthodox wisdom of
the Units and in a way there is a form of socialisation
in the Units. In order to be valued you adopt the norms
of the agency. I think there have been cases where
students have challenged the conventional wisdom, but
a student who is less self-confident and more uncertain
about his stance easily slips into a pattern which allows
him to pass a placement, but minimizes his learning
experience in the course of passing.

This pressure to adapt to the norms of the agency and the
chamelion-like skill of some students to blend with their work
environment presents some obvious dilemmas in terms of the
assessment of placements. Are certain attitudes and stances
struck by students just in order to survive and pass a placement? Some of the tutors' comments suggest that this may happen
and, in the case of the Crossroads units, the failure by the
fieldwork teachers to assess qualities, as well as skills (see
Chapter 11) tended to minimize any detailed scrutiny of this
question. Moreover, a number of the tutors commented on the
fact that the community work emphasis upon people's strengths
rather than their weaknesses - 'optimism about human potential'
could also result, in the case of fieldwork evaluation, in a
less than rigorous appraisal of all aspects of a student's
performance. Some tutors commented upon a 'lack of harshness'
in the evaluation of students and this assessment tends to be
confirmed by the record of student placements over the seven
years covered by this study. During this period, only two
students failed in a placement and one student withdrew before
the end of the placement period. It might well be significant
that the two students who failed did not initially opt to undertake a community work placement and the high commitment from
the majority of students who selected the placement may, partially, explain the high 'pass' rate. Not all the tutors agreed
with the 'lack of harshness' criticism.

Compared to other community work placements it has been
more possible to rely in Crossroads on supervisors
working with students on things they may not be doing
very well, in addition to encouraging what they already
do adequately. In some community work placements the
philosophy of the community worker about encouraging
the local people to delevop their own way of doing
things has spread to the student too much. If students
are having real difficulty I would want to depend on the
supervisor picking this up.

The Unit's policy of clearly indicating, in the final placement
report, whether a student had 'passed or failed' was also positively commented upon.

> One thing which is very useful in your evaluation form
> (and which we don't have for casework placements) is a
> clear statement whether the students have met an
> appropriate standard of work.

According to research reports, this policy contrasts sharply
with the practice adopted by some fieldwork workers in other
social work settings.

> Some fieldwork teachers were somewhat uncertain as to
> what they would like to happen but a number were clear
> they did not wish to play a part in the final decision
> (pass or fail). Some teachers went further in deying
> this role as assessors and claimed they and students
> shared a common role as learners.[3]

LOCAL VIEWS

There was a general appreciation that most of the students came
from the 'other side of the tracks' and needed a certain amount
of 're-education'. Some had unrealistic expectations of local
communities:

> I think they see how capable local people are - I think
> they learn that there are people in the community that
> can take a role of being leaders and showing the rest
> of the community what to do.

The less optimistic side was also stressed;

> The one thing they must learn almost immediately is the
> apathy of the community - you go to group meetings and
> there's only a handful at it.

A lack of understanding of community norms could result in
students (and community workers) working on the right issues,
but in the wrong way.

> I think they tackled some of the situations wrong.
> They didn't do it wilfully, they tried to accomplish
> a lot but it's the way they did it. I remember telling
> a student that he might get a door slammed in his face
> because he's carrying a piece of paper and looks like a
> Government official. If you stand there with paper and

the local person thinks here's some bugger looking for
money - maybe he's moved away from credit or rent arrears,
you don't know. We get a lot of this but students don't
think about it. Still you're always learning even if
it's only when you get a door slammed in your face.

On the whole, student manpower and enthusiasm was considered
valuable.

We were given a student and we detailed that student on
modernization and he did a tremendous job in this area.
He did all the leg work, door to door, talking to people.
We called meetings and got them organized into a sub-
group of the Tenants' Association so it helped the
tenants but it helped the student as well because he
was getting direct contact with the people. We built
a very strong sub-group because one neighbour discovered
he had similar problems to another - students are useful
in this development work. Another advantage of students
is that most of the groups I've been involved in, most
members have been workers so they don't have time during
the day - having students just makes that difference
between the group being successful or not.

The residents appreciated that the students' role and contribution varied according to the stage of local developments.

Some groups tend to use the student as general dogsbody -
arranging leaflets etc. It depends what stage they come
into the group. If it's a pretty well-established group
in many cases there isn't the same need for a student,
unless the group is particularly active or there is a
particular aspect of work suitable for a student at the
time. In a newly-formed group a student could be
invaluable.

A placement was most effective, for the local group, when there
was a specific project in mind;

I think the Unit should select which student goes to
which project but when a group gets students they should
have something in particular in mind for them - not just
appoint them to the Tenants' Association.

The crucial role of the field work teacher was engineering the
'fit' between the local organization and the student.

We've always been fortunate because the fieldwork teacher

has always been interested in the group. The fieldwork
teacher knows both sides of the coin – they know your
organization and its faults and difficulties, and they
know the student – his limitations. It is an advantage
to have the person in charge involved throughout because
the student is here for such a short time.

Thereafter, the student should be given considerable freedom.

The student should be given plenty of opportunity to
get to know the people he is working for – the fieldwork
teacher already knows them. Once a student gets a
particular responsibility it's only fair to let him
develop it in his own way.

Criticisms

Apart from tackling 'some situations in the wrong way' the
major criticisms of placements related to length and lack of
continuity.

The problem is lack of time and continuity. A student
just gets to know everyone, how the group works, how to
contact people and then you get a new student and obviously he doesn't have the contacts of the previous
student. Often people will have to get to know the
student before they will communicate with him.

The continuity of placements depended upon the priorities of
the units and was not directly controlled by local organizations.
On occasions, work which was initiated on placements was never
followed up, and, for good reasons, the local activists felt
that they had been used for a purely academic exercise.

I'll tell you what I don't like is community workers
using us as a vehicle for experiments and then disap-
pearing off. That could happen when students come –
they can create problems for you and then leave – take
the dampness survey – the first survey was done but
there's been no follow-up.

It was generally accepted that both students and community
groups could benefit from placements – 'You both learn' – but
some local activists were very critical and impatient when
students did not actively contribute in certain situations.

Sometimes they don't say much any time they're at a
meeting – they really don't. They don't impart much

knowledge to you.

The approach that goes down best with me is getting the
work done. I actually saw him doing what I thought he
should be doing - working with the kids - not just sitting
round the 'View' drinking coffee. I could see him putting
what he was learning into practice, but there are some
who are always sitting around doing paper work, or coming
along to a meeting and making an odd note about it.

Similar remarks are reported in other research studies.

Workers who wish to help you expend energy on you in
some way. As clients see it, listening does not involve
the expenditure of energy.[4]

These comments illustrate how friction and misunderstandings
can develop over the role and conduct of students on placements.
The local emphasis on 'getting work done' and expectations about
students being seen to be active - which can include 'speaking
out' at public meetings - can conflict with a professional concern about avoiding over assertiveness by outsiders, in order
not to pre-empt contributions from local residents. Thus, for
example, the students were often briefed by the Unit staff to
keep a low profile at local meetings and not to dominate proceedings. The balance between making contributions at meetings
and not pre-empting other speakers is a difficult one to strike,
and, in some cases, non-directiveness became indistinguishable
from passivity! Also, of course, the assumptions that students
had anything relevant to contribute - an assumption which local
activists tended to make - was not always correct. Students
who were at the start of their placement and working on complex
housing issues, related to redevelopment or dampness, rarely
had practical knowledge which was immediately relevant to the
local situation. They remained silent out of ignorance! This
non-activity was compounded, in the eyes of some local activists, by the internal and very visible work routine of the
units; staff and students sitting around, answering telephones,
talking, doing paper work and drinking coffee. This office
style was culturally alien to some local residents. It smacked
of white collar managers idling around while the workers sweated
on the shop floor. Despite the efforts of the staff to make
their offices as publicly accessible as possible, the internal
operation of the units still generated, for some people, a non-
work image. The real work was done 'out there'.

It's a good thing to have a community worker, but they
should be out more. I find they sit in the office and

> say I'm here if you want me'. I think they should go
> out and say 'I'm here whether you want me or not - do
> you want to talk about anything?' They should let
> people know they're available.

There were rational criticisms and it was the task of the
Crossroads staff to explain, why, in their work routines, the
students did not always conform to some local expectations.

SUMMARY

The educational aims and expectations of the staff were positively reflected in some of the comments made by the students
and tutors. The student group singled out, for particular
mention, the 'client's view of the world'; 'gaining more knowledge of local government and housing legislation' and, in a
minority of cases, 'the challenge made to their existing views
on the causes of social problems'. Some of the comments by
tutors and students about developing non-paternalistic relations
with clients also reflected the staff expectation about providing an 'alternative' work approach.

There were, however, some differences over points of emphasis
and what was singled out for special mention. The staff did
not emphasise 'research skills' which were commented on by a
number of tutors, and it would appear that the staff's expectations may, at times, have underestimated 'where the students
were at' when starting the placement. Some of the staff's
comments almost suggest a missionary zeal to convert the unin-
itiated, whereas many of the students were already viewing
social work within a structural perspective when they opted to
do the placement. The students' main interest was in testing
out how, in practice, alternative ideas worked. Both students
and local residents stressed the importance of placements having
a specific focus and the comments made, by some local residents,
clearly reveal a desire for students to be more open in expressing their views.

DOES SOCIAL WORK NEED COMMUNITY WORK?

Underpinning the funding of the Crossroads units was the assumption that community work placements could help equip social
workers for positions in local authority departments which, in
line with the philosophy of the post-Seebohm-Kilbrandon era in
social work, would provide a generic service which combined
casework, group work and community approaches. In this concluding section we want to examine the validity of this assumption - does social work practice need community work? We start

by comparing the feedback on the Crossroads units with the research carried out into social work by the DHSS[5] which, we will
suggest, provides clear evidence of the need for placements of
the type organized by Crossroads. Then we examine evidence
from research by Davies and Brandon,[6] which vigorously contests
the assumption that a creative link can be forged between social
work and community work.

Missing Links?

The exhaustive DHSS report views practice and training within
the context of the post Seebohm/Kilbrandon emphasis upon an
integrated approach to social work. The study is valuable in
clearly indicating that a gulf exists between this framework
and what many social workers actually do and many social work
educationalists actually teach. In the field, casework is still
regarded as the method of social work, rather than as one of a
number of relevant methods of working with clients.

> For social workers the meaning of generic seems to carry
> no suggestion of being able to use a range of methods,
> such as individual, family group or community work, nor
> offer a variety of techniques within one of these broader
> methods. Nearly all social workers we interviewed said
> only that the focus of their work was an individual or
> family.[7]

Our study suggests that even on training courses which are committed to a 'generic' approach, the familiar method, which for
most educationalists is casework, still tends to predominate.

> I think community work is part of social work training,
> but it's one thing for me to think it, it's another thing
> to actually show it. When you get inside a course a
> culture develops which certainly displays the values of
> the majority, and if the majority of experience is in a
> certain area - in this case, casework, - whether or not
> they mean to do it, the course turns out to be a casework
> course. We all say community work matters but in practice
> it is difficult to get it in. Naive though this seems,
> I didn't expect this to happen but really it's inevitable
> because we understand one another so much better in the
> areas of our own experience.   (Tutor)

There is evidence from the DHSS study that a student demand
exists for broader experiences and that, in addition, these
broader experiences would be welcomed by some local authorities.
Over half of the students interviewed wanted to work with

community groups and, more than was expected, actually had
ployment opportunities to work with community groups. Yet, only
a small minority of the students interviewed had community work
placements on their course, and most of these placements were
of a very limited duration (e.g. between one to four weeks).
The Report concludes that 'students tended to take too pessimistic a view of the possibilities of doing less conventional
kinds of work in local authority settings'.[8] This conclusion
could equally apply to the teaching staff on some courses. A
Catch-22 situation has developed, because some tutors believe
that casework is what the local authorities want, and are paying
for in the case of 'seconded' students. In our survey one tutor
commented;

> If there is any doubt I would want a student to concen-
> trate on casework because that is the work they will
> mainly be doing - that is the work employers are paying
> for.

It is not surprising, therefore, that the DHSS Report indicates
that students were ill-equipped for practising broader approaches to social work. It also suggests the potential contribution which community work could make to social work if a fully
generic approach was to be implemented. This becomes apparent
when we note what the DHSS study identifies as some of the
missing skills and deficient knowledge-areas in social work.
These include organizational expertise with reference to meetings and management and self-organization skills.

> The study of administration and organization seems to
> be unpopular with social work students. Perhaps these
> were taught at too abstract a level or maybe students
> were not helped to clarify the difference between theories
> of management and management of their own work.[9]

Social workers also lacked skills in dealing with the media and
tended to devalue advice and advocacy functions.

> Social workers in general are inept at putting their
> views in public. The skill of working with the individual
> offers them little help in talking to the public and in
> the hands of the media they are often innocents abroad.[10]

> The study did not attempt to quantify the amounts of
> social work time given to advice and advocacy. We are
> not able to identify precisely the areas of greatest
> pressure from work of this kind. What the study does
> show is that social workers generally accepted work of

this type whilst not in many cases having a very clear
conception of the place of such activity within social
work. It was seen as a necessary evil of work in a
Local Authority Department.[11]

If social work is to provide a generic service and move beyond
being an 'incomplete profession',[12] then a competence and commitment at intervening at organizational, management and political levels is essential. Community work placements offer
one potential focus for the acquisition and testing out of some
skills which are relevant to operating within the organizational
and political arenas of practice. It is interesting to note
that, in the feedback from the Crossroads students, the skills
and knowledge areas which were identified as positive learning
experiences were similar, and at times identical, to those
skills and knowledge areas which the DHSS study defined as
being missing and devalued in social work, i.e. organizational
skills, self-organization, fact-finding, insights into political
processes and the use of the media. Community work is also a
setting which can encourage the development of innovative skills
and qualities - traits which were identified in the DHSS study
to be sadly lacking in social work.

> There is quite bluntly, with some honourable exceptions,
> a lack of imagination and creativity which would lead
> to attempt to redefine objectives and roles through
> experiment and to provide organizational structures to
> facilitate innovation.[13]

In short, the Crossroads placements embraced experience, activities and skills which appear to be neglected in other practice
and educational settings.

The Brandon and Davies Research

Our arguments about the relevance of community work placements
for social work are directly contradicted by the research carried out by Brandon and Davies. As part of their well-publi-
cized study of assessment in fieldwork placements, Brandon and
Davies examined the performances and experiences of four
students in community work placements. Unfortunately, the
comments made on these placements are very sketchy within the
context of the overall study and many background details which
could be relevant are not included, such as the specific nature
and focus of the placements, the experience of the supervisor,
the adequacy of the teaching content (if any) on community work
in the courses which were involved. On the basis of these four
students, three of whom had already been considered of marginal

competence in earlier casework placements, Brandon and Davies
make some sweeping and very critical generalizations about the
value of community work placements within the context of social
work education.

> The research data suggest that the problem is in reality
> complex, and hinges on the question of whether community
> work practice and casework practice are truly compatible
> in one course; whether they demand similar skills, and,
> above all, whether the lessons learnt about one of them
> in a first placement can be transferred to the other in
> a second. If they cannot - and there is persuasive
> evidence in this study that they cannot - then it means
> that such students are receiving a fundamentally different
> fieldwork programme than those who receive two basically
> compatible placements, in which learning is cumulative
> from one to the other. Furthermore, there appears to
> be evidence that the quality of supervision in community
> work placements might be less reliable, and that the
> placement experience of students in some of them may
> bear little relevance for the work they will be expected
> to perform when eventually employed as social workers or
> probation officers.... Courses ought to be more cautious
> in the use they make of community work placements, and
> ought in particular perhaps to resist any specific demand
> by a student for one, unless strong educational arguments
> can be advanced to justify it.[14]

The Brandon and Davies research suggests a degree of separation
between social work and community work which is more absolute
than our own experience and research findings would indicate.
While we have suggested (see Chapter 11) that different combinations of skills and qualities are required for either change-
directed or integration-centred social work, we also noted that
certain skills and qualities are likely to be shared in common.
For instance, the qualities of 'patience', 'imagination' and
'hard work' are essential in any form of social work or community work. In our survey some of the course tutors also
identified common skills;

> For me the skills you are looking for are in general
> terms very much the sort of things we would look for in
> casework, although maybe a case worker wouldn't use the
> same language. Engagement skills - relationship skills
> are terribly important in case work; organizational
> skills - they may take a lower priority in case work,
> but particularly in a department with a heavy work load
> as most departments have now, they are vital; you help

fewer people if you are badly organized. Planning and
policy skills are important again; action skills and
making decisions with incomplete knowledge – important
because you often have to write an environmental report
on a child you've only seen twice. Communication
skills – vital with all sorts of people; political
skills – maybe some caseworkers wouldn't put it in,
but I think caseworkers in most settings should have
some political awareness. There are few settings where
social workers are not affected by political decisions
and they need to know how to get decisions made or changed.

Community work placements with Crossroads were generally regarded as satisfactory by social work tutors, and it seems
rather premature to single out for special mention unreliable
supervision in community work placements, when, as Brandon and
Davies themselves suggest, some 20% of all social work placements might be considered as being of an inadequate standard.
Given this overall shortcoming it would seem more appropriate
to concentrate upon defining clearer objectives and improved
standards for all social work placements rather than dis-
couraging the use of community work placements. Making connections between different placements can be problematic but,
as most of the tutors in the Crossroads survey indicated, this
task is essentially the responsibility of the social work
course tutors.

     The tutor is the person who knows the student for a
     period of time in different placements, so one of his
     important roles is to help to bring out the aspects of
     learning from more than one placement – to look at how
     learning on one placement can help the student's work
     in other situations. (Course Tutor)

Where tutors have little or no experience of community work
and courses include only a token amount of relevant teaching,
the task of making sense of different placement experiences
becomes, unfairly we would suggest, thrown back on the student.
Most students who completed placements with Crossroads suggested
that a community work placement was relevant for their social
work practice, and felt that the placement had been of value
to them when taking up employment, even though many of them
had experienced considerable difficulties and obstacles in
linking community and social work in their work situations.

CONCLUSION

Our experience and findings indicate that a community work
dimension is essential for social work if, in line with the
Seebohm and Kilbrandon recommendations, social work is to make
any serious claims to operate on a generic basis. On the other
hand, some alternative definitions of the nature of social
work - especially those which exclusively equate social work
with casework - will severely limit the scope for making
creative connections with community work.

Chapter Fourteen

A DEFENCE OF LOCAL COMMUNITY ACTION

The salient characteristics of the Crossroads approach to community work almost fit the identi-kit profile of a variety of
local community action which re-emerged in Britain during the
late 1960s and early 1970s: the emphasis on grass roots organizing and intensive neighbourhood based work; the uneasy ideological mixture of socialism and libertarianism; the commitment
to learning through collective action and a scepticism about
abstract theory; the focus on issue-centred groups and the mistrust of political parties and established organizations. This
style of local community action has been a prominent strand in
British community work over the last decade, and, after a
lengthy period of action and experimentation, it is now being
subjected to critical examination from many quarters. Local
community action has failed to live up to some of its early,
over-ambitious rhetoric - the poor have not 'transformed the
world' and 'power' is still far removed from the 'people'. This
has been one factor in the development of two ideologically
divergent schools of thought, which we have termed the social
planning approach and the radical left approach, both of which
are critical of local community action and suggest revised or
alternative models for community work practice.

In this final chapter we consider, in turn, the criticisms of
local community action which are suggested by these approaches
and we offer a defence, based upon our experiences of community
work in Glasgow.

THE SOCIAL PLANNING APPROACH

Criticisms of Local Community Action

The social planning approach currently represents a significant trend in the state sponsorship of community work[1] and also has, over recent years, received increased attention within the professional community work milieu. The criticisms of local community action, which are articulated by writers like Specht and Thomas,[2] include the following arguments:

Failure to influence social policy. By primarily focusing on the organization and development of community groups, the locality-based approach minimizes the possibilities, for both the worker and community groups, of directly influencing the policies of welfare institutions and the process of social policy-making. Local community action is often an exercise in frustration and disillusionment - 'large hopes and small realities'.

Failure to work for change 'from the inside'. The anti-state stance adopted by some locality-based workers ignores the potential for change and reform which can occur within state welfare institutions. Local authorities are not homogeneous, monolithic bodies which operate with a common mind. On the contrary, they are political arenas of conflicting demands and competing policy priorities. It is the responsibility of the community worker to be 'on the inside' influencing events in the interest of the consumer and client, rather than being negatively critical from the outside.

Lack of relevant skills. In terms of the development of community work skills and professional competence, the locality-based worker - who primarily focuses on relationship building and 'interaction' skills (working with local people) - is deficient in a range of other skills, technical expertise and sources of knowledge which are essential for the practice of community work. These missing attributes include skills which are particularly relevant to working in inter-organizational and intra-organizational settings, such as evaluation research, organizational analysis and programme planning skills.

Lack of professionalism. Finally, as Specht vigorously argues, much of the local community action in Britain has had more of the style and ethos of a social movement than of a profession which can legitimately command status, financial rewards and autonomy in work situations, from the wider society. If community workers are to claim payment and benefits from public funds, they need to develop an all round professional expertise and move beyond a concern for only disadvantaged groups. They must 'speak to and serve and win the support of the entire community'.[3]

The Social Planning Approach to Community Work

Whereas local community action focuses, in its goals and strategies, on the development of the social and political potential
of groups, the social planning approach is primarily concerned
with changing the organization of welfare institutions and producing a more sensitive fit between social policies and the
needs of clients. The community worker operates mainly at
inter-organizational and intra-organizational levels, working
to stimulate collaboration between established services and
seeking to modify the internal structure and policies of formal
institutions.

> As social planners, we should be able to bring a new
> vision and breadth to agencies and help release agency
> workers, especially in the social services, from a narrow-
> ness of approach caused both by their own specialist
> training and the burdens of their daily routines and
> responsibilities. Besides new concepts and perspectives,
> the social planner may also introduce alternative tech-
> nologies to agencies.[4]

There is nothing novel about the social planning approach to
community work. It has, for many years, been a central strand
in American community work, and, in Britain, a social planning
dimension has always existed in the work of co-ordinating bodies
within the voluntary sector, like Councils of Voluntary Service.
What is relatively new about the approach is its emergence,
over recent years, as a dominant feature in local authority
based community work, a trend which owes much to the re-organization of local government and the development of corporate
management policies. This trend was apparent in Glasgow when,
after the re-organization of local government, the Strathclyde
Region began to develop an ambitious community work programme
which was closely linked with the Region's 'areas of need' policy (see Chapter 2). By the late 1970s the Region's social work
department was employing over fifty community workers in the
city, with funding mainly coming from the urban aid scheme.
Although these staff operate at a variety of levels, - citywide,
district and local neighbourhoods - the guiding philosophy placed
a central emphasis upon the social planning task of producing a
more sensitive and responsive fit between the policies of local
government and the needs of local groups.

> Community workers working with local communities on a
> broad range of issues appear to us to carry out an impor-
> tant pivotal role between Councils and people (similar in
> many ways to that of an elected member in his constituency),

and they must be concerned to activate channels of
communication with local authority members and officers
in the same way as they do with community groups.[5]

Consistent with this linking role was an emphasis upon working
through institutional mechanisms and defining the processes for
change within boundaries which are acceptable to power holders.

We feel that community workers employed or supported by
the Council must seek to interpret 'conflict' in terms
of constructive challenge, and, through negotiation, to
reach a consensus, wherever possible, between the community's aspirations and the financial, political and
other constraints which bind the authorities so that
expectations are not unrealistically raised beyond the
capacity of the authorities to fulfil them.[6]

A Defence of Local Communuty Action

The social planning approach represents a significant move away
from the traditional community work focus on local organizing,
towards the full incorporation of community work within the
managerial structure of statutory services. For some observers
this move will represent a 'coming of age' for community
workers - a winning of their professional spurs and a hallmark
of official credibility. For others, like ourselves, the trend
is viewed with some criticism and suspicion.

Stereotypes of locality-based work. The social planning theorists are guilty, at times, of caricaturing the limitations of
local community action. Specht's criticism of British community
workers for allocating a low priority to working for social policy changes and their failure to develop skills in the 'struc-
turing' of change is not, in our experience, an accurate one.
As the case studies illustrate (see Part Two) much of locally
based community work is concerned with a dual process of organizing groups and attempting to change the policies and practices
of state welfare institutions. The external work of many community groups is directly concerned with social policy issues
and much time is devoted to plotting out strategies and developing 'action systems'. The skills required for this are precisely
those which Specht and Thomas argue are absent or ill-developed
in British community work, and it was the skills of organizational analysis and an improved knowledge of local government
which the Crossroads students identified as being valuable
learning experiences on their placements (see Chapter 13). The
crucial difference between the social planning approach and the
community action approach is not over whether there is an

an involvement in working for change in social policy, but,
rather, over the way in which social policy change should be
approached, and who should be involved in the process. It was
this very difference which brought Crossroads into conflict
with the local M.P. and caused him to comment that 'the difference between Crossroads and myself is not a question of helping
people - it's a question of the philosophy involved in it'.
The community action approach emphasizes change coming from
the mobilization of working class groups which operate outside
of formal power structure. The social planning approach, in
contrast, tends to emphasize change coming from professionals
and elected representatives in consultation with local groups.
Both approaches are concerned with changing social policy, but
they differ sharply in political analysis and the priority which
is given to different groups in the action process.

Influence on social policy. Although we would question the
criticism that local community action is not concerned with
changing social policy, the theorists of the social planning
approach are right to suggest that local community has only had
a marginal impact on the formulation and administrative practice
of major items of social policy, such as the supplementary benefits system or the financing of council housing. Linked with
this justified criticism is the implication that the scope for
the community worker to influence social policies is enhanced
within the social planning approach. While we would not doubt
that working at managerial levels does have considerable advantages in terms of access to information, making political contacts and command over technical resources, we would question
whether the influence of the worker is as substantial as some
of the literature tends to suggest. An experienced community
worker in Glasgow expressed similar doubts.

> This style of community work gives a lot of status and
> power to the community worker - 'Mr. Fix-it' - but takes
> away from the community the opportunity of learning them-
> selves. Most of their energy goes into creating 'old
> boy' networks with councillors and officials and it's
> impossible to measure the impact of that.

Working within state institutions should not be confused with
an effective ability to influence the major policy making functions of these institutions. The scale and hierarchical structure of local authorities, allied to the impact of corporate
management regimes, has resulted, as several observers have
noted,[7] in a tendency to concentrate formal policy making powers
in the hands of relatively small elites of senior officials and
politicians. While social workers and community workers can

enjoy considerable autonomy in their day to day work, they can
also be relatively detached from the major decision-making processes which are concerned with budgeting and the definition
of overall policy adjectives and priorities. Their professional
influence on policy making can be limited and, rather ironically,
aggressive community groups can, on occasions, reach the 'head
of the house' - the senior administrators and politicians -
more easily than can employees or even backbench councillors
who occupy a subordinate position in the power structure of
local government. These limitations on the influence of professional workers have been further reinforced by cutbacks in
public expenditure and the policy of the present Conservative
government of restricting the discretionary policy making powers
of local government.

Participation. A more serious question, for the theory and
practice of community work, arises over whether community workers should directly seek to influence policy-making and occupy
roles in the process of local government which, arguably, should
be filled by the representatives of local groups. Implicit in
much of the theory of social planning is the role of the community worker as an advocate for policy change - a professional
broker who, through negotiation and bargaining with other officials and politicians, has an active involvement in the
policy-making process. This role is sharply at variance with
much of the traditional community work theory which eschews
policy-making roles for the professional worker and emphasizes,
instead, the worker's role in enabling or organizing direct
representation from client and local groups. Working as the
link person between state agencies and community groups, the
social planner can easily become a surrogate spokesman for community opinion, acting as a mediator of local needs and a filter
for the flow of ideas and information. This was a role which
the Crossroads staff refused to perform, on the grounds that
local opinion should be articulated by local representatives
and that the presence of a community worker, in a broker role,
denied valuable learning experience for local representatives.
This role of 'speaking for' the community is made explicit in
a Strathclyde Region policy paper.

> It is essential to have a team of officers at local level
> to monitor the needs of an area from the viewpoint of the
> community and to speak for that community.[8]

We would suggest that the social planning approach can seriously limit and control the scope for direct representation by
community groups. This containment of participation can be
further reinforced by the social distance which can exist

between the community worker and local areas - community
workers employed at managerial levels do not, in our experience, operate from locally accessible offices - and, more importantly, by the practice in local government of interpreting
community consultation and participation mainly with reference
to the more formal and constitutional types of community organizations. Thus, for example, in Glasgow there was a tendency
for 'community consultation' to be defined primarily in terms
of contacts with the Community Councils, irrespective of whether
they were representative of dominant opinions within an area.

Conflict. As the above observations imply, the social planning
approach tends to operate within a political framework which
only permits disagreement within institutional boundaries. In
our typology of local group-power structure relations, the
social planning approach encompasses 'collaborative' and 'bargaining' relations, but effectively rules out those 'conflict'
relations which develop when working through the normal channels
of political and pressure group representation, are not perceived as a viable option by local groups (see Chapter 5). The
obvious question which arises, for both the community worker
and local groups, is what do you do when the normal channels
of consultation, bargaining and negotiation are exhausted and
fundamental disagreements still remain between the parties involved? These situations (such as those which arose over redevelopment and dampness in Gorbals and Govanhill), are not
readily amenable to a bi-partisan approach and are likely to
confront the community worker with an acid test of loyalty.
The social planning literature tends to hedge around this issue,
or hints, as Thomas does, that more sophisticated knowledge,
technical skills and professional competence can safeguard the
worker from 'the enervating effects of the bureaucracy on their
idealism'.[9] For the worker, who is caught in the crossfire of
local group-power structure conflicts, a dexterity at juggling
competing loyalties is certainly required but, in our experience,
we would seriously question how long this form of gymnastics
can be sustained without a serious loss of credibility in the
eyes of community groups. Improved training and skills will
not resolve the political contradictions which are inherent in
professional community work roles. Training can only make the
worker more aware of the likelihood of these conflicts arising.
Such contraditions require a political response and, for the
community worker, the most appropriate avenue for action is
through trade union and other collective responses both inside
and outside the workplace.

All approaches to community work have boundaries which define
and limit the degree of challenge to the state which it is considered legitimate for the workers, in their professional role,

to be identified with. For the Crossroads staff, this limit was
defined by a conflictual relationship, and did not embrace what
we have described as 'revolutionary or insurrectionary' relationships (see Chapter 5). In this respect the distinction
between the local community action approach adopted by Crossroads and the social planning approach is one of degrees and
not absolutes. Both operate within an essentially reformist
model of political change, but vary significantly with regard
to the activities and strategies which are defined as legitimate for community workers and local groups. By ruling out
conflict, in terms of confrontation and contest, the social
planning approach provides a more restricted political basis
for the practice of community work.

THE RADICAL LEFT APPROACH

Criticisms of Local Community Action

Although the social planning approach is a reflection of a
current trend in the state sponsorship of community work, it
is still relatively weakly represented in the British community
work literature. It is an approach which is more practised
than written or talked about. The reverse could be said to be
true of the radical left approach, examples of which have formed
a vigorous and dominant thread in much of the recent British
literature on community work,[10] but which rarely finds a clear-
cut expression in the work or philosophy of agencies which employ community workers. The radical left approach is more
written and talked about than practised. The 'radical left'
is a convenient shorthand expression to denote a range of criticisms about community work, and it is not a description of a
clearly defined and ideological cohesive school of thought.
Within the radical left critics of local community action are
to be found some strange bedfellows: Marxists of various types
and libertarians of widely different political persuasions.
All we have attempted to do here is to identify certain criticisms which are commonplace and recurring, irrespective of the
different political ideologies which might inform them.

Social control. The dominant role of state sponsorship in the
promotion of community work predisposes community work to exercise a social control function which belies the radical rhetoric
of many projects. Community work, like social work, is part
of the software of capitalism - an expression of repressive
tolerance which encourages citizen participation providing it
acts as a safety valve for working-class discontent and not as
an avenue for political activism.

Throughout the western world, societies are characterized
by one of the two major symbols of control in capitalist
society; the tank or the community worker.[11]

Political action. The locality focus of community work produces
material results which are of marginal value to working people,
encourages the development of a parochial 'community consciou-
ness' rather than a class consciousness, and fosters a divisive
set of relationships between different localities as they compete
with each other over scarce public resources.

Methods. The work of many community workers substitutes unre-
flective action and simplistic moral concerns for hard-headed
and detailed political analysis. The class dimension of community work and the political educational role of the worker
is confused by the emphasis which the community worker places
on 'non-directiveness' and their quixotic tilts at statutory
windmills serve to obscure the real targets of working-class
exploitation in Britain (e.g. big business).

Employment issues. A focus on those community and welfare
issues which are more immediately accessible for action - such
as housing, welfare rights and recreational provision - deploys
attention away from broader economic and employment issues and
contributes to a separation between community and industrial
action. Community action, taken in isolation, can be a diversion from building a united working class movement.

Prescription for Change

The prescriptions for community work which derive from these
criticisms are many and varied. Some deeply pessimistic critics
have concluded that community action will never arise above a
type of 'consumer consciousness' and advocate a concentration
on work-place organization as the only viable avenue open for
working-class political action.[12] Others have argued for a
forging of links with wider political movements - linking community groups to either the trade unions, the women's movement,
the revolutionary left or the Labour Party.[13] This focus on
building links is reflective of a shift in political perspective
from the optimism of the late 1960s, when some community workers
and activists were anticipating that independent action by the
poor and disadvantaged could build counter political movements
and institutions. Also, implied in much of the criticism is a
concern to rescue community work from the social welfare establishment. Whereas the social planners are anxious that the
political movement ethos of local community action will dilute
its professionalism, the radical left critics have the opposite

concern.

> Instead of socialist community work being seen as the
> lowest in the hierarchy of types of professional com-
> munity work and part of the social work, welfare, group
> therapy tradition, it must be totally disentangled from
> that tradition.[14]

With the social planning critique it was possible, within the
context of Glasgow, to pinpoint developments which clearly
reflected this approach and provided a revised model for the
practice of community work which went beyond local community
action. This is not possible for the radical left critique.
Although elements of the criticisms noted above did inform some
community work practice in the city (including that of Crossroads), there were no clear cut examples of community projects
which explicitly embodied a radical left approach and which
functioned, on a full time basis, over any period of time. Unlike some cities, Glasgow has had little recent history of political community organizing which falls outside of the traditional activities of Tenants' Associations and the work of
locality-centred voluntary agencies like Crossroads. Even in
the arena of forging links between community and industrial
action – an activity in which the city has a notable history
(see Chapter 2) – Glasgow has not produced the types of independent 'labour and community resource centres' which are concerned to link workplace and community-based groups.[15] These
centres, which represent one of the more creative and tangible
products of the radical left approach, have emerged in cities
like Coventry, Leeds and Bristol, but were not part of the
Glasgow scene during the 1970s. The absence of these developments can, in part, be attributed to the failure of Glasgow-
based community workers to stimulate much initiatives. Thus
the Crossroads staff were far more effective in organizing trade
union representation for themselves and other workers employed
by voluntary organizations in the West of Scotland than they
were in linking, on a regular basis, the activities of local
community groups to the wider trade union movement in the city.

A Defence of Local Community Action

The criticisms noted above are directly relevant to an examination of the work of Crossroads; the failure to link community
and industrial struggles; the emphasis on action at the expense
of political reflection and education; the willingness to 'take
on city hall' and ignore other political targets. These limitations, which closely mirror Corrigan and Leonard's caustic
Marxist critique of libertarian community work,[16] need to be

balanced against the participatory value of the local community
action approach and the tendency, on occasions, for the radical
left to pursue ideological elegance and purity at the expense
of working from 'where the people are at'.

Political Awareness. The tendency on the left to minimize the
political significance of local community action can both exag-
gerate these limitations and, at the same time, serve to over-
emphasize the positive features which are claimed for other
forms of working class activism, especially workplace organizing. Some of the gains derived from community action are far
more than of marginal significance for the people involved -
such as rehousing from a damp, insanitary, flat - and, while
the more militant areas may well win concessions in advance of
other areas, there is evidence to indicate that 'knock on'
effects do occur and that a process of mutual learning can
happen. The Gorbals Dampness Campaign not only won a 'special
case' status on rehousing and compensation but also provided a
political precedent and organizational example to other areas
in the city which suffered from dampness. This process is not
dissimilar to wage negotiations under 'free collective bargaining'. The alleged failure of local community action to generate
class consciousness and a socialist programme also has parallels
with workplace organizing. Beynon's sympathetic verdict on the
Ford Car workers echoes the comments of several writers who have
examined the political impact of community struggles.

> They have struggled bravely, and their resolve has
> frequently demanded admiration. Yet there is little
> evidence that they have been able to link their
> struggles positively with those of other workers.
> Their battle has produced no radical political demands.
> They have not been able to shift the basis of that
> struggle from the effects to the causes - to an attack
> upon the dominant logic of capitalist production.[17]

The Ford car workers, like the residents in Gorbals and Govanhill, are politically conscious and, in their daily lives, they
regularly experience the exploitation and vicissitudes of a
capitalist society. While their political consciousness may
not embody the politics of a Marx, Proudhon or Keir Hardie,
they do express, through their collective organizations -
whether trade unions, shop stewards' committees or Tenants'
Associations - attitudes and actions which are in opposition
to the prevailing power structure of society and are an expression of what has been described as the 'muted, defensive,
counter ideology' of the working class.[18] For left-wing critics
and community workers to dismiss this stance as merely being an

expression of 'community consciousness' or 'trade union consciousness' is both arrogant and patronizing.

Participation. One of the major strengths of local community
action is its potential to bring into collective action people
who are often excluded or alienated from any organized form of
political activity. For some groups, like housewives, pensioners and the unemployed, local community action represents
the most immediate and accessible arena for political involvement. How to retain this participatory value, and, at the same
time, broaden the organizational context and political content
of community action presents a major dilemma for the left. Some
of the prescriptions for change which have been advocated could
well sacrifice the participatory value at the expense of developing an improved organizational and political sophistication.
e.g. the argument which has been made in favour of community
workers concentrating upon building links with groups 'which
are prepared to raise socialist demands'[19] could well exclude
from consideration many individuals who are either inactive at
the present time or are members of organizations whose level
of political activity and consciousness does not conform to the
criteria of socialism which the community organizer might care
to apply. One possible outcome of this approach might be that
radical organizers could spend much of their time and energy
working only with a political élite within either the community
or industrial settings. This selective model of organizing
fits well into the orthodox Marxist theory of the revolutionary
vanguard, but it also implicitly excludes from an active involvement a large number of people who are on the margins of
organized politics and who, moreover, will tend to be among the
more disadvantaged and poor members of working class communities
Ironically, in our experience, this concentration on working
with the more politically conscious members of community organizations may not always produce a sharper and more decisive
form of collective action. As was indicated in the case studies
(see Chapters 7 and 8) a previous experience of left-wing politics may produce ritualistic forms of leadership in which the
rhetoric is 'radical' but the actions are conservative.

All community work is selective in terms of issues, groups and
strategies. We are not doubting here the legitimacy of selecting to work intensely with the more politically aware groups,
but, rather, we are questioning the implications this concentration might have for contact and work with those people in
working-class areas who are on the margins of politics and who
comprise the vast majority of residents. Community workers can,
in our view, be politically selective in another direction.
They can make strenuous efforts to encourage involvement from

those people who have been 'written off' by the formal political system, and who are also assigned a subordinate and passive
role in vanguard theories of change.

Social Control and the Welfare Establishment. The present
structure of the British welfare state is the product of more
than a century of class conflict, political compromise and
administrative innovation. Embodied within its legislation
and policies are elements of universal provision and elements,
which are being reinforced at the present time, of selective
provision which negatively discriminate against the poorer
sections of the working class. The welfare state is not, as
some optimistic Fabians once claimed, a triumph for socialism
but neither is it, as Marxist critics often imply, a triumph
for the incorporating powers of the capitalist state. To identify and locate community work only within the social control
dimension of the welfare state is to impose a unidimensional
analysis upon a multi-dimensional reality. It fails to define
community work (and likewise social work) within a political
arena where a constant battle is being fought between forces
for change and forces for reaction. Community work can certainly have a social control function and the history of British
community work is littered with examples, such as the conservative ideology of the Victorian settlement house movement, and
the soup kitchen and 'no politics' approach of some Councils
of Social Service during the depression years of the 1930s.[20]
But the hegemony of conservatism has not always been as all-
pervasive as some critics have suggested.[21] Just as the Bev-
eridge Report, the foundation of the modern welfare state,
contained a mixture of progressive and conservative measures,
so the personal social services have embraced a variety of
approaches and political ideologies. The balance between these
competing elements is never static and equal. It changes according to wider political trends and gains which are won during
one period can swiftly disappear during later periods of reaction. In a sense, this has been the recent history of community work in Britain. A period of trial and error experimentation, informed by a mixture of political motives, was
initiated during the late 1960s and this has been followed by
a period of backlash and political re-assessment. While the
limits of radical action have now become more sharply defined
and the sponsorship trend is away from the more controversial
styles of community work, it is too simple to argue that this
was always what was intended to happen. If the sponsors of
community work had only wanted to encourage a 'bread and cir-
cuses' variety of community work, it is puzzling why so many
of the early projects were given, at least initially, so much
autonomy in their day to day running and management. Community

work in Britain has been of an essentially pluralistic nature
and this has been reflected in its sponsorship, as well as in
the activities of different projects. This pluralism can be
advantageous in providing a legitimacy for the more radical
varieties of community work and the freedom to manoeuvre which
it granted is sorely missed, when, as at the present time, the
trend in central government is towards a more clear cut and
ideologically pure form of welfare policy.

While we have raised critical questions about the political con-
strains which can operate in state agencies, it is too sweeping
a judgement to suggest that community work loses all its radical
potential by an association with state welfare and social work.
This view assumes that the work of the employees within the
social service is uniformly conservative and that employment
settings permit little freedom for developing counter-ideologies
and approaches. Also, how do you escape from these possible
sources of incorporation? The prospect of the Labour movement
generating its own finance for radical community organizing has
yet to be realized. Apart from those activists who operate
purely on a voluntary basis, or who fund projects through private means, the alternative left projects are faced, especially
when they have to pay salaries, with having to bargain for state
funds or, as a short term alternative, with negotiating grants
from the larger charitable trusts. Is money which comes from
charitable trusts, or even the EEC, any less-constraining than
are funds from the welfare establishment?

CONCLUSION

The social planning approach and the radical left approach provide the outline for a broader organizational and conceptual
framework for community work, at the risk of limiting the scope
and opportunities for participation, especially from those working people who are on the margins of collective action. This
is not an argument for retaining an exclusively localized-base
for community work. Rather, it is a warning that value conflicts
and choices will arise when attempts are made to overcome the
political and social policy limitations of local community
action. Frustration with the piecemeal nature of the practical
results should not become an excuse for relegating local organ-
izating to a secondary place, or for community workers, whether
in the interests of corporate management or socialism, assuming
a more directive stance in relation to local groups. If community work has a distinctive role to play, in both social work
and the labour movement, it is in terms of the commitment to
participatory ideals in the struggle for social change. Community workers who abandon this commitment, for whatever reason,
only serve to reproduce a form of paternalism which is all too
familiar to working people.

APPENDIX 1

STUDENT QUESTIONNAIRE

NAME: AGE:
                                            (during placement)

TRAINING INSTITUTION:

COURSE: LENGTH OF COURSE:

Were you seconded/direct grant/other?

Did you have previous work experience prior to training?

Did you request a community work placement?

    If so, why?

Did you request a placement with Crossroads?

    If so, why?

Did you complete another community work placement during
training?

    If so, where?

A. EVALUATION OF THE PLACEMENT AS AN EDUCATIONAL EXPERIENCE

1. Your Project

    a) What was your main project?

    b) Did you have any choice in the selection of your
       project?   How?

    c) How important was your project? Indicate how important
       the work done during your placement was for the various
       interested parties - use this scale: 1. Very important;
       2. Important; 3. Of little importance.

           YOU

           AGENCY

           LOCAL GROUPS

2. <u>Supervision</u> is either individual supervision only; group supervision only; or a mixture of the two. What type of supervision did you have?

   What comments do you have on this supervision?

3. <u>Recording</u>

   Students are asked to keep a daily log, weekly review of activities and process recordings of meetings. What comments do you have about this type of recording?

   If you completed a case study, could you comment on its usefulness?

4. <u>Evaluation of the Placement</u> for the College/University is written by the student him/herself as well as by the field-work teacher. Sometimes all students on placement discuss the student's evaluation and very occasionally local people are involved. What comments do you have about these methods of evaluation?

5. <u>What did you learn from this Placement?</u>

   a) <u>Knowledge</u>: Did the placement give you increased knowledge about certain areas of work? Could you list, in order of priority, the most valuable areas of learning.

   b) <u>Skills</u>: What community work skills did you have an opportunity to develop during this placement? Could you list, in order of priority.

      In your opinion, what are the most important skills in community work practice?

   c) <u>Values</u>: Did this placement make you consider your personal values which underline your approach to social work? If so, please describe.

      Did it raise any questions about 'professional' social work for you?

      To whom did you feel accountable? - staff/management/local people/yourself/a combination (please expand if you pick this option)?

      In a situation of conflict, to whom did you feel ultimately responsible?

      Do you consider that a student should be exposed to ethical dilemmas on Placement (e.g. Crossroads stance against the eviction of persons from dangerous buildings forced students to make a personal decision whether to be involved in civil disobedience tactics)?

6. What specific advantage does a student unit have for training?

   What disadvantages?

7. What are the specific advantages to you as a student of your fieldwork teacher and the agency trying to combine the educator/activist roles?

   What disadvantages?

   On balance, is it a good idea?

8. Involvement of local people

   How important was the involvement of local people in terms of your educational experience? Please give examples:-

   How do you see the role of local people in student training?

9. What did you contribute to the local area during placement? - please assess your contribution.

   What are the advantages to local groups of having students on placement?

   And the disadvantages?

   On balance, is it a good idea?

10. Was this a satisfactory placement in your terms?
          Why?

    Indicate how important the following factors are in your answer (rank 1 to 4 as illustrated in question 1(c)):-

             fieldwork teacher

             total staff of unit

             other students

             local people

             placement experience

             other

    How should the placement be reorganized to provide you with a more satisfactory placement?

B. LINKS WITH COLLEGE AND UNIVERSITY

1. Please describe the links between training body and placement.

    What comments do you have on this? (Be specific, if possible.)

2. Please describe the theory relevant to community work
    practice available on the course.

    What comments do you have on this?

    How could the course be reorganized to allow you to cope
    more effectively with a community work placement?

C. LINKS BETWEEN COMMUNITY WORK AND SOCIAL WORK

1. In your opinion, what are the links between community
    work and social work?

2. Is a community work placement of value to a person intend-
    ing to work in other settings? If so, how?

3. What does this placement provide that is not generally
    available in a social work placement? If appropriate,
    could you compare and contrast this placement with others
    during training.

D. EXPERIENCE SINCE TAKING UP EMPLOYMENT

    Most of you have now been working for some time. Could
    you briefly list your employment since completing the
    course? Could you also comment upon:-

1. In what ways (if any) this placement was useful to you
    once you started working?

2. In retrospect, are there experiences you now consider of
    value from your placement or training which you considered
    of less relevance at the time?

3. If you were now to repeat your training, would you approach
    this placement differently? Describe.

    What would you want included: a) in this placement?
                                   b) in the training course?

E. EVALUATION OF CROSSROADS

    I am going to be asking officials, politicians, and
    especially local people how they would evaluate the
    community work service provided by the student units.
    As you were all observers of the staff and service given,
    I would be interested in your observations on the service
    Crossroads provided.

1. Briefly describe how you saw Gorbals Group/Crossroads and
    the relationship of staff to overall management. Were

local people involved with the student units, or with
overall management, formally or informally? Please
comment.

2. What effect had the student unit on the local area?
    Could you describe?

3. What would you describe as a 'successful' community work
    project? e.g. increased resources to an area; personal
    development of local people, better services to an area;
    increased political awareness; others. Could you rank in
    order of importance. Was Crossroads a successful community
    work project and why?

F. ANYTHING ELSE YOU WANT TO INCLUDE

APPENDIX 2

QUESTIONNAIRE FOR TUTORS

TRAINING INSTITUTION:

Approximately how many students have you tutored who completed a community work placement either with the Govanhill Unit or Gorbals Unit?

A. Evaluation of Placement as Educational Experience

1. What were the strengths of the placement:

    a) for the student?

    b) for the tutor and University/College?

    AND the weaknesses:

    a) for the student?

    b) for the tutor and the University/College?

2. What specific advantages and disadvantages does a student unit have for training, compared to an individual placement?

3. Supervision: The Student units used group supervision, individual supervision, and often a mixture of the two. Could you comment on the supervision of students on placement with the Units?

4. Recording: Students kept a daily log, notes of every meeting attended, and sometimes completed a case study. Could you comment on the recording expected by the Units?

5. Evaluation of the placement was written by the student himself as well as by fieldwork teacher. Sometimes all students on placement discussed the student's evaluation and very occasionally local people were involved. Could you comment on this method of evaluation?

6. What were the main areas in which students seemed to have advanced their understanding or practice ability?

7. Crossroads' stance against eviction of persons from dangerous buildings forced students to make a personal decision whether to be involved in civil disobedience tactics. Do you consider that a student should have to make a practical decision about an ethical dilemma on a placement, and why?

8. How do you see the role of clients or client groups in community work placements?

B. <u>Links between placement and Training Institution</u>

1. Please describe the links between the training body and the placement, and comment upon this and the role of tutor and purpose of student visits. How could the links be improved: a) during placement? b) on an on-going basis?

2. What are the special problems of tutoring students on community work placements?

3. What problems do students experience when undergoing community work placements, and how could the course be better organized to allow the students to cope more effectively?

C. <u>Links between Community Work and Social Work</u>

1. In your opinion, what are the links between community work and social work?

2. Is a placement with the student units attached to Crossroads of value to a person intending to work in other settings? If so, how?

3. What does this placement provide that is not generally available in other placements? If appropriate, could you compare and contrast this placement with others used by the training institutions.

4. Is a 'pass' in a community work placement of equal standing to a 'pass' in a casework placement?

D. Anything else you want to include.

This section to be filled in by the tutor who is responsible for community work teaching.

E. Community Work Teaching on the Course

1. Please describe the theory relevant to community work practice available on the Course (or Courses). Is teaching purely theoretical or does it include some practice-centred sessions, e.g. practical exercises, role playing, simulation games, etc.?

2. How many sessions are allocated to the teaching of community work on your Course? Are these sessions for all students or are they for those students who have a particular interest?

3. What is the timing of the teaching of community work compared to the timing of community work placements? What briefing does a student receive before going on placement?

4. Placement Policy: Are all students encouraged to undertake a community work placement or only those who express an interest?

5. In general, do other community work supervisors find general meetings of fieldwork teachers helpful (we didn't!)? Are there any special meetings for supervisors of community work students?

REFERENCES

Chapter One   INTRODUCTION

1. *Social Work (Scotland) Act* HMSO, 1968. Also see; *Social Work and the Community* HMSO, 1966.
2. D.N. Thomas, Research and Community Work, *Community Development Journal* Vo.15, No.1, 1980.
3. M. Key, P. Hudson, and J. Armstrong *Evaluation Theory and Community Work* Young Volunteers Force, 1976.
4. ibid., p 11.
5. P. Marris, Experimenting in Social Reform. In D. Jones and M. Mayo (Eds) *Community Work One* Routledge and Kegan Paul, 1974, p 257 .
6. M. Key et al., op.cit. p 16 .

Chapter Two   GORBALS AND GOVANHILL

1. T. Johnston *The History of the Working Classes in Scotland* E.P. Publishing, 1974.
2. ibid., p 281.
3. S. Checkland *The Upas Tree* University of Glasgow Press, 1976, p 20 .
4. For details see; N. Milton *John Maclean* Pluto Press, 1973, p 175-183.
5. H. McShane and J. Smith *No Mean Fighter* Pluto Press, 1978, p 44 .
6. For details see; L. Flynn (Ed) *We Shall Be All* Bookmarks, 1978.
7. P. Corrigan and N. Ginsburg, Tenants Struggle and Class Struggle. In *Political Economy and the Housing Question* Political Economy of Housing Workshop, Octopress, 1975.
8. W. Hannington *Unemployed Struggles 1919-1936* Lawrence and Wishart Ltd. 1979, p 71-72.

9. For details see; R. Bryant, Conflict and Community Work:
    A Case Study *Community Development Journal* Vol.14, No.2,
    1979.
10. Glasgow Corporation *Housing and Social Deprivation* 1973.
11. T. Brennan *Reshaping the City* Grant, 1959, p 60/61 .
12. ibid., p 60.
13. ibid., p 65.
14. ibid., p 63.
15. *Glasgow Herald* 19 November, 1974.
16. *Glasgow Herald* 1879.
17. B. Holmes *Govanhill Area Survey to Locate Housebound,
    Chronic Sick and Disabled* Crossroads Youth and Community
    Association, 1978.
18. J. Shannon *Placement Report* 1971.
19. Glasgow Corporation *Govanhill: Report for Planning Action
    and Local Consultation in the Govanhill Community* 1974.
20. Glasgow Corporation *Areas of Need in Glasgow* 1973.
21. Strathclyde Regional Council *Strathclyde: areas for
    priority treatment* 1975.
22. Strathclyde Regional Council *Multiple Deprivation* 1976.
23. S. Holterman *Census Indicators of Urban Deprivation*
    Working Note No.6, Department of the Environment, 1975.
24. S. Checkland, op.cit., p 47.
25. V. Cable, Glasgow: Area in Need. In G. Brown (Ed) *The
    Red Paper on Scotland* EUSPB, 1975.
26. J. Firn, External Control and the Regional Policy. In
    G. Brown (Ed) *The Red Paper on Scotland* op.cit.
27. V. Cable, op.cit.
28. For example see; P. Townsend *Poverty in the United Kingdom*
    Penguin Books, 1979, Ch.15.
29. S. Checkland, op.cit., p 95-96.
30. J.H. Rae *Social Deprivation in Glasgow* Glasgow District
    Council, 1973.
31. Quoted in R. Bryant, Housing and Community Action *Focus*
    No.48, 1976.
32. K. Carmichael, A City in Need *Scotsman* 7 June, 1972.
33. V. Cable, op.cit., p 244.
34. K. Carmichael, op.cit.

Chapter Three   CROSSROADS

1. For details on The Gorbals Group see; R. Ferguson *Geoff -
    The Life of Geoffrey M. Shaw* Famedram Publishers, 1979.
2. For details see; B. Kenrick *Come out of the Wilderness -
    The Story of East Harlem Protestant Parish* Harper and
    Brothers, 1962.
3. G. Shaw *Report on Work of Gorbals Experiment, for the Home
    Mission Committee of the Presbytery of Glasgow* 1968, p 1.
4. ibid., p 12.

5. For details see: R. Bryant, 'The View' A Community News-
    paper *Community Development Journal* Vol.13, No.1, 1978.
6. W. Fyffe, The Inadequacy of Authority *Glasgow Herald*
    5 April, 1965.
7. G. Shaw, op.cit., p 7.
8. B. Holmes, R. Bryant and D. Houston. Student Unit in
    Community Work: An Experimental Approach. *Social Work
    Today* Vo.4, No.14, 1975.
9. J. Ecklein and A. Lauffer *Community Organisers and Social
    Planners, A Volume of Case and Illustrative Materials*
    John Wiley & Sons, 1972, p 92.
10. A. Robertson *Submission to the Industrial Tribunal*
    November, 1976.
11. Crossroads Youth and Community Association *Staff Contract*
    August, 1976.

Chapter Four   COMMUNITY WORK AND TRAINING

1. B. Holmes, R. Bryant and D. Houston *Student Unit in Commun-
    ity Work. An Experimental Approach* op.cit.
2. J. O'Brien *Neighbourhood Organization and Interest Group
    Processes* Princeton University Press, 1975.
3. R. Holman *Power for the powerless: the role of community
    action* British Council of Churches, 1972, p 9.
4. R. Bryant, Community Action *British Journal of Social Work*
    Vol.2, No.2, 1972.
5. R. Holman *Poverty: Explanations of Social Deprivation*
    Martin Robertson & Co. Ltd., 1978, p 288 .
6. P. Friere *Pedagogy of the Oppressed* Penguin Books, 1972.
7. J. Smith, Possibilities for a Socialist Community Work
    Practice. In *Towards a definition of Community Work*
    Association of Community Workers, 1978.
8. P. Friere, op.cit., p 43.
9. For more details on the organization of placements see:
    B. Holmes and R. Bryant, Fieldwork Training in Community
    Work. In C. Briscoe and D. Thomas (Eds) *Community Work:
    Learning and Supervision* Allen and Unwin, 1977.
10. See, for example, G. Williams *Supervision in Community
    Work Placements* Aberdeen Association of Social Service,
    1972.
11. We would not claim any originality for this typology of
    skills. It is based upon a model suggested by Professor
    Slavin. See: J. Rothman and W. Jones, *A New Look at Field
    Instruction* Associated Press, 1971, p 69.
12. C.W. Mills *The Sociological Imagination* Oxford University
    Press, 1959, Ch.1.

Chapter Five   INTRODUCTION TO CASE STUDIES

1. For example: R. Bryant and R. Morran, Social Facilities
    in High Flats - A Glasgow Project *Scottish Journal of
    Youth and Community Work* Vol.4, No.3, 1977. B. Holmes
    *Govanhill Area Survey to locate housebound, chronic sick
    and disabled* op.cit.
2. H. Specht, Disruptive Tactics. In R.H. Kremer and
    H. Specht, (Eds) *Readings in Community Organization Practice*
    Prentice Hall, 1969. R.L. Warren, Types of Purposive
    Change at the Community Level. In R.H. Kramer and
    H. Specht (Eds) *Readings in Community Organization Practice*
    op.cit.
3. A. Barr *The Practice of Neighbourhood Community Work*
    Department of Social Administration and Social Work,
    University of York, 1977.
4. A. Barr, op.cit., I.A. Spergel*Community Problem Solving:
    The Delinquency Example* The University of Chicago Press,
    1969.
5. H. Specht *Disruptive Tactics* op.cit., p.383.
6. ibid., p.384.
7. H. Griffiths, Community Reaction and Voluntary Involvement.
    In J. Darby and A. Williamson (Eds) *Violence and the
    Social Services in Northern Ireland* Heinemann, 1978.
8. R.N. Morris and J. Mogey *The Sociology of Housing*
    Routledge and Kegan Paul, 1965, p 44.
9. M. Rein and R. Morris, Goals, Structures and Strategies
    for Community Change. In R.H. Kramer and H. Specht (Eds)
    Readings in Community Organization Practice op.cit.
10. ibid., p 200.
11. ibid., p 192.
12. ibid., p 196.

Chapter Six   DAMPNESS: ORGANIZING A MASS CAMPAIGN

1. *Sunday Mail* November, 1975.
2. E.E. Schattschneider *The Semi-Sovereign People* Holt,
    Rinehart and Winston, 1960, p 72.
3. The sections of this chapter on 'The Problem' and 'The
    Campaign' draw upon reports by J. Gracie (student),
    D. Anderson (student) and J. Bain (Job Creation worker).
4. For details of this building system, see: R.M.E. Dimont,
    Tracoba *The Architect and Building News* 26 June 1963.
5. For details see: National Building Agency *Technical
    Report on Hutchestown 'E' Scheme* April, 1977.
6. H. Specht, Disruptive Tactics. In R.H. Kramer and
    H. Specht (Eds) *Readings in Community Organization
    Practice* op.cit.
7. For details see: R. Bryant, Rent Strike in the Gorbals

Community Development Journal Vol.17, No.1, 1982.
8. S.D. Alinsky *Reveille for Radicals* Vintage Books, 1969.
9. R. Bryant *The Dampness Monster* Scottish Council of Social Service, 1979, p 32.
10. S.D. Alinsky, op.cit., p 54.
11. R. Bryant *The Dampness Monster* op.cit., p 55.
12. For an example of the problems which can arise when community workers are members of delegations see: S. Jacobs *The Right to a Decent House* Routledge and Kegan Paul, 1976, Ch.8.
13. N. Van Hoffman, The Good Organizer. In J. Ecklein and A. Lauffer (Eds) *Community Organizers and Social Planners* op.cit.
14. Glasgow District Council *The Dampness Issue: Position Statement* 1980.

Chapter Seven   CHANGE AND RITUALISM

1. This section draws upon a student report by M. May, 1973.
2. *The View* July/August, 1973.
3. M. Rein and R. Morris *Goals, Structures and Strategies for Community Change* op.cit.
4. S. Jacobs *The Right to a Decent House* op.cit., Ch.11.
5. M. Rein and R. Morris, op.cit.
6. Govanhill Working Party Minute, 29 June, 1974.
7. For details on the Govanhill Housing Association see: M. Thornley, Tenement Rehabilitation in Glasgow. In R. Darke and R. Walker (Eds) *Local Government and the Public* Leonard Hill, 1977.
8. *The View* March, 1974.
9. S. Arnstein, A Ladder of Citizen Participation *Journal of the American Institute of Planners* No.35, 1969.
10. *The View* June, 1974.
11. M. Rein and R. Morris, op.cit.

Chapter Eight   FROM APATHY TO ACTION

1. For details see; R. Bryant *Conflict and Community Work: A Case Study* op.cit.
2. The sections on the 'Public Meeting' and 'The Week of Action' are extracts from a student report by Mary Hemmings, 1976.
3. J.S. Coleman *Community Conflict* Glencoe Free Press, 1957, p 12.
4. North Tyneside CDP *North Shields: Organizing for Change in a Working Class Area* Final Report, Vol.3, 1978, p 82.
5. Crossroads Youth and Community Association *Staff Policy Statement* November, 1975.

Chapter Nine THE POLITICS OF SPONSORSHIP

1. For details of this review see the following: P. Morris,
    Voluntary Bodies Under the Microscope *Community Care*
    12 January, 1977. R. Bryant, Local Authorities and
    Voluntary Organizations: A Scottish Review *Social Service
    Quarterly* Winter, 1978.
2. For a discussion of non decision-making see: P. Bachrach
    and M. Baratz *Power and Poverty: Theory and Practice*
    Oxford University Press, 1970.
3. P. Corrigan and P. Leonard *Social Work Practice Under
    Capitalism: A Marxist Approach* MacMillan Press, 1978, p 36.

Chapter Ten LESSONS FROM EXPERIENCE

1. J.L. Ecklein and A.A. Lauffer (Eds) *Community Organizers
    and Social Planners* op.cit., p 10.
2. P. Friere *Pedagogy of the Oppressed* op.cit.
3. For details see: T.R. Batten *The Non-Directive Approach in
    Group and Community Work* Oxford University Press, 1967.
4. J. Rothman, An Analysis of Goals and Roles in Community
    Organization Practice. In R.M. Kramer and H. Specht (Eds)
    Readings in Community Organization Practice op.cit.
5. See, for example, A. Barr *The Practice of Neighbourhood
    Community Work* op.cit.
6. J. Rothman, op.cit., p 266-267.
7. See, for example, P. Corrigan and P. Leonard *Social Work
    Practice Under Capitalism: A Marxist Approach* op.cit.,
    M. Repo, Organizing 'The Poor' Against the Working Class.
    In J. Cowley, A. Kaye, M. Mayo and M. Thompson (Eds)
    Community or Class Struggle? Stage 1, 1977.
8. P. Corrigan and P. Leonard, op.cit., p 39.
9. The history of friendly societies and the co-operative
    movement are amongst the more obvious examples of working
    class organization centred around community and welfare
    issues. See: S. Yeo, Working Class Association, private
    capital, welfare and the state in the late 19th and 20th
    centuries. In N. Parry, M. Ruskin and C. Satyamurti (Eds)
    Social Work, Welfare and the State Arnold, 1979.
10. H. Salmon *The Hillfields Community Association: A Case
    Study* Coventry DCP, Occasional Paper, October, 1972, p 25.
11. H. Specht *Community Development in the U.K.* Association of
    Community Workers, 1975.
12. See, for example, North Tyneside CDP *North Shields:
    Organizing for Change in a Working Class Area* Final Report
    Volume 3, 1978, especially the section on 'Action on Play'.
13. H. Salmon *The Hillfields Community Association* op.cit., p 2.
14. See, for example, R. Holman *Poverty: Explanations of
    Social Deprivation* op.cit., C.A. Valentine *Culture and*

Poverty The University of Chicago Press, 1968.
15. D.J. O'Brien *Neighbourhood Organization and Interest-Group Processes* op.cit., p 98.
16. P. Bachrach and M.S. Baratz *Power and Poverty* op.cit.
17. D.J. O'Brien, op.cit., p 8.
18. ibid., p 39.
19. ibid., p 92.
20. M. Rein and R. Morris *Goals, Structures and Strategies for Community Change* op.cit., p 201.
21. See, for example, M. Mayo (Ed) *Women in the Community* Routledge and Kegan Paul, 1977.
22. J. Freeman *Tyranny of Structurelessness* Leeds Women ORA, 1973, p 2.
23. ibid., p 7.
24. C. Kirwood, Community Democracy. In G. Brown (Ed) *The Red Paper on Scotland* op.cit., p 95.

Chapter Eleven   WHAT MAKES A GOOD COMMUNITY WORKER?

1. *Concise Oxford Dictionary* Fifth edition, Oxford Univ. Press, 1964.
2. See, for example, H. Salmon, Ideology and Practice. In P. Curno (Ed) *Political Issues and Community Work* Routledge and Kegan Paul, 1978.
3. H. Liddell and R. Bryant, A Local View of Community Work. In M. Mayo and D. Jones (Eds) *Community Work One* op.cit., 1974.
4. P. Friere *Pedagogy of the Oppressed* op.cit.
5. See, for example, E. Meyer and N. Timms *The Client Speaks* Routledge and Kegan Paul. 1970.
6. Quoted in C.F. Thomason *The Professional Approach to Community Work* Sands & Co., 1969, p 111.
7. See, for example, R. Leaper *Community Work* NCSS, 1968. G. Goetschius *Working with Community Groups* Routledge and Kegan Paul, 1969. P. Baldock *Community and Social Work* Routledge and Kegan Paul, 1974. F. Milson *An Introduction to Community Work* Routledge and Kegan Paul, 1974.
8. Gulbenkian Foundation *Community Work and Social Change* Longmans, 1968.
9. Social Work Curriculum Study *The Teaching of Community Work* CCETSW, 1975.
10. Gulbenkian Foundation *Current Issues in Community Work* Routledge and Kegan Paul, 1972.
11. Association of Community Workers *Knowledge and Skills for Community Work* 1975.
12. S.D. Alinsky *Rules for Radicals* Random House, 1971, Ch.4.
13. ibid., p 71.
14. See, for example, R. Deacon and M. Bartley, Becoming a Social Worker. In H. Jones (Ed) *Towards a New Social Work* Routledge and Kegan Paul, 1975.

Chapter Twelve WHAT IS A SUCCESSFUL COMMUNITY WORK PROJECT?

1. H. Liddell and R. Bryant *A Local View of Community Work* op.cit.
2. Quoted in C. Kirkwood, Community Democracy. In G. Brown (Ed) *The Red Paper in Scotland* op.cit.
3. For details see C. Clarke et al *Planning for Community Councils* University of Strathclyde, 1975.
4. S. Alinsky *Reveille for Radicals* op.cit.
5. For details see: P. Morris *Voluntary Bodies Under the Microscope* op.cit.

Chapter Thirteen WHAT DO STUDENTS GAIN FROM COMMUNITY WORK PLACEMENTS?

1. See, for example, O. Stevenson, P. Parsloe, M. Hill et al *Social Service Teams: The Practitioner's View* HMSO, 1978.
2. During the period from 1975 to 1978 the fieldwork teachers post with the Govanhill Unit was split between two part-time staff.
3. O. Stevenson, P. Parsloe and M. Hill, op.cit., p 356.
4. J. Mayer and N. Timms *The Client Speaks* op.cit., p 86.
5. O. Stevenson, P. Parsloe and M. Hill, op.cit.
6. J. Brandon and M. Davies *The Limits of Competence in Social Work: An Assessment of Marginal Students in Social Work Education* British Journal of Social Work, Vol.9, No.3, 1978.
7. O. Stevenson, P. Parsloe and M. Hill, op.cit., p 339. For further evidence of the dominance of the casework method see: S. Rees *Social Work Face to Face* Edward Arnold, 1978.
8. O. Stevenson, P. Parsloe and M. Hill, op.cit., p 371.
9. ibid., p 351.
10. ibid., p 358
11. ibid., p 263
12. N. Gilbert and H. Specht, The Incomplete Profession. In H. Specht and A. Vickery (Eds) *Integrating Social Work Methods* Allen and Unwin, 1977.
13. O. Stevenson, P. Parsloe and M. Hill, op.cit., p 328.
14. J. Brandon and M. Davies *The Limits of Competence in Social Work* op.cit., p 341.

Chapter Fourteen A DEFENCE OF LOCAL COMMUNITY ACTION

1. See, C. Cockburn *The Local State* Pluto Press, 1977.
2. D.N. Thomas, Community Work, Social Change and Social Planning. In P. Curno (Ed) *Political Issues and Community Work* op.cit., H. Specht *Community Development in the U.K.* op.cit.
3. H. Specht, op.cit., p 15 .

4. D.N. Thomas, op.cit., p 248 .
5. Strathclyde Regional Council *Policy Review Group on Community Development Services* 1978.
6. ibid.
7. See, for example, C. Cockburn, op.cit.
8. Strathclyde Regional Council, op.cit.
9. D.N. Thomas, op.cit., p 255 .
10. See, for example, S. Bolger, P. Corrigan, J. Docking and N. Frost *Towards Socialist Welfare Work* MacMillan Press, 1981. P. Hain (Ed) *Community Politics* John Calder, 1976. P. Corrigan and P. Leonard *Social Work Practice Under Capitalism* op.cit. J. Cowley, A. Kaye, M. Mayo and M. Thompson *Community or Class Struggle?* op.cit.
11. P. Corrigan, Community Work and Political Struggle. In P. Leonard (Ed) *The Sociology of Community Action* Sociological Review Monograph, University of Keele, 1975, p 57.
12. See, for example, P. Saunders *Urban Politics* Penguin Books, 1979, Ch.3.
13. For contrasting perspectives on this debate see: D. Corkey and G. Craig, CDP Community Work or Class Politics? and J. Smith, Hard Lines and Soft Options: A Criticism of Some Left Attitudes to Community Work. In P. Curno (Ed) *Political Issues and Community Work* op.cit.
14. J. O'Malley *The Politics of Community Action* Spokesman, 1977, p 172.
15. For details see: Network of Labour and Community Research and Resource Centres: More Resources, Not Less *Community Development Journal* Vol.17, No.1, 1982.
16. P. Corrigan and P. Leonard, op.cit., Ch.3.
17. H. Beynon *Working for Ford* Penguin Books, 1973, p 317.
18. B. Moorhouse, M. Wilson and C. Chamberlain, Rent Strikes - Direct Action and the Working Class. In R. Miliband and J. Saville (Eds) *The Socialist Register* 1972, Merlin Press, p 153.
19. D. Corkey and G. Craig, op.cit. p 42.
20. For evidence of the social control function of community work see: N. Dennis, The Popularity of the Neighbourhood Community Idea *Sociological Review* VI, (2) 1958.
21. For examples of reformist currents within the history of social work and community work see: R. Lees *Politics and Social Work* Routledge and Kegan Paul, 1972. D. Leat, Social Theory and the Historical Construction of Social Work Activity: The Role of Samuel Barnett. In P. Leonard (Ed) *The Sociology of Community Action* op.cit.